FLOYD CLYMER'S MOTORCYCLIST'S LIBRARY

The Book of the
B.S.A.
(GROUPS B, C, M.)

A PRACTICAL GUIDE ON THE HANDLING AND MAINTENANCE OF ALL 1945 TO 1959 FOUR-STROKE SINGLES, EXCEPT THE 1954-9 250 c.c. AND ALL "GOLD STAR" MODELS

BY

W. C. HAYCRAFT
F.R.S.A.

FIFTEENTH EDITION
1961

ANNOUNCEMENT

By special arrangement with the original publishers of this book, Sir Isaac Pitman & Son, Ltd., of London, England, we have secured the exclusive publishing rights for this book, as well as all others in THE MOTORCYCLIST'S LIBRARY.

Included in THE MOTORCYCLIST'S LIBRARY are complete instruction manuals covering the care and operation of respective motorcycles and engines; valuable data on speed tuning, and thrilling accounts of motorcycle race events. See listing of available titles elsewhere in this edition.

We consider it a privilege to be able to offer so many fine titles to our customers.

FLOYD CLYMER
Publisher of Books Pertaining to Automobiles and Motorcycles

2125 W. PICO ST.   LOS ANGELES 6, CALIF.

INTRODUCTION

Welcome to the world of digital publishing ~ the book you now hold in your hand, while unchanged from the original edition, was printed using the latest state of the art digital technology. The advent of print-on-demand has forever changed the publishing process, never has information been so accessible and it is our hope that this book serves your informational needs for years to come. If this is your first exposure to digital publishing, we hope that you are pleased with the results. Many more titles of interest to the classic automobile and motorcycle enthusiast, collector and restorer are available via our website at www.VelocePress.com. We hope that you find this title as interesting as we do.

NOTE FROM THE PUBLISHER

The information presented is true and complete to the best of our knowledge. All recommendations are made without any guarantees on the part of the author or the publisher, who also disclaim all liability incurred with the use of this information.

TRADEMARKS

We recognize that some words, model names and designations, for example, mentioned herein are the property of the trademark holder. We use them for identification purposes only. This is not an official publication.

INFORMATION ON THE USE OF THIS PUBLICATION

This manual is an invaluable resource for the classic motorcycle enthusiast and a "must have" for owners interested in performing their own maintenance. However, in today's information age we are constantly subject to changes in common practice, new technology, availability of improved materials and increased awareness of chemical toxicity. As such, it is advised that the user consult with an experienced professional prior to undertaking any procedure described herein. While every care has been taken to ensure correctness of information, it is obviously not possible to guarantee complete freedom from errors or omissions or to accept liability arising from such errors or omissions. Therefore, any individual that uses the information contained within, or elects to perform or participate in do-it-yourself repairs or modifications acknowledges that there is a risk factor involved and that the publisher or its associates cannot be held responsible for personal injury or property damage resulting from the use of the information or the outcome of such procedures.

WARNING!

One final word of advice, this publication is intended to be used as a reference guide, and when in doubt the reader should consult with a qualified technician.

PREFACE

THE purpose of this handbook is to provide in a concise, readable form *all* essential information necessary to enable you to obtain the maximum mileage, maximum efficiency, minimum fuel consumption, and lowest running costs from your B.S.A.

B.S.A. motor-cycles need no introduction as they have a firmly established reputation for up-to-date design, precision finish, high performance with reliability and economy, and last but by no means least, good looks.

The present edition of THE BOOK OF THE B.S.A. deals comprehensively with the maintenance and overhaul of the following B.S.A. four-stroke singles—

1. The 1945–53 249 c.c. S.V. Model C10.
2. The 1945–53 249 c.c. O.H.V. Model C11.
3. The 1950–3 249 c.c. O.H.V. Model C11 de luxe.
4. The 1945–55 496 c.c. S.V. Model M20.
5. The 1945–58 591 c.c. S.V. Model M21.
6. The 1945–59 348 c.c. O.H.V. Models B31, B32.
7. The 1949–59 499 c.c. O.H.V. Models B33, B34.
8. The 1949–57 499 c.c. O.H.V. Model M33.

It should be noted that the M33 engine is identical in design to the "B" series engines and that Model C11 de luxe is identical to Model C11 throughout except in regard to the finish.

The only 1945–59 B.S.A. motor-cycles not covered in this handbook are the two-stroke models, the twin-cylinder O.H.V. models, the "Gold Star" O.H.V. singles, and 1954–9 249 c.c. models (C10L, C11G, C12, C15).

Throughout most of the text the instructions are dated to prevent any possible misunderstandings. Where such instructions are *not* dated, they apply to *all* 1945 and subsequent models. To facilitate engine strip (B31–B34, M33), I have included some close-up photos taken when dismantling a 1952 B31 "springer." I have subsequently owned a similar 1955 model.

In conclusion I thank B.S.A. Motor Cycles Ltd. of Birmingham, 11, for their generous assistance with regard to data, and for permitting various B.S.A. illustrations to be reproduced.

W. C. H.

CONTENTS

CHAP.		PAGE
	Preface	
I.	HANDLING A B.S.A.	1
II.	ALL ABOUT CARBURATION	13
III.	CARE OF LIGHTING SYSTEM	27
IV.	B.S.A. LUBRICATION	49
V.	GENERAL MAINTENANCE	69
	Index	147

CHAPTER I

HANDLING A B.S.A.

It is not possible in this maintenance handbook to deal with actual riding except in the briefest outline and considerations of space at the author's disposal make it necessary for him to concentrate on the layout and handling of B.S.A. controls and to omit dealing with the technique of riding, legal matters, etc. Do not fail to read a copy of the official booklet, *The Highway Code*. Also always wear a crash helmet. It is likely to prevent serious injury in the event of an accident.

Outline of Preliminaries. It is assumed that you have bought outright or have paid a deposit on a brand-new or a good second-hand mount and wish to get on the road forthwith. Before you can do this, however, you must attend to the following preliminaries—
 1. Insure against *third-party* risks. See that you get the vital "Certificate of Insurance." With a new machine you cannot obtain this until the machine has been registered and a registration number allocated to it. Pending this, obtain an insurance "cover note." If your B.S.A. is worth a lot, it is advisable to take out a full comprehensive insurance policy. If it is bought on a hire-purchase system, you will *have* to do this.
 2. Obtain the registration book and registration licence (Form R.F.1/A for renewal; Form R.F.1/2* for original registration or change of ownership). All except the 250 c.c. coil ignition B.S.A. models are taxed at the rate of £3 15s. per annum (£1 5s. extra for a sidecar). The 250 c.c. models are taxed at £1 17s. 6d. per annum (10s. extra for a sidecar).
 3. Take out a "provisional" (six months) or a three-year driving licence, form D.L.1. in either case; sign the driving licence immediately you get it. You are not eligible for a three-year licence until you are 16 (for group G) and have complied with one of the following conditions—
 (*a*) You have held a licence (other than a provisional or Visitor's licence) authorizing the driving of vehicles of the class or description applied for within a period of ten years ending on the date of coming into force of the licence applied for.
 (*b*) You have passed the prescribed driving test (this includes a test passed whilst serving in H.M. Forces) during the said period of ten years.

* On Form R.F.1/2 you must state the engine and frame number (e.g. ZB31–24473 and ZB315–20334) situated on the rear-side of the crankcase and on the near-side of the steering-head lug—at the top of the front down-tube, respectively.

4. Unless your B.S.A. is a very early model (registered prior to 1st October, 1937) fit a reliable speedometer to show within ± 10 per cent accuracy when 30 m.p.h. is being exceeded. On all models of recent manufacture a speedometer is fitted as standard equipment above the

Fig. 1. Typical of the B.S.A. Single-cylinder Range Combining Good Looks and a Gentlemanly Performance in Traffic with a Sports Performance on the Open Road

Vivid acceleration, splendid steering, and a 73 m.p.h. full throttle speed with 95 m.p.g. fuel consumption, are good characteristics of the 1959 350 c.c. O.H.V. Model B31 shown above. It is one of six O.H.V. singles and has a sports engine, improved gearbox, "swinging arm" rear suspension, full-width light alloy hubs, and (an optional extra) complete enclosure of the secondary chain.

front forks (*see* Fig. 4), or on 1953-9 350-600 c.c. models on a streamlined headlamp cowl (*see* Fig. 2).

5. Fit "L" plates to the front and rear of the machine if you are eligible for a "provisional" licence only.

6. If you carry a pillion passenger, see that she or he sits *astride* a proper pillion seat securely *fixed* to the machine. If you hold only a "provisional" licence, the pillion passenger must hold a current driving licence covering group G.

7. Use an "ignition suppression" type sparking plug or terminal cover (*see* page 74) if the machine was originally registered after 1st July, 1953, so that it does not cause interference to television and radio sets.

Note that all the official forms previously referred to can be obtained from a money-order post office.

The Riding Position. The standard riding position on a new B.S.A. is generally found to be satisfactory for a man of average build, but to suit those not of average physique, a combined adjustment of the handlebars, footrests, and some of the handlebar controls, can be made. See that the riding position is really comfortable. The footrest hanger bosses are serrated internally and the hangers can be moved to alternative positions. The handlebars are readily adjustable (four bolts). A shaped foam-rubber pad beneath a saddle top improves comfort.

To Adjust the Footrests. On "swinging arm" models first remove the exhaust pipe and silencer (together) to enable the footrest shaft to be

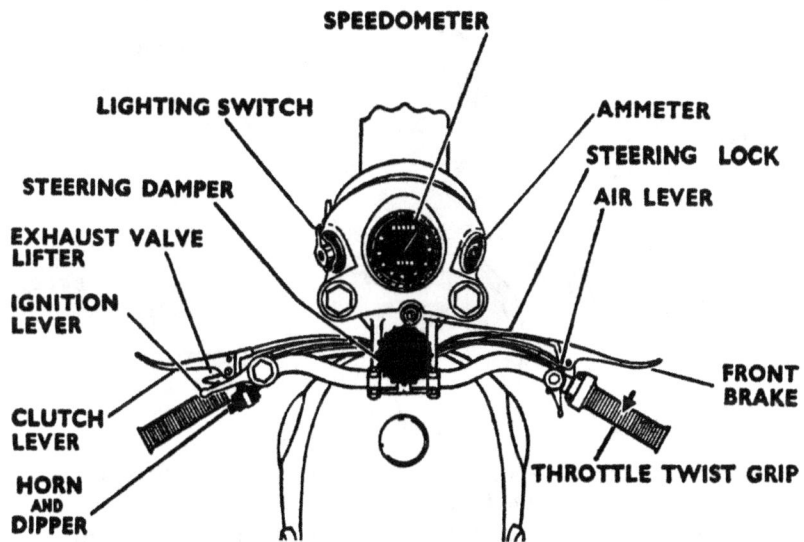

FIG. 2. LAYOUT OF HANDLEBAR CONTROLS, ETC., ON 1953-8 S.V. AND 1953-7 O.H.V. "MAGDYNO" MODELS

The steering lock (operated by a Yale key) was introduced in 1955. On 1953-5 models the horn and dipper switches were separate as shown in Fig. 4. Note the remarks below Fig. 4.

tapped out from the near-side after nut removal. Then fit both footrest hangers to the detachable serrated sleeves as required.

LAYOUT AND USE OF CONTROLS

The controls (mostly on the handlebars) may conveniently be divided into three groups: (1) engine controls, (2) motor-cycle controls, and (3) electrical controls. Before attempting to start up, you should, if you have never previously handled a B.S.A., get quite familiar with the controls.

It is assumed that you are familiar with general principles and understand the functions of the controls which are more or less the same on all motor-cycles. If you are a complete novice it is a good plan to sit on the saddle and "twiddle" the various levers while thinking about what would happen if the engine were running.

On "Magdyno" Models. The layout of the handlebar controls is clearly shown in Figs. 2 and 4. This layout applies to all 1945-58 "Magdyno" models; there is some variation in the positions of the speedometer, ammeter, and lighting switch. On 1953-8 models the speedometer,

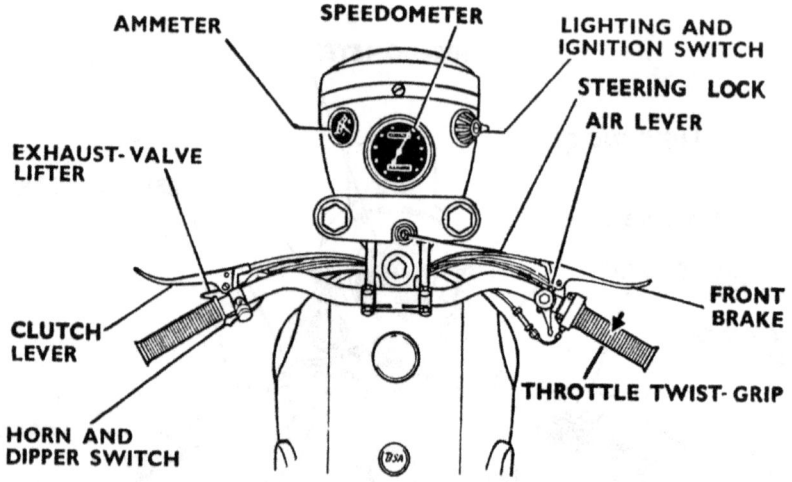

Fig. 3. Layout of Handlebar Controls, etc., on 1958-9 Coil Ignition O.H.V. Models B31, B33

The 1958-9 350 c.c. and 500 c.c. O.H.V. models with Lucas alternator and rectifier (instead of a "Magdyno") have no ignition lever, but an ignition switch. A steering damper is not fitted.

ammeter, and lighting switch are housed in a headlamp cowl (*see* Fig. 2), while on most pre-1948 models the speedometer is mounted on the petrol tank. On some 1947 models, however, with girder-type front forks (e.g. M20, M21), the speedometer is located above the front forks.

Those handling a B.S.A. for the first time should note the following points—

1. All handlebar controls (excluding 1954-6 ignition levers) are operated by *inward* movement.

2. The throttle twist-grip (which controls engine speed) has a full movement of approximately *one-quarter* of a complete turn. With the throttle-stop correctly set to provide good tick-over, the throttle slide does not close completely. On most B.S.A. models it is essential to use a very small throttle opening (about one-sixteenth to one-eighth of the total twist-grip movement) for starting from cold; otherwise some difficulty may be experienced.

3. The air lever (which enables the mixture of air and petrol to be varied) must be kept closed completely for starting from *cold* but at all other times it should normally be *wide open*. Slight closing when travelling slowly under load, to ward off a tendency for pinking, may sometimes be desirable, but it is generally best to use the ignition lever to forestall pinking.

4. The ignition lever (which moves the contact-breaker base on the

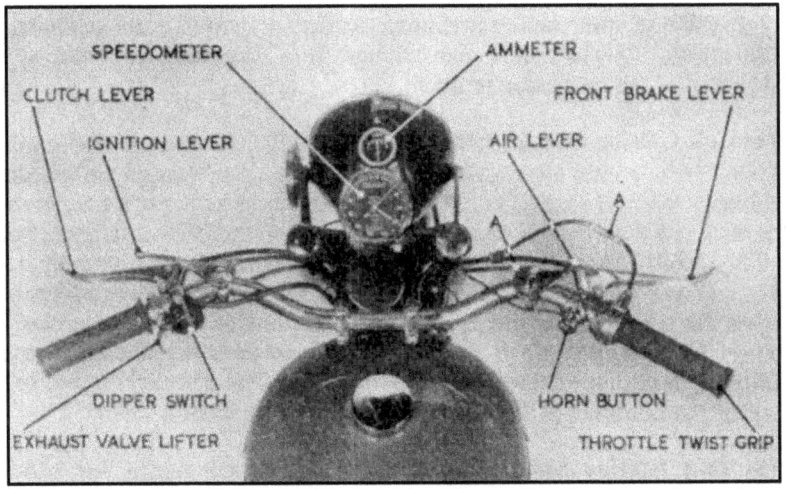

Fig. 4. Layout of Handlebar Controls, etc., on 1945-52 S.V., O.H.V. "Magdyno" Models

Except for switch layout, it applies (*see* text) to all 1945-57 single-cylinder S.V. and O.H.V. "Magdyno" models. Note that on all machines the handlebars, footrests (including "swinging arm" models), and control levers are adjustable for position. A cable adjustment is also provided at *A*. (For lighting switch details, *see* page 36.)

magneto portion of the "Magdyno") should always be kept fully, or nearly fully, advanced while riding, except when pinking occurs. For pinking, less frequent now with branded fuels, the ignition should be temporarily retarded a shade, but note that this automatically reduces the power output. At the first opportunity after temporary retardation, the ignition lever should be *advanced as far as possible*. For starting purposes, however, it is always advisable to retard the ignition lever slightly to prevent the risk of kick-back.

5. Never use the exhaust-valve lifter (which raises the exhaust-valve off its seat) for any purpose other than starting and stopping the engine. It is permissible, however, to use it occasionally when descending hills, provided that the throttle is shut right back and the air lever is kept wide open.

6. The clutch lever (which disconnects and re-connects the drive from

the engine to the rear wheel) must always be used *fully* and *progressively*. Use it only when moving off and during each gear change. For comfort, slip some rubber tube on to the lever (also the front-brake lever).

7. The foot gear-change pedal on the off-side of the gearbox provides four gear ratios and "neutral" which lies between first and second gears. Note that "neutral" can only be obtained *after* engaging first gear. All downward changes (*see* Fig. 7) are made by upward movement of the pedal with the toe, and all upward changes are made by downward movement of the toe. The gear-change pedal returns to the same (horizontal) position after each gear change is effected, ready for the next change to be made. During each gear change it is necessary to make a *full* movement of the gear-change pedal.

On Coil Ignition Models (1945-53). On the 250 c.c. coil ignition models (C10, C11) the control layout is similar to that on the "Magdyno" models, previously referred to, but as may be seen in Fig. 5 no separate air lever is provided and the exhaust-valve lifter is omitted, the 250 c.c. engine being readily kicked over compression. The ignition lever is also absent, automatic advance-and-retard mechanism being specified. On all coil ignition models the switch gear incorporates an ignition key. This enables the ignition to be switched off when the machine is left standing, thereby preventing a discharge from the battery through the primary circuit in the event of the contacts of the contact-breaker being closed.

On Coil Ignition Models (1958-9). The control layout for Models B31, B33 is shown in Fig. 3. No ignition lever is provided, the advance and retard being automatically controlled. As on the 1945-53 250 c.c. models, an ignition key is provided in the centre of the lighting switch mounted on the off-side of the headlamp cowl. It has three positions: EMG (emergency), OFF, and IGN (ignition on). The EMG and IGN positions are on the left- and right-hand sides respectively of the OFF position.

In the event of the battery being exhausted, the engine can be started after temporarily turning the ignition key to the EMG position. Starting is normally effected with the ignition key turned to the IGN position. Whenever the engine is stopped, the key should be turned to the OFF position to prevent battery discharge.

The 1945-54 Petrol Taps. The single petrol tap fitted to the underneath of the tank (on 1945-54 "Magdyno" models), on the near-side at the rear, is most ingenious and maintains a reserve supply of petrol in the simplest way imaginable. In Fig. 6 are shown two taps to explain clearly its method of working.

With the tap shown on the left: the small reserve lever is moved away from the marking "RES" and the hole at the base of the vertical tube (projecting into the tank-filter) is shut, thus forcing the petrol to enter the tap body via the top orifice of the tube, and a reserve petrol supply is automatically maintained within the tank to the level of the top of the tube.

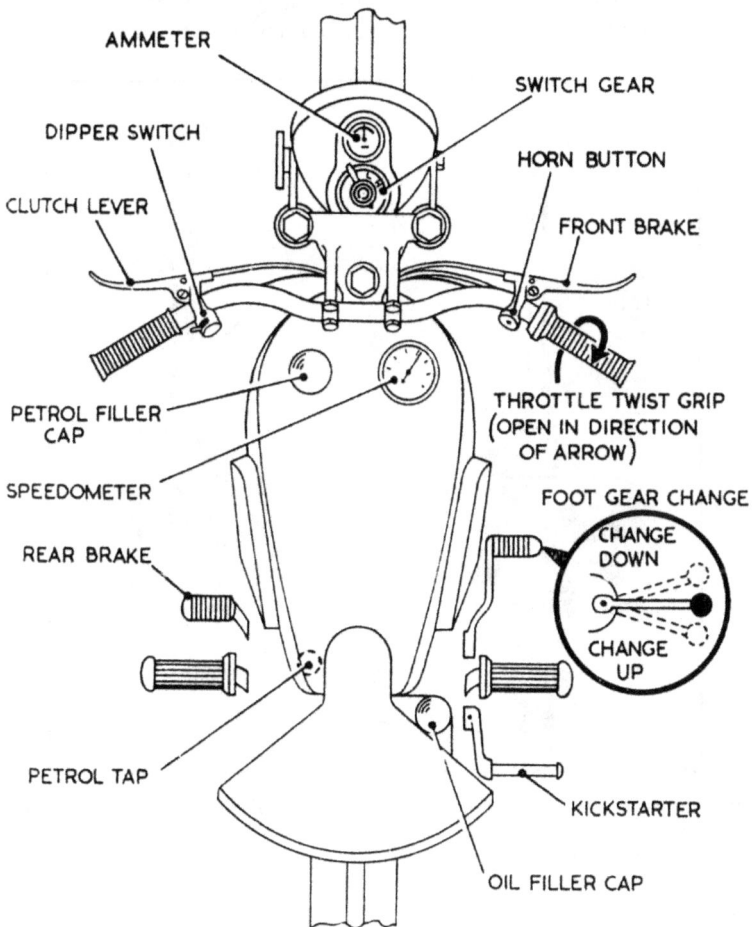

FIG. 5. LAYOUT OF CONTROLS ON B.S.A. COIL IGNITION MODELS C10, C11

On the 1945 250 c.c. Models C10, C11 (with girder-type forks) and the corresponding 1953 Models (with telescopic forks) the speedometer is mounted on the front forks as shown in Fig. 4, instead of on the tank. Note that the ignition switch in the centre of the lighting switch is turned *clockwise* to switch on.

With the tap shown on the right: the reserve lever has been moved fully towards the marking "RES," and the hole at the base of the vertical tube is open, thus causing the reserve petrol supply in the tank to by-pass the vertical tube and enter the tap body through the open hole near the bottom of the tube and tank.

On 1945-54 "Magdyno" models, to turn on the petrol push the *hexagonal* button marked "ON"; to turn off the petrol push the *serrated* button marked "OFF." On 1945-53 coil ignition models with no reserve tap, to turn on the petrol, turn the button *anti-clockwise* and pull the button out. To turn off the petrol, turn the button *clockwise* and push inwards.

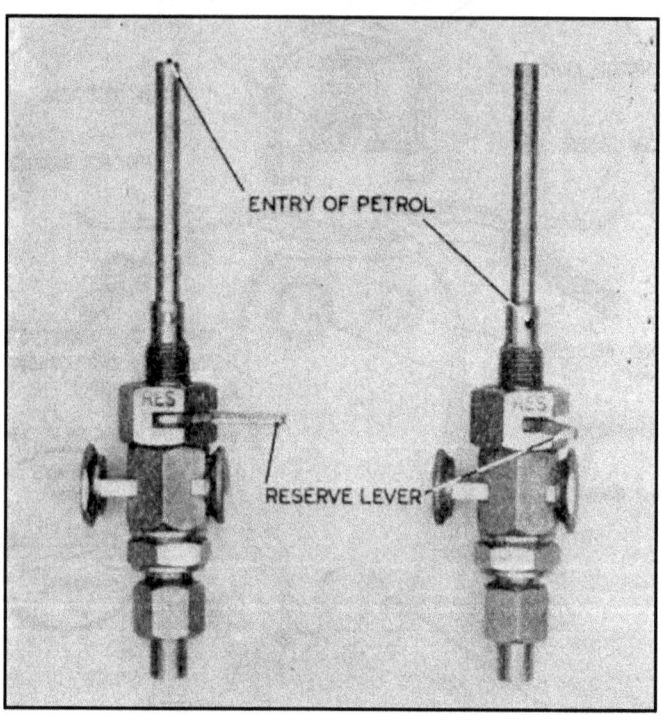

Fig. 6. Showing (Left) Petrol Tap with Reserve Lever Set for Running on Main Supply, and (Right) for Running on Reserve Supply when Main Supply is Exhausted (1945-54 "Magdyno" Models)

Modified Petrol Tap. On all 1955-8 "Magdyno" models and the 1958-9 Models B31, B33 to turn the push-and-pull type petrol tap on or off, pull the serrated button out or push it in respectively. To switch over to the reserve petrol supply from the main supply, turn the button *clockwise* and pull it out about $\frac{1}{8}$ in. further to lock in position.

Starting Up. Before attempting to start up, make quite sure that there is sufficient engine oil of the correct type and grade in the oil tank, gearbox, and oil-bath chain case (*see* Chapter IV), and that the motor-cycle parts have been adequately lubricated, and the battery attended to.

HANDLING A B.S.A.

The oil tank has a maximum capacity of 3¼ to 5½ pints (according to the machine). Also check that the tyre pressures (*see* page 129) are correct and that there is sufficient petrol in the tank, the capacity of which varies from 2½ to 4 gal.

Push your B.S.A. forward off its rear or centre stand, or keep it jacked up. If the machine is moved off its stand it is advisable to stand astride the machine, as this helps to balance it. On a "Magdyno" or 1958-9 coil-ignition model with a reserve petrol tap, verify that the reserve lever (or button, 1955-9) is correctly positioned, and turn on the petrol (*see* page 8).

On a coil ignition model always verify that the ignition is switched on (turn ignition key *clockwise*). On a "Magdyno" or coil model with a separate air lever, close this completely if starting from *cold*, and retard the ignition lever (where fitted) so that it is about half fully advanced.

Open the throttle very slightly (say, one-eighth) by *inward* movement of the throttle twist-grip. See that the foot gear-change mechanism is in "neutral," i.e. between first and second gears. It is advisable to actually verify that the operation of the kick-starter does not rotate the wheel. If the engine is quite cold, momentarily depress the tickler on the carburettor float-chamber, but do not flood the carburettor so that petrol begins to drip. If the engine is warm, do not flood the carburettor at all, and leave the air lever (where fitted) partly (say, one-third) open.

Next, start up the engine. On a 250 c.c. coil ignition model give the kick-starter a vigorous kick downwards, when the engine should respond. On all models over 250 c.c. depress the kick-starter until compression stops the engine, raise the exhaust-valve lifter, and then give the kick-starter pedal a vigorous downward kick. At the same time release the exhaust-valve lifter. The engine should start up at the first or second attempt, but if it fails to do so, repeat the starting procedure. As soon as the engine of a "Magdyno" model fires, advance the ignition lever fully, or nearly fully, and open the air lever slowly as far as possible until the engine runs evenly at a moderate speed.

Engaging First Gear. Disengage the clutch by squeezing the handlebar lever, and move the foot gear-change pedal *upwards* to its *full* extent. If you fail to engage first gear readily with the motor-cycle stationary, rock the machine gently to and fro while maintaining slight pressure on the foot gear-change pedal. Continue doing this until you *feel* that first gear is engaged.

Moving Off. Open the throttle slightly by turning the throttle twist-grip *inwards*, and gently and progressively engage the clutch by releasing the handlebar lever. As the clutch engages and the motor-cycle gathers momentum, open the throttle a little more. Should any slight pinking occur, on a "Magdyno" model, immediately retard the ignition very slightly, or close the air lever a shade. For all normal running after the engine has warmed up ("Magdyno" models) it is important to keep the ignition lever fully advanced and the air lever wide open, so long as this does not entail any tendency for the engine to "knock."

Making Upward Gear Changes. Momentarily close the throttle, disengage the clutch, and *depress* the foot gear-change pedal to its *full* extent. As far as possible, combine these three actions in one *smooth* movement. Pause a second before disengaging the clutch. Quickly but progressively re-engage the clutch and simultaneously open the throttle again, immediately the desired gear change is effected. When changing up into second, third, or fourth gear, avoid imposing undue pressure on the foot gear-

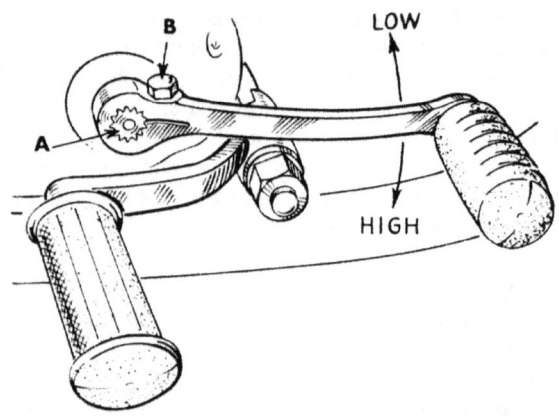

FIG. 7. THE B.S.A. POSITIVE-STOP FOOT GEAR-CHANGE

After making each gear change, the lever and pedal always return to the same position. The lever is adjustable on the splined shaft *A* after loosening the pinch-bolt *B*.

change pedal, because this can cause damage and is quite unnecessary, but maintain light pressure until the clutch is re-engaged.

Making Downward Gear Changes. Simultaneously open the throttle slightly, pause a second, disengage the clutch, and with toe pressure *raise* the foot gear-change pedal upwards to its full extent. Then quickly and progressively re-engage the clutch.

When making a gear change, hold the foot gear-change pedal in position with the toe until the gear is *felt* to engage and the clutch has been re-engaged. Make all gear changes quietly and smoothly. An accomplished motor-cyclist does not advertise to the whole street that he is making a gear change.

Note that when changing down quickly from fourth or third gear into first gear it is not essential to disengage the clutch, to throttle up the engine and to *re-engage the clutch* during each gear change. It is sufficient to slow down to a low speed, disengage the clutch, and make two or three full upward movements of the gear-change pedal in quick succession, according to whether third or fourth gear respectively was previously engaged. Each time you raise the gear-change pedal "blip" the engine, i.e. throttle up slightly.

To Obtain "Neutral." It is necessary to change down into first gear, stop,* and then with the clutch still disengaged, *slightly* and very gently *depress* the foot gear-change pedal with the toe. In this instance do not move the pedal to its full extent, otherwise you will miss "neutral" and engage second gear. A "light touch" is required, and you should be careful to re-engage the clutch gradually in case first gear should have been accidentally engaged.

To Stop the Machine. Close the throttle, apply both brakes simultaneously, and change down into neutral.

To Stop the Engine. With neutral engaged and the throttle shut right back (giving generally a slow tick-over), raise the exhaust-valve lifter, or (on coil-ignition models) switch off the ignition.

Run in Engine Carefully for 1,000-1,500 Miles. *The advice given below is the most important advice in the book.* Except with bench-tested "Gold Star" engines, all B.S.A. engines must be handled very, very carefully for the first 1,000-1,500 miles. Attend to all routine maintenance operations with special care. After the first 250 miles drain and refill the oil tank with fresh oil and clean the filter (*see* pages 54, 55). Repeat this at 1,000 miles (thereafter at 2,000 miles). Change the oil in the gearbox after the first 500 miles and thereafter every 2,000 miles (*see* page 51).

During the running-in period the throttle should not be opened wide; a new or reconditioned engine should be nursed very carefully, otherwise it may be permanently spoiled and never deliver its full power. When new, bearing surfaces appear dead smooth but actually they are covered with fine tool marks which are invisible to the naked eye. Until these disappear, and a mirror-like gloss and hardness spread all over, local friction is very apt to occur and the oil film may break down at one or more places, possibly causing a seizure. To speed on a new machine is a great temptation, but for some time, be content with *one-third* of full throttle and always avoid rapid acceleration.

Make a point of not using more than *half* throttle in any gear until running-in is nearly completed. On 250 c.c. coil-ignition models (C10, C11)

* A really accomplished rider can obtain "neutral" *before* coming to a complete standstill, but a novice is not advised to attempt to obtain "neutral" while the machine is moving.

do not exceed 30-35 m.p.h. in top gear, and correspondingly lower speeds in the other gears. By making full use of the gearbox, aim at making the engine run "light" as much as possible. As the running-in period nears completion, progressively increase the throttle openings, but do not run on full throttle until 1,500 miles have been covered.

During Running-in. Avoid rapid acceleration, particularly if the engine is not pulling under load, and above all never allow the engine to labour when hill climbing through not changing down to a lower gear in good time.

Check the various routine adjustments (*see* Chapter V) such as plug and contact-breaker gaps, tappet clearances, clutch adjustment, etc., somewhat more often than usual, and also check external nuts and bolts for tightness (*see* page 72). *Always keep the oil tank well topped-up* (*see* page 49), and change the engine oil, drain the crankcase, and clean the filters at the intervals stated on page 54. Change the gearbox oil at the periods specified on page 61.

Use Upper-cylinder Lubricant during Running-in Period. B.S.A. Motor Cycles, Ltd., recommend the addition during running-in of some upper-cylinder lubricant to the *petrol* each time the tank is replenished. Where an upper-cylinder lubricant is not available, it is a good plan to add about one egg-cupful of engine oil to every two gallons of petrol.

The Speedometer Trip. To turn the trip to zero, pull out the spring-loaded flexible control under the instrument and turn it *clockwise*. On releasing the control, it automatically disengages. This applies whether the speedometer is mounted above the front forks (1945-52) or set in the headlamp cowl (1953 onwards).

Steering Head Lock. All 1955 and later models have a thief-proof locking device built into the steering head. To lock the steering when parking the machine, insert the Yale key into the key-hole (*see* Fig. 2) and turn the key when the steering is moved over to the *left* to almost its full extent. Be very careful not to lose the key (always keep it on a chain ring), and note the important advice on page 64 regarding the application of oil.

CHAPTER II

ALL ABOUT CARBURATION

ALL B.S.A. models are sent out from the works with the carburettors carefully tuned and with jet sizes, throttle valve, and needle position giving the best all-round performance. Normally it is not wise to alter the maker's setting. A slow-running adjustment is, however, sometimes required and after a considerable mileage it may be desirable to alter the jet needle position. About every six months the carburettor should be dismantled, thoroughly cleaned, and inspected.

This chapter deals with the standard needle-jet Amal carburettor (fitted to most 1945-55 models over 250 c.c.) and also with the later "Monobloc" type Amal instrument. Some understanding of how the Amal carburettor functions is desirable.

STANDARD NEEDLE-JET AMAL CARBURETTOR

How it Works. The carburettor fitted to all engines (except when a "Monobloc" type is used) is of the two-lever needle-jet type, the mixture at slow or idling speeds being controlled by a readily adjustable pilot jet, whilst at higher speeds the mixture is controlled by means of a needle attached to the throttle slide and working in a needle-jet. This carburettor is for all practical purposes automatic, the air lever being closed only to facilitate starting from cold; but under very adverse circumstances it may be necessary to close it partly while riding. External adjuster screws are provided for slow-running and throttle-stop adjustment. The essential details of the Amal carburettor are shown in Figs. 8 and 11; and below is an outline of how the carburettor functions.

In Fig. 8, showing a sectional view of the instrument, A is the carburettor body or mixing chamber, the upper part of which has a throttle valve B with taper needle C attached by a needle clip. The throttle valve regulates the quantity of mixture supplied to the engine.

Passing through the throttle valve is the air valve D, independently operated and serving the purpose of obstructing the main air passage for starting and mixture regulation. Fixed to the underside of the mixing chamber by the union nut E is the jet block F, and interposed between them is a fibre washer to ensure a petrol-tight joint.

On the upper part of the block is the jet-block barrel H, forming a clean through-way. Integral with the jet block is the pilot jet J, supplied through the passage K. The adjustable pilot air-intake L communicates with a chamber, from which issues the pilot outlet M and the by-pass N. A

14   THE BOOK OF THE B.S.A.

throttle stop (*see* Fig. 9) is provided on the mixing chamber, by which the position of the throttle valve for tick-over is regulated independently of the cable adjustment.

The needle-jet O is screwed in the underside of the jet block, and carries at its bottom end the main jet P. Both these jets are removable when the jet plug Q, which bolts the mixing chamber and the float chamber together,

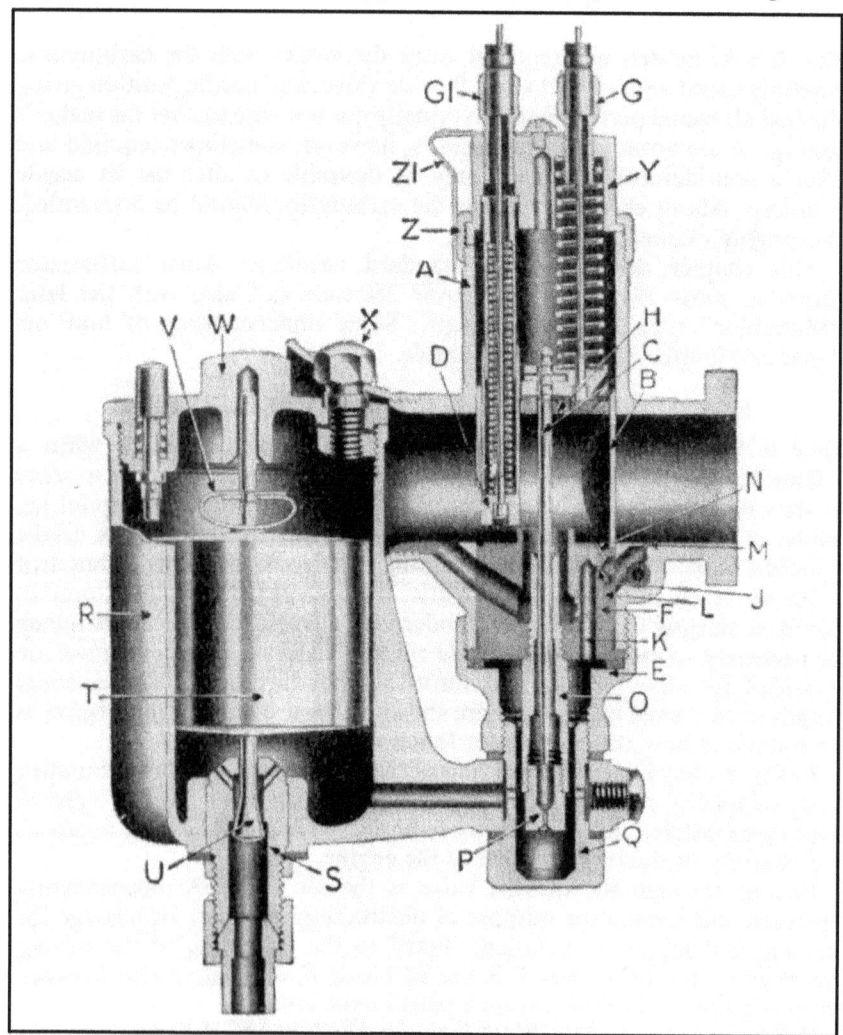

FIG. 8. SECTIONAL VIEW OF AMAL STANDARD NEEDLE-JET SEMI-AUTOMATIC CARBURETTOR (1945-55 "B" AND "M" MODELS)

On B.S.A. four-stroke models the adjusters shown at G, $G1$, are omitted, the cable adjustment being as shown at A in Fig. 4.

is removed. The float chamber, which has bottom feed, consists of a cup R supplied with petrol through union S. It has the float T and the needle valve U attached by the clip V. The float chamber cover W has a lock screw X for security.

The petrol tap having been turned on, petrol will flow past the needle valve U until the quantity of petrol in the chamber R is sufficient to raise the float T, when the needle valve U will prevent a further supply entering the float chamber until some in the chamber has already been used by the engine.

The float chamber having filled to its correct level, the fuel passes along the passages through the diagonal holes in the jet plug Q, when it will be in communication with the main jet P, and the pilot feed-hole K; the levels in the needle and pilot jets are the same as that maintained in the float chamber.

Imagine the throttle valve B very slightly open. As the piston descends, a partial vacuum is created in the carburettor, causing a rush of air through the pilot air-intake L and drawing fuel from the pilot jet J. The mixture of air and fuel is admitted to the engine through the pilot outlet M.

The quantity of mixture capable of being passed by the pilot outlet M is insufficient to run the engine. This mixture also carries excess of fuel. Consequently, before a combustible mixture is admitted, throttle valve B must be slightly raised, admitting a further supply of air from the main air-intake.

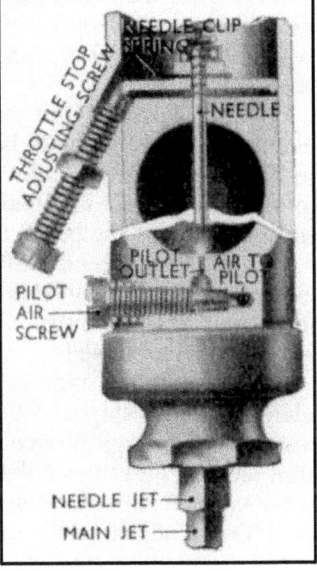

FIG. 9. THROTTLE STOP AND PILOT AIR SCREW

The further the throttle valve is opened, the less will be the depression on the outlet M, but, in turn, a higher depression will be created on the by-pass N, and the pilot mixture will flow from this passage as well as from the outlet M.

The mixture supplied by the pilot and by-pass system is supplemented at about one-eighth throttle by fuel from the main jet P, the throttle valve cut-away determining the mixture strength from here to one-quarter throttle. Proceeding up the throttle range, mixture control by the needle position occurs from one-quarter to three-quarters throttle, and from this point the main jet is the only regulation.

The air valve D, which is cable-operated on the two-lever carburettor, has the effect of obstructing the main through-way and, in consequence, increasing the depression on the main jet, enriching the mixture. Two cable adjusters A are provided on the handlebars (see Fig. 4).

"MONOBLOC" TYPE AMAL CARBURETTOR

Functioning of Instrument. The "Monobloc" type Amal carburettor differs from the standard type of instrument used on S.V. and O.H.V. singles prior to 1955 in several fairly important respects, but its general functioning is similar. The "Monobloc" design includes: a horizontal float chamber made integral with the carburettor body; a float needle of moulded nylon; a top petrol-feed; a needle jet with "bleed" holes giving two-way compensation; and a detachable pilot jet which can be easily cleaned.

Fig. 10 illustrates the essential parts of the instrument. The float chamber (13) and float needle (9) maintain a constant level of petrol in the needle jet (14) and the pilot jet (17). The selection by the makers of the appropriate jet sizes and main-bore choke ensures a proper atomizing and proportioning of the petrol and air sucked into the engine.

The air valve (3) is normally kept fully raised, and the throttle valve (24), controlled by the handlebar twist-grip, regulates the volume of mixture, and therefore the power. At all throttle openings a correct mixture is automatically obtained.

The "Monobloc" type carburettor, like the standard type instrument, operates in four stages. When opening the throttle from the fully closed position to one-eighth open (for tick-over) the mixture is supplied by the pilot jet (17), and the strength of the mixture is determined by the setting of the knurled pilot air-adjusting screw (20) which has a coil locking-spring to facilitate adjustment. As the throttle is opened slightly farther, the main jet system comes into action, the mixture being augmented by the main jet (16) through the pilot by-pass.

The amount of cut-away on the atmospheric side of the throttle valve regulates the petrol-to-air ratio between one-eighth and one-quarter throttle. The needle jet (14) and the jet needle (23) take over the mixture regulation between one-quarter and three-quarter throttle, and the mixture strength is determined by the relative position of the needle in the clip (4) attached to the throttle valve (24). When the throttle is opened beyond three-quarters, the mixture strength is determined only by the size of the

Key to Fig. 10

1. Mixing-chamber cap
2. Mixing-chamber cap ring
3. Air valve
4. Jet-needle clip
5. Jet block
6. Air passage to pilot jet
7. Tickler assembly
8. Banjo securing-bolt
9. Float needle
10. Float
11. Float-chamber cover screws
12. Float-chamber cover
13. Float chamber
14. Needle jet
15. Main-jet holder
16. Main jet
17. Pilot jet
18. Throttle-stop adjusting screw
19. Jet block locating-screw
20. Pilot air-adjusting screw
21. Mixing chamber
22. Fibre seal
23. Jet needle
24. Throttle valve
25. Throttle return-spring

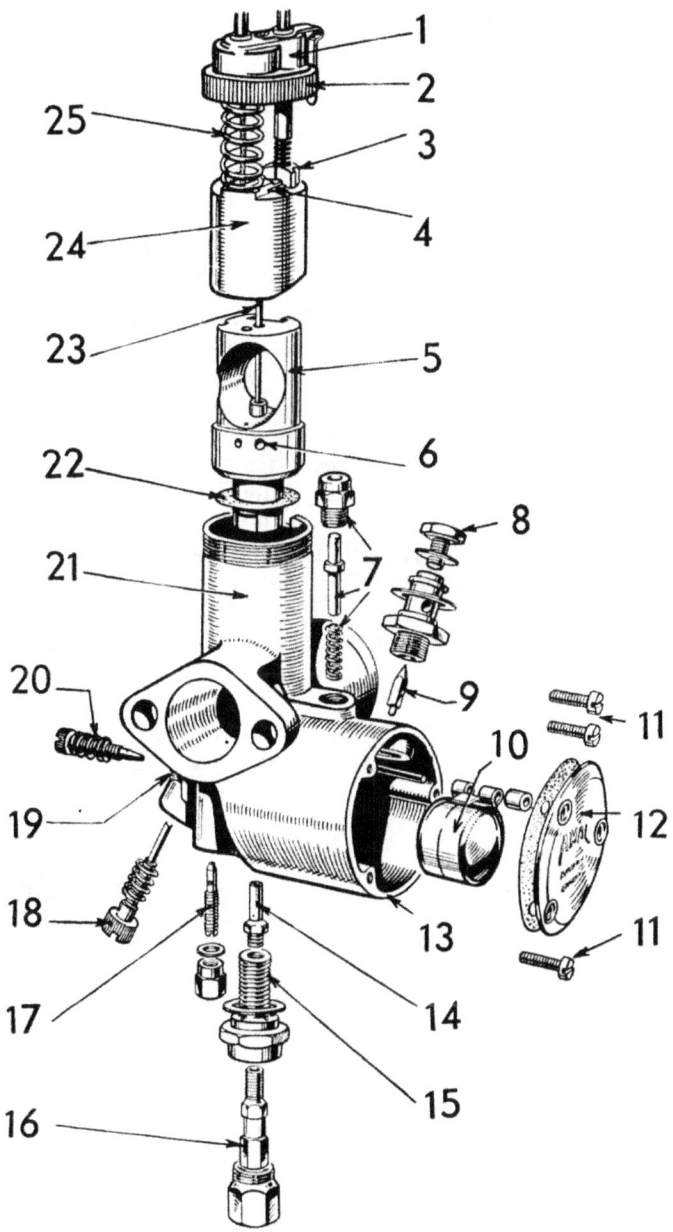

Fig. 10. Exploded View of Amal "Monobloc" Type Carburettor (1955 Onwards)

main jet. Note that the main jet (16) does not spray petrol direct into the carburettor mixing chamber, but discharges through the needle jet into the primary air chamber. From there it enters the main choke through the primary air choke. The latter has a two-way compensating action in conjunction with the "bleed" holes in the needle jet. Pilot and main jet behaviour are not affected by this two-way compensation which governs only acceleration at normal cruising speed.

TUNING THE CARBURETTOR (STANDARD AND "MONOBLOC" TYPE AMAL)

The same tuning instructions apply to the standard and "Monobloc" type instruments. Normally it is unwise to interfere with the maker's carburettor setting (*see* Tables I, II) unless there is a very special reason for doing so. However, it is sometimes desirable to make a slow-running adjustment with the pilot air-adjusting screw.

To obtain good slow-running, observe the following instructions—

To vary the strength of the normal running mixture, it is necessary to adjust the height of the needle in the throttle valve, or else to fit a larger or smaller size main jet. The condition of the sparking plug provides an excellent guide to the condition of the mixture.

Altering Slow-running Adjustment. This should be effected with the engine already warmed up, the throttle twist-grip closed and the throttle slide abutting the throttle-stop screw. The air lever should be fully open and the ignition lever (where automatic ignition-advance is not provided) should be set to obtain the best slow-running (half to two-thirds advanced).

TABLE I

AMAL (STANDARD) CARBURETTOR SETTINGS FOR 1945-54

B.S.A. Model	Main Jet Size	Throttle Valve	Needle Position	Needle Jet
C10 (1945–53)	90	4/4	2	0·105
C11 (1945–53)	80	4/4	3	Std.
B31 (1945–54)	150	6/4	3	Std.
B32 (1945–54)	150	6/4	3	Std.
B33 (1949–54)	200	29/4	3	Std.
B34 (1949–54)	200	29/4	3	Std.
M20 (1945–54)	170	6/4	2	Std.
M21 (1945–54)	160	6/4	2	Std.
M33 (1949–54)	200	29/4	3	Std.

Table II

AMAL ("MONOBLOC") CARBURETTOR SETTINGS FOR 1955-9

B.S.A. Model	Main Jet Size	Pilot Jet Size	Throttle Valve	Needle Position
B31, B32 (air filter)	200	30	376/3½	2
B31, B32 (no filter)	260	30	376/3½	2
B33, B34 (air filter)	210	25	376/3½	3
B33, B34 (no filter)	260	25	376/3½	3
M20 (1955 only)	240	30	376/3½	3
M21 (1955-7)	250	30	376/5	2
M33 (1955-8)	260	25	376/3½	3

Loosen the lock-nut (omitted on the "Monobloc" type carburettor) which secures the throttle-stop screw, and *screw in* the pilot-air adjusting screw until the mixture is excessively rich and the engine commences to run unevenly. Now weaken the mixture by *unscrewing* the pilot-air adjusting screw until the engine runs evenly. Avoid excessive weakening of the mixture which would probably cause the engine to spit back through the carburettor or even stop when the throttle is opened. With the pilot-air adjusting screw properly set, it may be found that the engine is running excessively fast. In this case unscrew the throttle-stop until the engine runs at an even and steady tick-over.

Where a considerable throttle-stop adjustment has to be made, further adjustment of the pilot-air adjusting screw may be required in order to obtain a perfect slow-running mixture. Avoid an excessively slow tick-over, as this is apt to induce low-temperature condensation on the cylinder walls and cause variable starting under variable atmospheric conditions.

It is important to avoid excessive richness of the slow-running mixture, especially if much riding is done on small throttle openings; if the mixture is too rich, considerable running on the pilot jet will occur *while riding*, with consequently a high fuel consumption.

Aim at obtaining the best tick-over on a mixture bordering on the weak side. The engine should be quite near the point of spitting-back. When perfect slow-running has been obtained, tighten the lock-nut (standard type carburettor) on the throttle-stop screw without disturbing the position of the screw.*

---

* Rev the engine up and down sharply several times and note whether the exhaust is nice and crisp, with no "flat spots" as the twist-grip is rotated. It is essential to obtain good acceleration as well as good tick-over. When making this test, the ignition lever (where fitted) must be *fully advanced*. Never run the engine fast with the ignition lever even slightly retarded.

Altering Jet-needle Position. The tapered jet needle secured by a clip to the throttle valve regulates the mixture between about *one-quarter and three-quarter full throttle.* The tapered jet needle and the needle jet gradually wear, through continuous movement of the throttle, and this slowly enriches the mixture within the throttle range just referred to, thereby increasing the petrol consumption. The remedy is to lower the tapered jet needle *one notch* by securing it in No. 2 position or, in the event of bad wear existing, in No. 1 position (top groove). If an excessively rich mixture persists after lowering the jet needle so that it is in the top notch, renew both the jet needle and the needle jet. The size of the main jet (below the needle jet) determines the mixture strength from *three-quarter to full throttle.*

Poor Slow-running. If it is found impossible to obtain good slow-running by making the pilot air adjustment as described on page 18, it is possible that there are air leaks, due to a poor joint at the carburettor attachment to the cylinder and/or a worn inlet-valve guide. Badly seating valves will also weaken the mixture. Defects in the ignition system may also be responsible for poor tick-over. The sparking plug may be oily, or the points set too close (*see* page 74). Possibly the spark is excessively advanced or the contact-breaker needs attention (*see* page 77). See that the H.T. pick-up brush on "Magdyno" models is bedding down and in good condition; also that the slip-ring is clean. Examine the H.T. cable for signs of shorting.

Obstructed Pilot-jet. If the pilot-jet adjustment does not obtain the desired results and the engine will not idle nicely with the throttle almost closed, the air lever wide open, and the ignition (if manual control is provided) half to two-thirds advanced, it is possible that the pilot jet is obstructed. The jet on the standard type carburettor is actually a duct drilled in the jet block, is very small, and can readily become choked.

To obtain access to the pilot jet on the standard type carburettor, remove the jet plug and float chamber (*see* Fig. 8), and detach the jet block by pushing or tapping it out of the carburettor body. The pilot jet can then be cleared by blowing. On the "Monobloc" type carburettor it is only necessary to remove the cover nut below the pilot jet (17) shown in Fig. 10, and unscrew the pilot jet.

HINTS ON MAINTENANCE (1945-59)

To Dismantle Standard Type Carburettor. Periodic cleaning is necessary to maintain efficient functioning of the instrument. It is best to disconnect the petrol pipe and then remove the carburettor from the face of the inlet port after unscrewing the carburettor-flange nuts. Referring to Fig. 8, unscrew the mixing-chamber cap lock-ring (*Z*), held by spring (*Z*1); detach the mixing-chamber cap (*Y*). Then pull out the air valve (*D*), omitted on

Models C10, C11, and the throttle valve (*B*), with the jet needle (*C*) attached. To inspect the two valves, or slides, and the jet needle, it is not *necessary* to detach the two slides from the control cables.

Should you desire to detach the air valve (*D*) from the control cable (*G*1), compress the spring and release the nipple from the base of the slide. To remove the throttle valve (*B*) from the control cable (*G*), compress the spring and permit the cable nipple to vacate the hole in which it seats. Then release the spring and allow the nipple to pass through the larger size hole.

In order to remove the taper jet needle (*C*) from the drum-shaped throttle slide, remove the spring clip which is located at the top of the slide. The normal position for the jet needle is given in Table II. Raising or lowering the needle enriches or weakens the mixture respectively.

Next take the float chamber (*R*) off the carburettor. Remove the jet plug (*Q*) from the union nut (*E*). Be careful not to lose either of the two fibre washers (one above and one below the float-chamber lug). Unscrew the lock-screw (*X*) and turn the float-chamber cap (*W*) until this can be removed from the float chamber. To remove the float itself, compress the spring clip (*V*) and withdraw the float (*T*) from the float chamber. On removing the float from the float chamber, the needle (*U*) will come away from the bottom. Take care not to mislay the two fibre washers (one above and one below the float-chamber lug union).

Now remove the needle jet (*O*), thereby exposing the main jet (*P*). Afterwards remove the main jet from the needle jet. Finally unscrew the mixing-chamber union nut *E* and detach the jet block *F*. Should this be stiff, tap it out gently, using a wooden stump inside the mixing chamber.

To Dismantle "Monobloc" Type Carburettor. Close the two-level petrol tap and disconnect the petrol pipe by undoing the banjo bolt (8) over the float chamber (*see* Fig. 10). Referring to Fig. 10, unscrew the mixing-chamber knurled cap-ring (2) on top of the carburettor and also remove the two nuts securing the carburettor flange to the face of the inlet port. Then remove the body of the carburettor (21), complete with the integral float chamber (13). While removing the carburettor, pull the air valve (3), and the throttle valve (24) from the mixing chamber and tie them up temporarily out of the way. As mentioned in the instructions for the standard type carburettor, it is rarely necessary to disconnect the slides from the cables. Check that the flange washer is sound.

Further dismantling is straightforward. Referring to Fig. 10, to remove the jet needle (23), withdraw the jet-needle clip (4) on top of the throttle valve, and remove the needle. To obtain access to the float (10), remove the three screws (11) securing the float-chamber cover (12). Lift out the hinged float (10) and withdraw the moulded-nylon needle (9). Lay both aside for cleaning. The float-chamber vent, by the way, is embodied in the tickler assembly (7), and the top-feed union houses a filter element of fine gauze which is readily accessible for cleaning.

To remove the main jet (16), remove the main-jet cover and unscrew

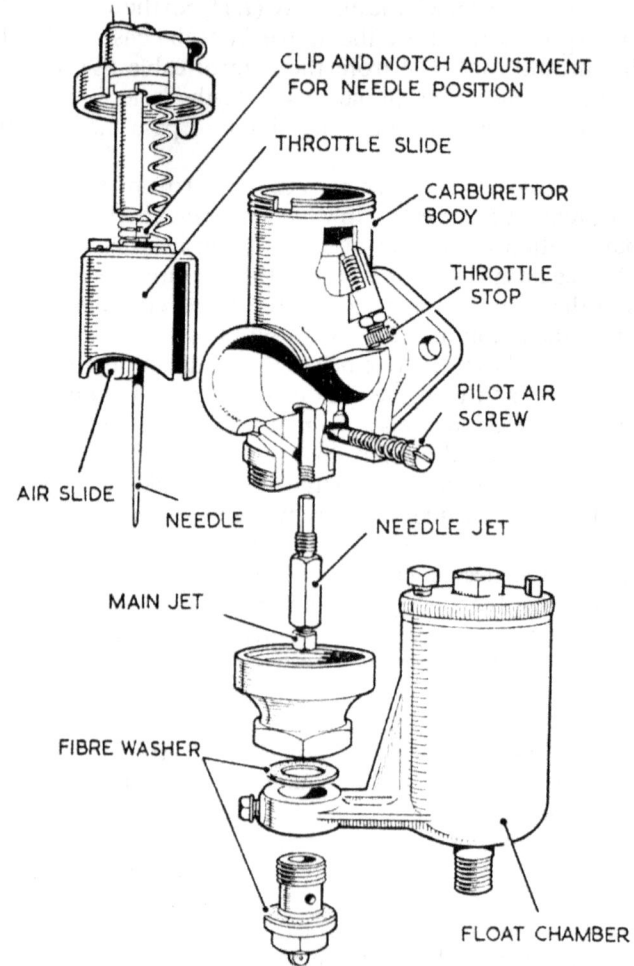

FIG. 11. VIEW OF AMAL STANDARD NEEDLE-JET CARBURETTOR PARTLY DISMANTLED

On the 250 Model C10, C11 the air slide is omitted.

the jet from the jet holder (15), which should also be unscrewed. Remove the jet-block locating screw (19) to the left of and slightly below the pilot air-adjusting screw. Then push or tap out the jet block (5) and fibre seal (22) through the large end of the mixing chamber (21). To remove the pilot jet (17), remove the pilot-jet cover nut and unscrew the jet.

ALL ABOUT CARBURATION 23

Cleaning the Carburettor. Wash all the carburettor components thoroughly clean with petrol and blow through the various ducts and passages to make sure that they are quite clear. Avoid using a fluffy rag for drying purposes. Pay special attention to the small pilot-jet passages in the jet block on both the standard and "Monobloc" type instruments. See that all impurities are removed from inside the float chamber. On the "Monobloc" type carburettor do not forget to clean the detachable pilot jet and the filter gauze inside the top-feed union for the float chamber.

Inspecting Components. When dismantling the carburettor it is advisable to make a close inspection of the various parts if the carburettor has been in continuous service for a considerable period.

1. THE FLOAT CHAMBER. Examine the components very carefully and check that the vent is unobstructed. The float must be in perfect condition. Clean the moulded-nylon needle on the "Monobloc" type carburettor very thoroughly, and be careful not to damage it. On a standard type carburettor hand-polish the valve part of the float needle by rotating the needle on its seat while pulling it vertically upwards. If a distinct shoulder is visible on the needle where it seats, renew the needle at once. Check for any sign of bending or distortion of the clip.

2. THE THROTTLE VALVE. Test this for fit in the mixing chamber. Should excessive play exist, renew the slide forthwith. See that the new slide has the correct amount of cut-away.

3. THE JET-NEEDLE CLIP. The spring clip securing the tapered needle to the throttle valve must grip the needle firmly, and free rotation must *not* occur, as this causes the needle groove to wear. Always be careful to replace the needle with the clip in the correct groove (*see* pages 18, 19).

4. THE JET BLOCK. Before tapping this home in the mixing chamber verify by blowing that the pilot-jet ducts are clear and that the jet-block fibre seal is in good condition.

5. THE CARBURETTOR FLANGE. Examine this for truth with a straight-edge. Distortion sometimes occurs, and this may cause an air leak. If the flange face is slightly concave, file and rub down the face with emery cloth until it is dead flat and smooth. Alternatively have it faced dead true on a grinder.

Assembling Standard Type Carburettor. Referring to Fig. 8 refit the jet block (F) with the fibre washer on its under side, and screw on lightly the mixing-chamber union nut (E). Screw in the needle jet (O) and the main jet (P). Open the air lever $\frac{7}{8}$ in. (omitted on 250 c.c. models) and the throttle twist-grip half way; grasp the air slide (where fitted) between the thumb and the finger and make sure that the jet needle enters the central hole in the adaptor body (H). Slightly turn the throttle slide until it enters the guide, when on pushing down the slides, the air valve should enter its guide. If not, slightly move the mixing-chamber cap (Y), when the air valve will slide into position. Screw home the mixing-chamber knurled cap-ring (Z). No force is necessary.

Replace the carburettor-flange washer, offer up the carburettor body to the cylinder head, and secure in position by tightening evenly the two nuts. Replace the float and needle in the float chamber, holding the needle against its seating with a pencil until the float (T) and needle clip (V) are slipped into position. See that the spring clip enters the needle groove. Then screw home the float-chamber cover securely and lock in position by tightening the lock-screw (X).

Insert the jet plug (Q) in the union nut (E) and very firmly tighten the union nut with a suitable spanner. Remove the jet plug and fit the float chamber and secure with the jet plug. Be sure there is a fibre washer above and below the float-chamber lug as shown in Fig. 8. When the float chamber has been correctly positioned, tighten the jet plug firmly. Finally reconnect the petrol pipe and tighten the union nut at the base of the float chamber. In the event of the pilot-jet adjustment having been disturbed, re-tune as described on page 19.

Assembling "Monobloc" Type Carburettor. Do this in the reverse order of dismantling. Referring to Fig. 10, screw home the pilot jet (17) and the pilot-jet cover nut, not omitting to replace its washer. Push or tap home the jet block (5) and fibre seal (22) through the large end of the mixing chamber (21). Check that the fibre-seal fitted to the stub of the jet block is in good condition. Then fit the jet-block locating-screw (19). Screw the main-jet holder (15) into the jet block, after checking that the washer for the holder is sound. Next screw the main jet (16) into the main-jet holder.

Replace the moulded-nylon needle (9) in the float chamber (13), and fit the hinged float (10) with the *narrow* side of the hinge uppermost. Afterwards fit the float-chamber cover (12) and secure by means of the three screws (11). Verify that the cover and body faces are undamaged and quite clean. Renew the washer.

If previously removed, attach the jet needle (23) to the throttle valve (24) and secure with the jet-needle clip (4), making sure that the clip enters the correct groove (*see* Table II on page 19).

Position the carburettor-flange washer, and offer up the carburettor to the face of the inlet port after easing the air (except on 250 c.c. models) and throttle valves (3) and (24) down into the mixing chamber (*see* previous hints concerning the standard type carburettor). When easing the throttle valve home, make sure that the tapered jet needle (23) really enters the hole in the jet block (5). Secure the carburettor flange firmly to the engine by means of the two nuts, and tighten these evenly. Tighten down firmly the mixing-chamber knurled cap-ring (2) and see that the throttle slide works freely when this is tightened down.

Finally reconnect the petrol pipe by tightening the banjo securing-bolt (8) over the float chamber (13).

The Vokes Air Filter (Rigid or Plunger-sprung Models). This is illustrated in Fig. 12. The filter assembly (*see* Fig. 12) is attached by an elbow (3)

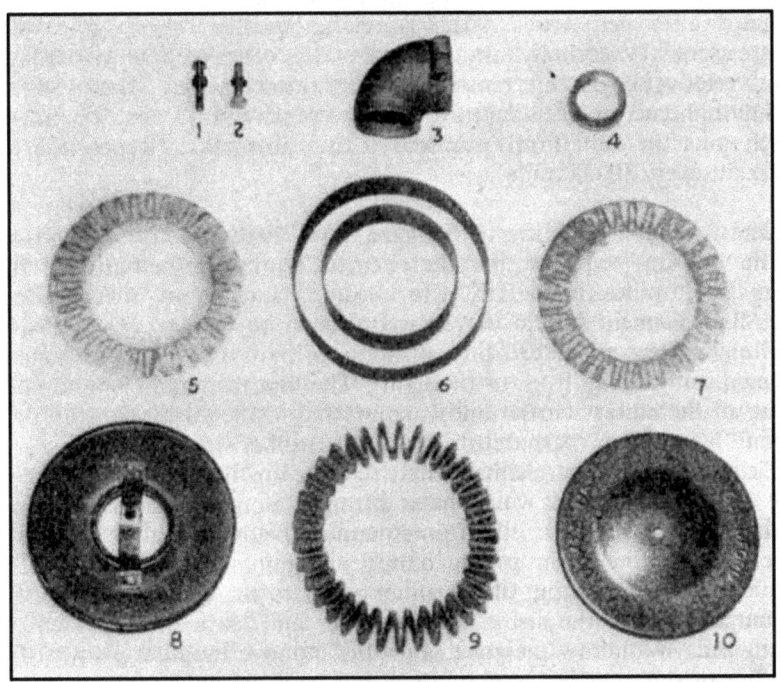

FIG. 12. VOKES AIR FILTER AND ATTACHMENT SHOWN DISMANTLED

1. Screw and washer holding filter assembly together
2. Pinch-bolt and washer for securing elbow (3) to adaptor (4)
3. Elbow connecting plate (8) and adaptor (4)
4. Adaptor for connecting elbow (3) to carburettor air-intake
5. Felt sealing-washer
6. Perforated sheet-metal rings for filter element (9)
7. Felt sealing-washer
8. Inner plate screwing on to elbow (3)
9. Three-ply filter element (fabric in middle)
10. Outer-plate secured to plate (8) by screw (1)

and adaptor (4) to the air-intake of the carburettor. At about every 5,000 miles, unscrew the complete filter assembly from the elbow. Having removed the filter assembly, remove the external centre screw and washer (1) and dismantle the filter as shown in Fig. 12 (items (5) to (10)).

The three-ply element (9) is of the "oil-dip" type, protected by two sheet-metal perforated rings (6). Wash the three-ply element thoroughly in petrol, allow to dry, and then submerge it in light, clean engine oil (grade, about SAE 20) for a few minutes. Allow the surplus oil to drain off for about fifteen minutes, and then re-assemble the three-ply element and protective rings between the two end-plates (8) and (10).

When assembling the filter, be very careful to locate the two felt sealing washers (5), (7) correctly. The ends of the three-ply element and protective rings should at no point overlap the felt washers (5), (7) on either their inner or outer peripheries. After assembling the filter, tighten the external centre screw (1) securely, and then screw the complete filter assembly on to the elbow (3). Do not remove the elbow unnecessarily. It must be kept firmly tightened to the adaptor (4) by the pinch-bolt (2), and the adaptor itself must be kept firmly screwed to the air-intake. Renew the filter element every 10,000 miles.

The C. & W. Air Filter ("Swinging Arm"Models). This filter is also of the "oil-dip" type and the filter element requires to be removed about every 5,000 miles (in the U.K.) for cleaning and dipping in suitable oil. The filter element should be renewed after a big mileage when cleaning no longer frees embedded dirt, or spots of light are visible through the element on holding it up to the light. The filter assembly is mounted in front of the battery carrier and is connected to the air-intake stub of the Amal "Monobloc" carburettor by a short rubber sleeve.

To remove the filter element, first free the air-filter cover by removing the two securing-bolts which pass through elongated slots; the lower bolt secures the cover to the frame member below the saddle; the other one attaches the cover to the battery clamping-strap. Disconnect the rubber sleeve connecting the air-filter cover to the air-intake stub of the carburettor; slip the sleeve off the cover and leave the other end undisturbed. Withdraw the cover and then remove the filter element from it after prising out the wire circlip with a screwdriver.

Wash the filter element very thoroughly in petrol, dry it, and then submerge it completely in thin oil (about SAE 20) for a few minutes. Remove the element, allow all surplus oil to drain off, and afterwards secure the element to the air-filter cover by means of the circlip. Then replace the cover on the machine, attaching it to the frame member below the saddle and to the battery strap by means of the two securing-screws. Finally reconnect the rubber sleeve to the filter cover.

CHAPTER III

CARE OF LIGHTING SYSTEM

LUCAS electric lighting equipment has been specified on all 1945 B.S.A. models onwards. This comprises, except on the 1945-53 250 c.c. Models C10, C11, and the 1958-9 Models B31, B33, a "Magdyno," headlamp, tail lamp, and a lead-acid battery. Models C10, C11 have coil ignition, a Lucas E3H dynamo being used. Coil ignition is also provided on the 1958-9 Models B31, B33, but here no dynamo is fitted; a Lucas alternator is housed in the oil-bath chain case.

The Lucas "Magdyno." This consists of a magneto and a 6-volt dynamo strapped together to form a single unit. The dynamo can if necessary be detached and the magneto half only used. In this case a protective cover (obtainable from the makers) must be fitted over the gears to exclude dirt. All 1945 and later "Magdynos" and dynamos have compensated-voltage-control fitted. With this arrangement the cut-out is mounted separately from the dynamo, only two brushes are fitted, and charging is entirely automatic (*see* page 29).

DYNAMO MAINTENANCE

When removing the metal cover-band, it is not necessary to disconnect the negative or positive* lead of the battery at the battery end, but always disconnect the battery lead when making any required adjustments to the wiring circuit. To disconnect, push back the rubber shield and unscrew the cable connector, being careful not to touch the frame with the cable and cause a short circuit. When reconnecting, make sure the rubber shield is pulled well over the connector. Disconnect at terminals (screw type).

If at any time the motor-cycle is ridden with the battery disconnected, or in any way out of service, it is possible to run with the switch in any position without causing damage to the electrical equipment.

The Commutator Brushes. Every 10,000 miles remove the dynamo cover (the metal cover-band) and inspect the brushgear and commutator. It is very important to make sure that the brushes move freely in their holders. This can be easily ascertained by holding back each retaining spring and gently pulling each flexible lead, when the brush should move without sluggishness. It should also return to its original position directly

---

* Positive lead on pre-1950 models with negative earth system.

the lead is released. When testing a brush in this way, release it gently and see that the spring is clear of the brush holder, otherwise the brush may get chipped. The brushes should be clean and "bed" over the whole surface; that is, the face in contact with the commutator should appear uniformly polished. Dirty or sticking brushes may be cleaned, after removal, with a cloth moistened with petrol. See that they are replaced in their original positions.

If the brushes become so badly worn that it is necessary to remove them, this can easily be done as follows: release the eyelet on the brush lead by unscrewing the hexagonal nut or screw at the terminal; then, holding

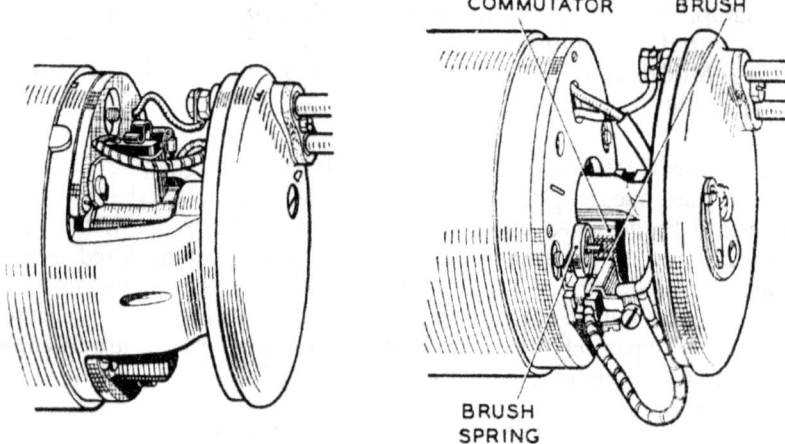

Fig. 13. Commutator End of Lucas E3L and E3H Dynamo or Dynamo Portion of the "Magdyno"

Some thin machine oil should be put in the lubricator (E3H dynamo) about every 2,000–3,000 miles. The driving-end bearing is packed with H.M.P. grease on assembly.

back the spring lever out of the way, withdraw the brush from its holder. Renew with genuine Lucas brushes.

The brush springs should be inspected occasionally to see that they have sufficient tension to keep the brushes firmly pressed against the commutator when the machine is running. It is particularly necessary to keep this in mind when the brushes have been in use a long time and are very much worn down. Owners are cautioned that it is unwise to insert brushes of a grade other than that supplied with the dynamo, or to change the tension springs. The arrangement provided has been made only after many years' experience, and will be found to give the best results and the longest life. When the brushes become so worn that they no longer "bed down" on the commutator, new brushes should be fitted by a Lucas service depot; this will ensure that the brushes are properly "bedded."

CARE OF THE LIGHTING SYSTEM

The Commutator must be Clean. The surface of the commutator segments should be kept clean and free from oil or brush dust, etc. Should any grease or oil work its way on to the commutator through over-lubrication, not only will it cause sparking but, in addition, carbon and copper dust will collect in the grooves between the commutator segments.

The best way to clean the commutator, without disconnecting any leads, is to remove from its box-holder one of the main brushes and, inserting a dry duster, hold it by means of a piece of wood against the commutator surface, at the same time causing the armature to be rotated. If very dirty, moisten the duster with petrol. If the commutator has been neglected for a long period, it may need cleaning with fine glasspaper, which is more difficult to do. The segments should be *dark bronze* and highly polished.

Lubrication of the Dynamo. *See* pages 28 and 57.

The Dynamo Terminals. On the "Magdyno" (Fig. 13) with separate voltage-control unit the positive dynamo terminal is marked "D" and the shunt-field terminal "F" on the cover. To connect up, first slacken the fixing screw on the terminal block and remove the clamping plate. Then withdraw the metal sleeve from each terminal. The cables should then be passed through the clamping plate holes and bared at the ends for $\frac{3}{8}$ in. Now fit the sleeves over the cables, bend back the wires over them and push the sleeves home into the terminals, finally screwing down the clamping plate. *Note: yellow sleeving goes to terminal "D."*

To Remove Dynamo ("Magdyno" Models). Loosen the "Magdyno" securing-strap and remove the small nut (on the off side) securing the dynamo to the top of the gear housing.

Compensated Voltage Control. This is used for all Lucas dynamos. Wiring diagrams: *see* pages 41-6. The control unit (Model MCR1) comprises the cut-out and voltage control (working on the trembler principle) neatly housed in a box on the rear mudguard, or in the tool box on "swinging arm" models. It keeps the battery properly charged automatically, the dynamo output varying according to the state of charge of the battery and the load.

With C.V.C. equipment the lighting switch is provided with only three positions—"Off," "L," and "H" (*see* page 36). In all three positions the dynamo gives a controlled output, thus relieving the rider of much responsibility. The regulator begins to operate when the dynamo voltage reaches about 7.3 volts. During daylight running when the battery is well charged the ammeter may indicate a charge of only 1 or 2 amp, for the dynamo gives only a trickle charge.

The regulator provides for an increase of dynamo output as soon as the lamps are switched on. The effect of switching the lamps on after a long run with the battery voltage high is often to cause a temporary discharge reading at the ammeter, but fairly soon the voltage falls and the regulator responds, thereby causing the output of the dynamo to balance the load of the lamps.

When the battery is in a discharged state, the regulator increases the dynamo output and restores the battery to its normal state of charge in the shortest possible time.

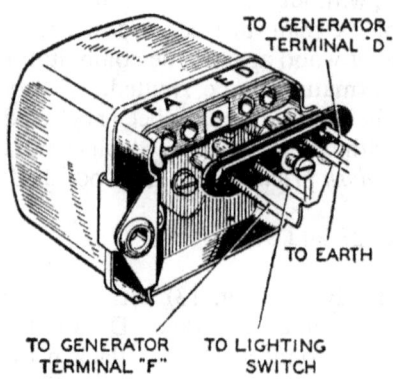

Fig. 14. Lucas Cut-out and Regulator Unit Connexions

Do Not Tamper with the C.V.C. Unit. The unit is sealed by the makers, and does not need adjustment once it is correctly set. The only conceivable trouble is from the contacts oxidizing or welding together, owing to accidental crossing of the dynamo field and positive leads. Be careful if making wiring alterations (*see* page 39). Referring to Fig. 14, make sure that the C.V.C. unit connexions are correct, tight, and that the insulation is sound.

Should you fit a "Lucas-Nife" battery in place of the lead-acid type, you must fit a new regulator to ensure a good charging rate with a discharged battery. You are advised to have the changeover made at a Lucas service depot and to visit a depot whenever any serious electrical fault develops.

Absence of Fuses. In order to simplify the system as far as possible, no fuse is provided. If all the connexions are kept clean and tight, there is no possibility of any excess current.

Ammeter. This gives a reading of the amount of current flowing into or from the battery and shows whether the equipment is functioning satisfactorily. It is of the centre-zero type and mounted as shown in Figs. 2-4.

THE ALTERNATOR AND RECTIFIER

The Lucas Alternator. On 1958-9 Models B31 and B33 there is no dynamo, a Lucas 60-watt alternator being fitted. As may be observed in Fig. 15, the stator of the alternator is mounted on three distance pillars projecting from the crankcase casting. The rotor is attached to the engine shaft, the engine-shaft shock-absorber hitherto fitted being omitted.

Because the alternator unit has no rotating windings, commutator, brushgear, or oil seals, no maintenance whatever is called for other than to see that the three snap-connectors in the output cables are tight and clean, and the leads unfrayed. If it should be necessary for any reason to remove the rotor, note that keepers need not be fitted to the rotor poles.

Fig 15. The Lucas Alternator Unit Housed Inside the Oil-bath Chain case on the 1958-9 350 c.c. and 500 c.c. O.H.V. Models B31, B33
(*By courtesy of "The Motor Cycle."*)

The Lucas Rectifier. Electrical connexion is made between the coils of the six-coil stator and a full-wave rectifier clamped above the tool compartment. The rectifier consists of four plates (coated on one side with silenium) and operates like a non-return valve, allowing current to pass in one direction only. The alternating current from the alternator is thus converted into uni-directional (d.c.) current for charging the battery. The only rectifier maintenance necessary is to keep the connexions tight and clean, and occasionally to check that the nut securing the rectifier unit is absolutely tight. The nut which clamps the rectifier plates together must under no circumstances be slackened.

Should it be necessary for any reason to disconnect the leads from the rectifier, they must be reconnected correctly as indicated in Fig. 16.

Fig. 16. The Lucas Rectifier Connexions

CARE OF THE BATTERY (LEAD-ACID TYPE)

It is of the utmost importance that the battery should receive regular attention to keep it in good condition.

The following are the most important maintenance hints for a Lucas battery—

1. Keep the electrolyte level with the tops of the separators.
2. Add only distilled water, never tap water.
3. Test the condition of the battery by taking occasional readings of the specific gravity of the acid with a hydrometer.
4. Never leave the battery in a badly discharged condition.

Battery Removal. Removal of the battery is desirable before topping-up its cells. On rigid-frame models and those provided with plunger-type rear

FIG. 17. BATTERY LOCATION ON "SWINGING ARM" MODELS

springing the battery is mounted on the near side of the machine; to remove the battery it is only necessary to unscrew and remove the battery clamping-screw, and pull aside the hinged metal strap.

On 1954 and later "swinging arm" models the battery is mounted beneath the dual seat (*see* Fig. 17). To remove the battery, first remove the two bolts from under the rear of the dual seat and withdraw the dual seat backwards from the forward locating bar. Then remove the two small bolts securing the battery strap, disconnect the battery terminals, and lift the battery out.

Topping-up the Cells. Examine the acid level about every four weeks, and even more frequently in tropical climates. Take off the battery lid; remove the vent plugs. Inspect the hole in each vent plug and make certain that it is not obstructed. A choked vent plug hole will result in an increase of pressure in the cell owing to "gassing," and this may cause trouble.

CARE OF THE LIGHTING SYSTEM 33

Wipe the top of the battery clean with a rag and also verify that the rubber washer often fitted beneath each vent plug, to prevent leakage, is in position. After wiping the top of the battery, either destroy the rag or wash it thoroughly, using several changes of water. See that a supply of clean distilled water is to hand.*

Be careful not to hold a naked light near the vents. If the level is below the tops of the separators, add *distilled* water as required to bring the level correct (*see* Fig. 18). This should be done just *before* a

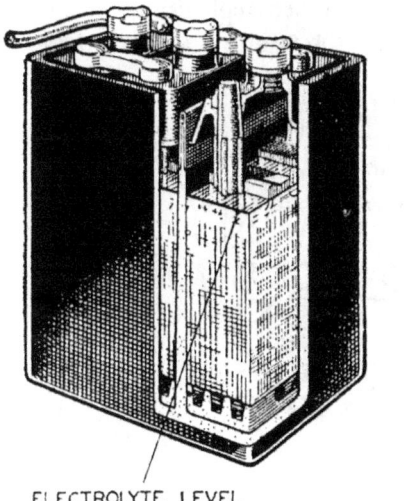 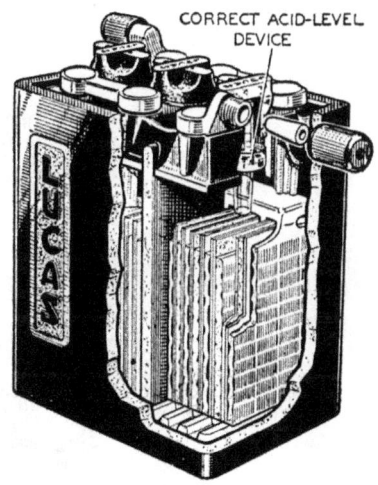

ELECTROLYTE LEVEL

FIG. 18 AND 18A. TWO TYPES OF LUCAS BATTERY FITTED TO B.S.A. MODELS

The battery shown on the left is fitted to 1945-53 models and differs from the battery on the right (fitted to most 1954-9 models) in that no acid-level device is used.

charge run, as the agitation due to running and the gassing will thoroughly mix the solution.

Where no acid-level device (*see* Fig. 18A) is provided, insert the nozzle of a Lucas battery filler into each cell as shown in Fig. 19 until the nozzle rests on the separators. Hold the filler in this position until air bubbles stop rising in the glass container. The cell is then topped-up to the correct level (shown in Fig. 18).

To top-up a Lucas battery of later type having an acid-level device, pour distilled water round its flange (not down the tube) until no more drains through into the cell. This occurs when the level of the electrolyte reaches the bottom of the central tube and prevents further escape of air displaced

* The distilled water, unlike the sulphuric acid, is lost gradually by evaporation. It is obtainable from garages and chemists.

by the topping-up water. Lift the tube slightly to permit the small quantity of water in the flange to drain into the cell; the level of the electrolyte will then be correct. Alternatively use the method just described.

Do not add acid to the electrolyte unless some of the solution has been accidentally spilled. In this case add diluted sulphuric acid of specific gravity equal to that in the cells. Finally replace the vent plugs, fit the battery, and strap it down securely. See that the battery leads are firmly and correctly reconnected.

Replenishing the Lucas Battery Filler. When replenishing the Lucas battery filler with distilled water, see that the screw-on nozzle is replaced

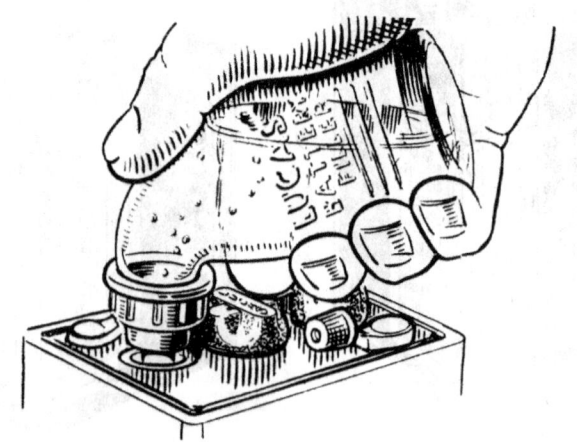

FIG. 19. TOPPING-UP A CELL WITH THE LUCAS BATTERY FILLER

correctly. Be sure that the rubber washer is fitted over the valve with the small peg in the centre of the valve engaging the hole in the projecting boss of the washer.

Checking Specific Gravity. Motor-cyclists seldom bother about this procedure, but checking the S.G. readings of the electrolyte is desirable by yourself or at a garage if some loss of acid is known to have occurred, or if the general condition of the battery is suspect. Fig. 20 shows the correct method of using a Lucas hydrometer to check the S.G. reading of the electrolyte in each cell. S.G. readings should not be taken immediately after topping-up the battery, as the electrolyte will not then be thoroughly mixed.

After a sample has been taken and checked, it must, of course, be returned to the cell. The taking of S.G. readings with a hydrometer is the most efficient way of ascertaining the state of charge of the battery. The S.G. readings should be approximately the *same for all three cells*. Should the reading for one cell differ substantially from the readings for the others, probably some acid has been spilled or has leaked from the cell concerned. There is also a possibility of a short-circuit between the battery plates. In the latter case it will be necessary to return the battery to a Lucas service depot for attention.

Under no circumstances must the battery be permitted to remain in a discharged condition for long, or serious deterioration will occur. A

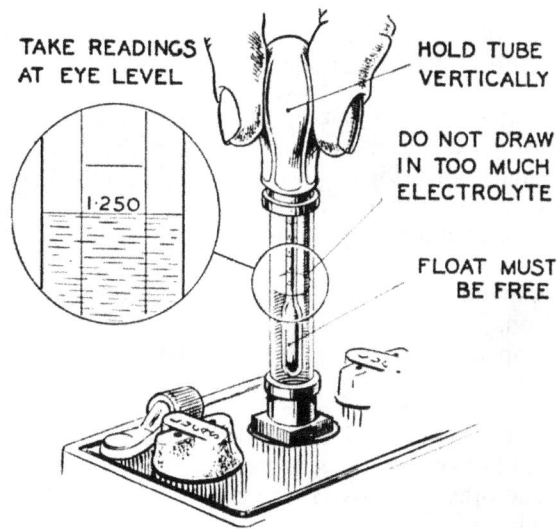

Fig. 20. Lucas Hydrometer being used to Check Specific Gravity of Battery Electrolyte

low state of charge is often caused through parking the machine for long periods with the lighting switch in the "L" position, unaccompanied by much daylight running. After checking the S.G. readings wipe the top of the battery and remove any spilled electrolyte; replace the three vent plugs and the battery lid.

Table III

SPECIFIC GRAVITY READINGS FOR LUCAS BATTERIES

Temperature	Fully Charged	Requires Charging
80° F 60° F	1·285 1·295	1·235 1·245

Battery Connexions. Always keep the battery connexions clean, free from corrosion, and tight; otherwise the ammeter readings will *not* indicate the true state of charge of the battery. To prevent corrosion they should be smeared with petroleum jelly.

Storage. If the equipment is laid by for several months, the battery must be given a small charge from a separate source of electrical energy about once a month, in order to prevent any permanent sulphation of the plates. In no circumstances must the electrolyte be removed from the battery and the plates allowed to dry, as certain chemical changes take place which result in permanent loss of capacity.

Lucas Lighting Switch Positions. Automatic-voltage-control is provided on all 1945 and later B.S.A. models, and therefore the dynamo or alternator charges the battery when the engine is running with the lighting switch in any of its three positions which are as follows—

Off: Headlamp, tail lamp, speedometer, and sidecar lamp (where fitted) switched off.

L: Headlamp pilot bulb, tail lamp, speedometer, and sidecar lamp (where fitted) on.

H: Headlamp main bulb, tail lamp, speedometer, and sidecar lamp (where fitted) on.

Adjusting the Headlamp Position. If the headlamp is incorrectly aligned and/or the main bulb is out of focus, maximum road illumination will not be obtained, and other road users may be inconvenienced by dazzle. It is easy to rectify both faults.

The best method of checking the alignment of the headlamp is to stand your B.S.A. facing a light-coloured wall at a distance of approximately 25-30 feet. Switch on the main driving light and note if the beam is projected straight ahead and parallel with the ground.

Take vertical measurements from the centre of the headlamp, and from the centre of the illuminated circle on the wall, to the ground. Both measurements should be equal. If they are unequal, loosen the two fixing bolts securing the headlamp in the front-fork mounting brackets (where fitted) and tilt the headlamp until the centre of the beam is truly parallel with the ground. Afterwards tighten the two headlamp fixing bolts firmly.

Correct Focusing. On all new B.S.A.s the double-filament main bulb is carefully focused to give the best illumination. Provided that Lucas bulbs of the correct wattage and number are fitted as replacements, subsequent re-focusing should not be necessary, unless the focusing adjustment has been disturbed. Some 1950-1 and all 1952-9 models have a Lucas headlamp with a main bulb which is permanently "pre-focused."

Narrowly converging and widely diverging beams are highly undesirable

CARE OF THE LIGHTING SYSTEM

as they illuminate the road poorly and are liable to dazzle other road users. Adjust the focus of the headlamp immediately if its *beam* is not uniform, is too wide, is of short range, or has a dark centre. To focus the headlamp (where a focusing adjustment is provided) it is necessary to remove the lamp front from the lamp body; then slacken the screw on the bulb holder clamping-clip as illustrated in Fig. 21. The bulb holder can then be moved backwards or forwards on the reflector axis until the headlamp is

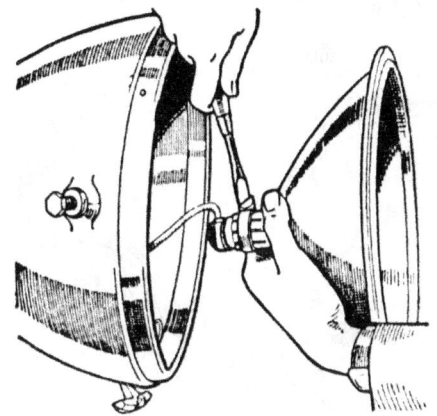

FIG. 21. SLACKENING THE BULB HOLDER CLAMPING-CLIP ON TYPICAL LUCAS FOCUSING-TYPE HEADLAMP
A focusing-type headlamp is fitted to most pre-1952 B.S.A. models.

focused correctly. Focus the headlamp against a light-coloured wall approximately 25–30 feet away from the headlamp. See that the bulb holder clamping-screw is firmly re-tightened after making a final adjustment. For correct bulb renewals, *see* page 39.

Cleaning Lucas Lamps. The reflector is most important. Never scratch its surface during handling, and avoid finger-marking the surface, readily done on earlier Lucas headlamps with detachable reflectors.

Never clean a reflector with metal polish. Lucas reflectors have a colourless and transparent protective covering. To clean any finger marks (except on Lucas light-units), polish the surface gently with a chamois leather or with a clean, *very soft* dry cloth such as a Selvyt.

Clean the black surfaces of the lamp body with a good car polish, and polish the chromium-plated rim with a chamois leather or a soft, dry cloth, after first washing off any dirt with water.

BULB RENEWAL

When fitting a new bulb to a Lucas headlamp, see that the new bulb is of Lucas manufacture. Lucas bulbs are specially designed for use with Lucas reflectors; another make of bulb may *not* always give the best results.

Focusing Type Headlamps. Where a double-filament main (focusing-type) bulb is concerned, it is important to make sure that the bulb is fitted with the dipped-beam filament *above* the centre filament, and it is sometimes desirable to check the focus of the headlamp (*see* page 36).

Non-focusing Type Headlamps. To obtain access to the bulbs on all 1952-9 headlamps of the sealed-unit type and provided with a "pre-focus" main bulb, remove the headlamp rim, complete with light unit assembly

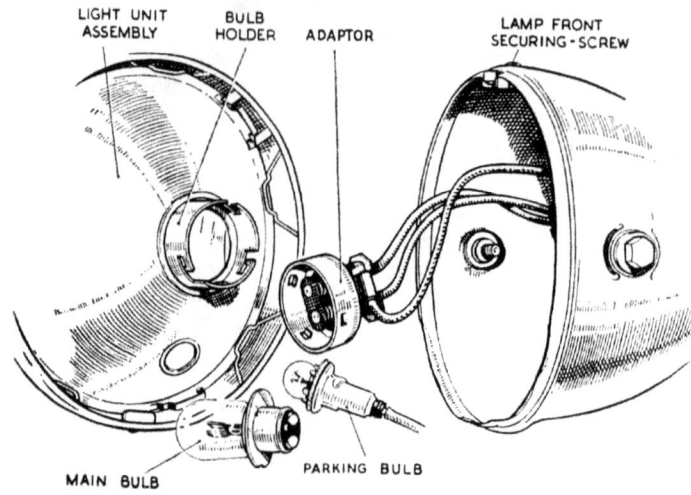

FIG. 21A. TYPICAL LUCAS HEADLAMP WITH LIGHT-UNIT ASSEMBLY AND "PRE-FOCUS" MAIN BULB

The reflector is sealed to the glass and, in the event of either being damaged, the complete unit must be renewed. An underslung (external) parking bulb is provided on 1952-4 headlamps.

(*see* Fig. 21A); to do this loosen the screw on top of the headlamp shell and pull the rim away at the top.

The Lucas "pre-focus" bulb (No. 312) has a broad locating flange; it can be fitted in the bulb holder in one position only, a notch on the flange engaging a projection inside the bulb holder. The adaptor which secures the "pre-focus" bulb comprises a bayonet-fitting cap, and this also can be fitted in one position only, its prongs not being symmetrical.

Referring to Fig. 21A, to replace a "pre-focus" main bulb, turn the adaptor *anti-clockwise*, pull it off, and remove the bulb from the holder in the rear of the reflector. Fit the new bulb in the holder, engage the projections on the inside of the adaptor with the slots in the bulb holder, press on the adaptor, and secure it by turning *clockwise*.

Where an underslung parking bulb is fitted (1952-4 headlamps) it is important to see that the metal carrier-plate for the bulb is pressed home

CARE OF THE LIGHTING SYSTEM

firmly. Twin pilot lamps (*see* Fig. 22) can readily be obtained and fitted by those who dislike the underslung type of parking bulb which gives rather poor illumination when using it for riding in built-up areas with normal street lighting.

Bulbs for 1945-7 Lamps. For the 1945-7 Lucas DU and D type headlamps, and the Lucas tail lamps, the correct bulb renewals are—

Main bulb: 6-volt, 24-watt, double-filament, Lucas No. 168.
Pilot (also instrument panel) bulb: 6-volt, 3-watt, Lucas No. 200.
Tail-lamp bulb: 6-volt, 6-watt, Lucas No. 205.

Bulbs for 1948-50 Lamps. For machines fitted with the Lucas MU42 headlamp (used on most 1948-50 magneto-ignition singles, and also on 1948-53 coil-ignition Models C10, C11), the correct bulb renewals are—

Main bulb: 6-volt, 24-watt, double-filament, Lucas No. 168.
Pilot bulb: 6-volt, 3-watt, Lucas No. 200.
Tail-lamp bulb: 6-volt, 6-watt, Lucas No. 205.

Bulbs for 1950-1 Lamps. For late 1950 "B" and "M" models, and all 1951 models (except C10, C11) with the Lucas SSU700P headlamp, the correct bulb renewals are as follows—

Main bulb: 6-volt, 30/30-watt, double-filament, Lucas No. 169.
Pilot bulb: 6-volt, 3-watt, Lucas No. 200.
Tail-lamp bulb: 6-volt, 6-watt, Lucas No. 205.

Bulbs for 1952-9 Lamps. For some 1950-1 models and all 1952-9 models (except "C" Series models) having the Lucas SSU700P/1, SS700P (1955-7), or later type headlamp (with "pre-focus" main bulb), the correct bulb renewals are as follows—

Main bulb: 6-volt, 30/24-watt, double-filament, Lucas No. 312.
Pilot bulb: 6-volt, 3-watt, Lucas No. 988.
Tail lamp bulb: 6-volt, 6-watt, Lucas No. 205.
Stop-tail lamp bulb (where fitted): 6-volt, 18/6-watt, Lucas No. 384.

If a "Britax" stop-tail lamp is fitted, a Lucas No. 205 bulb is suitable for the tail light. For a speedometer light fit a 6.5-volt, 0.3-amp bulb.

WIRING OF THE EQUIPMENT

Before making any alteration to the wiring, or removing the lighting switch from the back of the Lucas headlamp, disconnect the positive lead (negative lead with positive-earth system) at the battery to prevent the possibility of short circuits. For wiring see Figs. 23-29.

All cables to the headlamp are taken directly into the switch, which can be easily withdrawn from the lamp body when the fixing screws are removed (pre-1953 models without a cowl).

The various lighting cables are identified by means of coloured sleeves, or by colours on the harness. When making a connexion, proceed as follows: bare about $\frac{3}{8}$ in. of the cable, twist the wire strands together, and turn back about $\frac{1}{8}$ in., so as to form a small ball. Remove the grub-screw from the appropriate terminal and insert the wire so that the ball fits in the terminal post. Now replace and tighten the grub-screw; this will

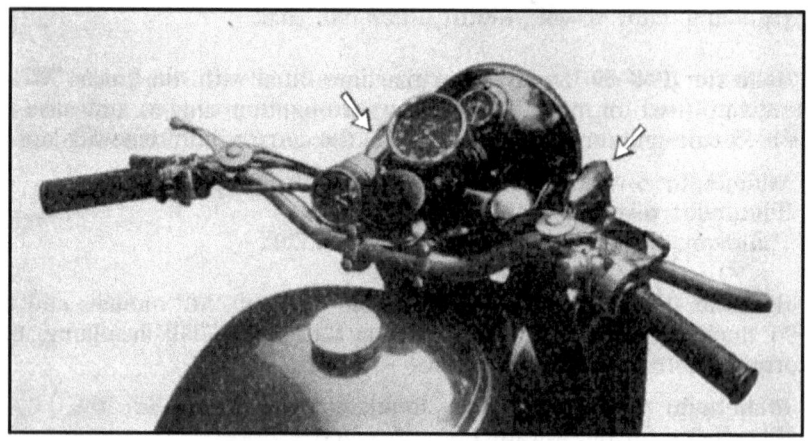

FIG. 22. TWIN PILOT LAMPS ON AUTHOR'S 1952 B.S.A.
If desired, Lucas or other proprietory dual lights can readily be fitted to replace an underslung pilot light.

compress the ball to make a good electrical connexion. See that the rubber sleeves are pulled well over the various connectors.

When removing Petrol Tank. On an earlier B.S.A. with an instrument panel it is not advisable to disconnect the wiring at the panel itself. Leave this end intact and disconnect the wires at the headlamp, dipper switch, horn, tail lamp, and compensated-voltage-control unit.

SLEEVE COLOURS, FIGS. 23 AND 25

1. Red	7. Red and black	20. White
2. Red and yellow	8. Yellow	22. White and brown
3. Red and blue	12. Yellow and purple	23. White and purple
4. Red and white	13. Yellow and black	28. Green and black
5. Red and green	14. Blue	33. Black
6. Red and brown	15. Blue and white	

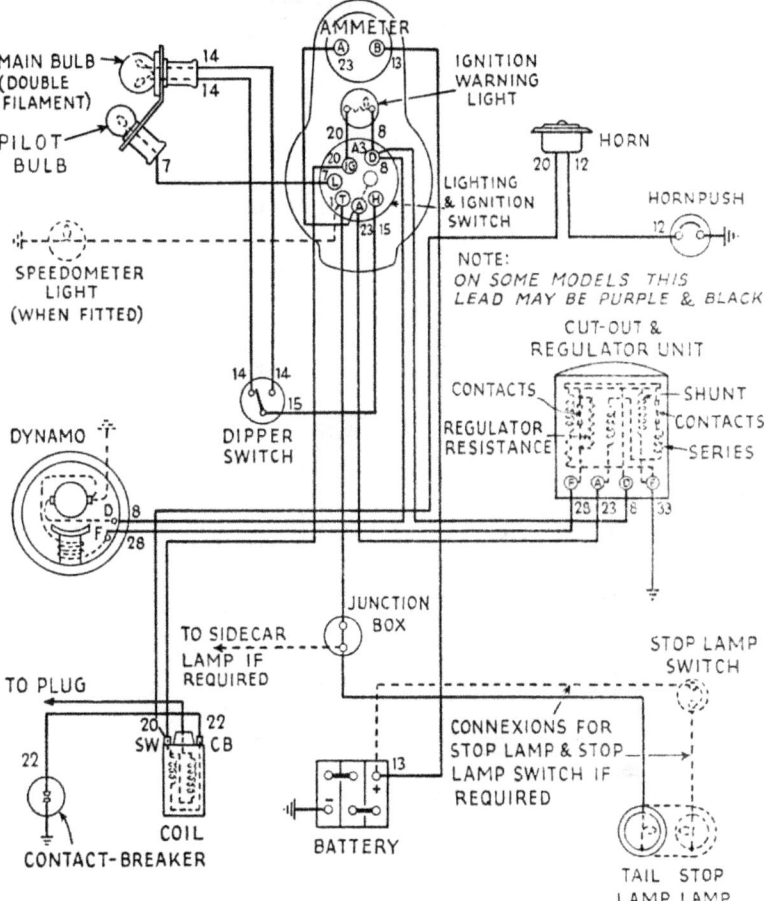

FIG. 23. WIRING DIAGRAM FOR LUCAS COIL IGNITION AND DYNAMO LIGHTING WITH COMPENSATED VOLTAGE CONTROL (1945-51)

This diagram with negative earth applied to 1937-50 and early 1951 C models (C10, C11). All internal connexions are shown dotted and the cables are identified by coloured sleeves.

(*See* Key on page 40.)

(*B.S.A. Motor Cycles, Ltd*)

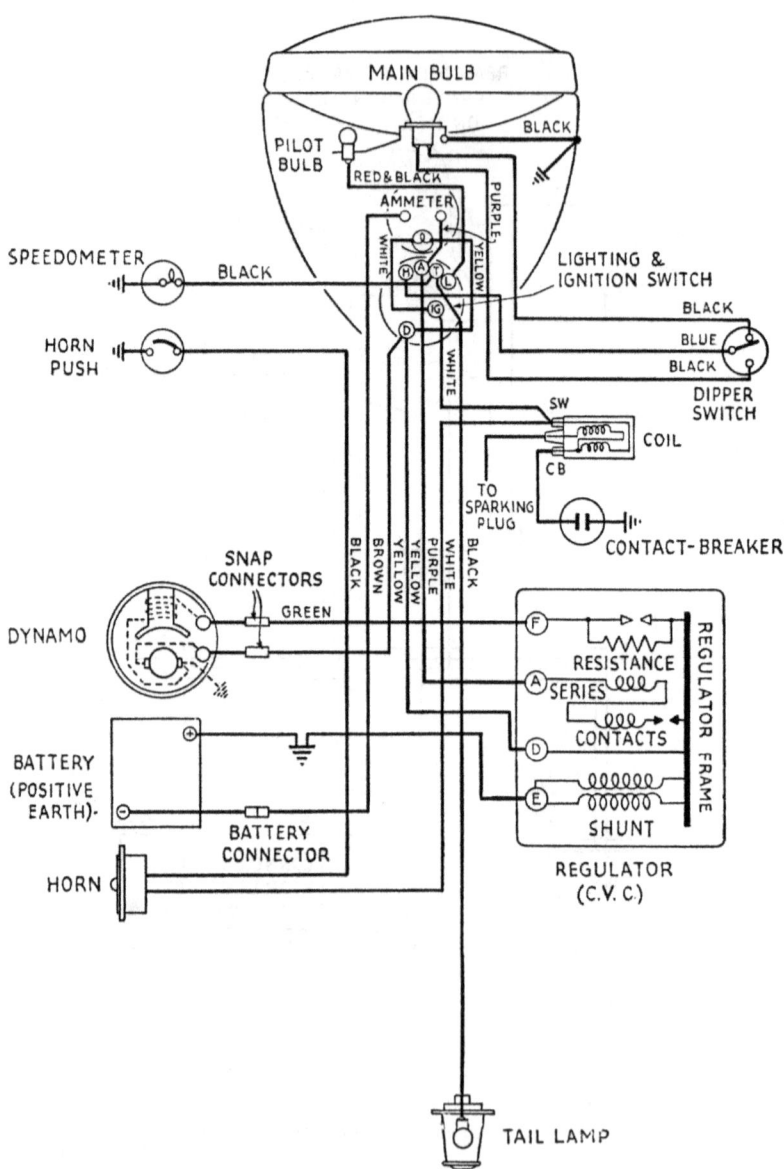

FIG. 24. WIRING DIAGRAM FOR LUCAS COIL IGNITION AND DYNAMO LIGHTING WITH COMPENSATED VOLTAGE CONTROL (LATE 1951 TO 1953)

This diagram with positive earth applies to late 1951 and all 1952-3 models C10, C11. A coloured cable harness is used in place of coloured sleeves for cable identification.

(*B.S.A. Motor Cycles, Ltd.*)

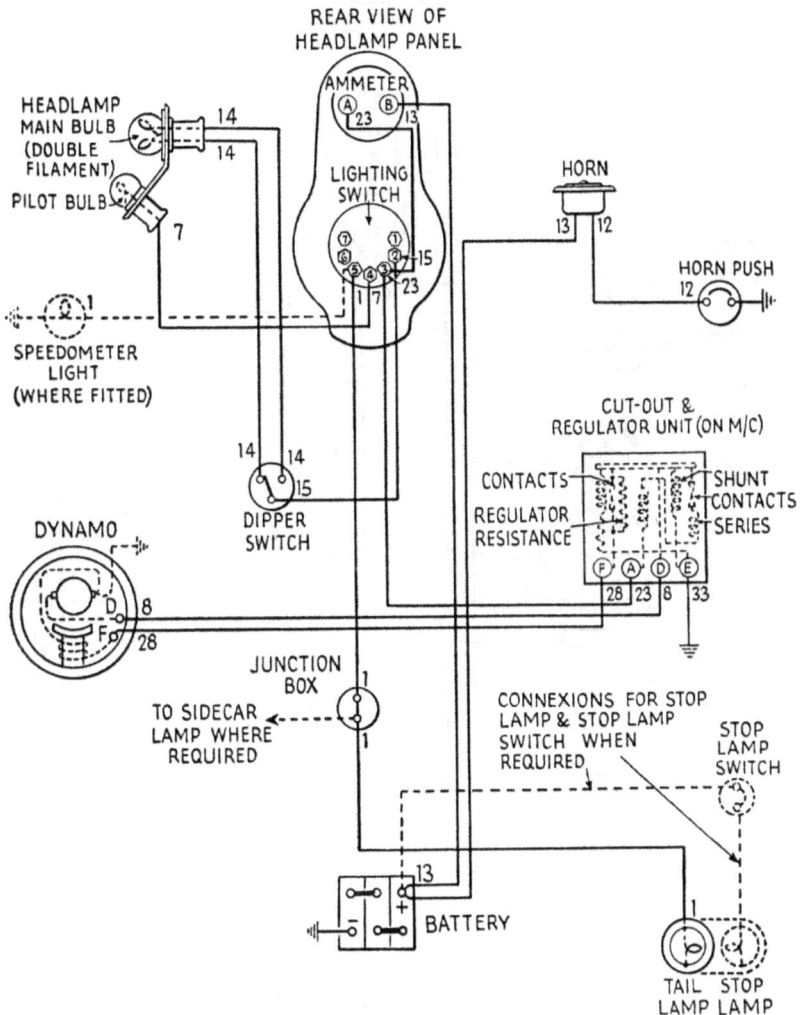

Fig. 25. Wiring Diagram for Lucas "Magdyno" Lighting Equipment, with Compensated Voltage Control (1945 to 1950)

Applies to all 1945-9 and early 1950 "B" and "M" models. All internal connexions are shown dotted and a negative earth is used. On late 1950 and subsequent "B" and "M" models a positive earth is used, and the appropriate diagrams are shown in Figs. 26-9. (The key to the sleeving colours is on page 40.)

(Joseph Lucas, Ltd.)

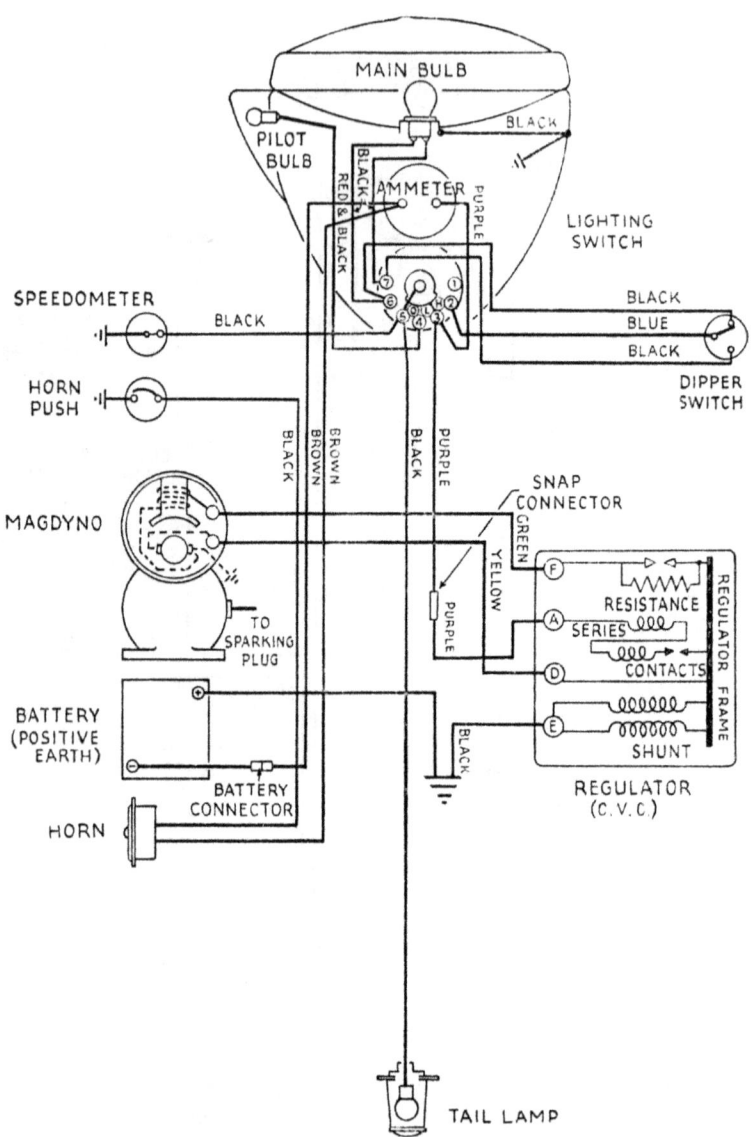

Fig. 26. Wiring Diagram for Lucas "Magdyno" Lighting Equipment with Compensated Voltage Control (Late 1950 to 1952)

The diagram applies to late 1950-52 "B" and "M" models with positive earth and SUU700P or SSU700P/1 headlamp.

(*B S.A. Motor Cycles, Ltd.*)

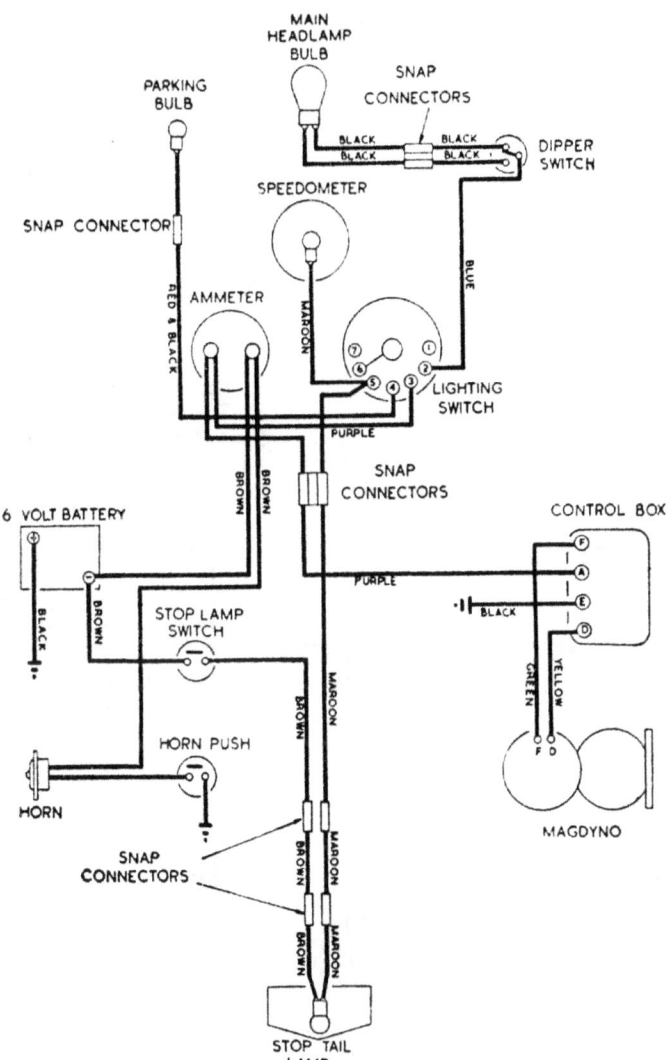

FIG. 27. WIRING DIAGRAM FOR LUCAS "MAGDYNO" LIGHTING EQUIPMENT WITH COMPENSATED VOLTAGE CONTROL (1955 "SWINGING ARM" MODELS)

This (positive earth) diagram applies to 1955 "B" models with SS700P headlamp and cowl embodying the ammeter, lighting switch, and speedometer. It also applies to 1955 models with plunger-type rear suspension, but in this instance the horn is connected to the negative terminal of the battery. The wiring diagram is also applicable to 1953-4 machines with cowled headlamps, but for the above-mentioned horn connexion modification and compensated-voltage-control (C.V.C.) unit terminals which are marked consecutively F.A.D.E. instead of F.A.E.D.

(B.S.A. Motor Cycles, Ltd.)

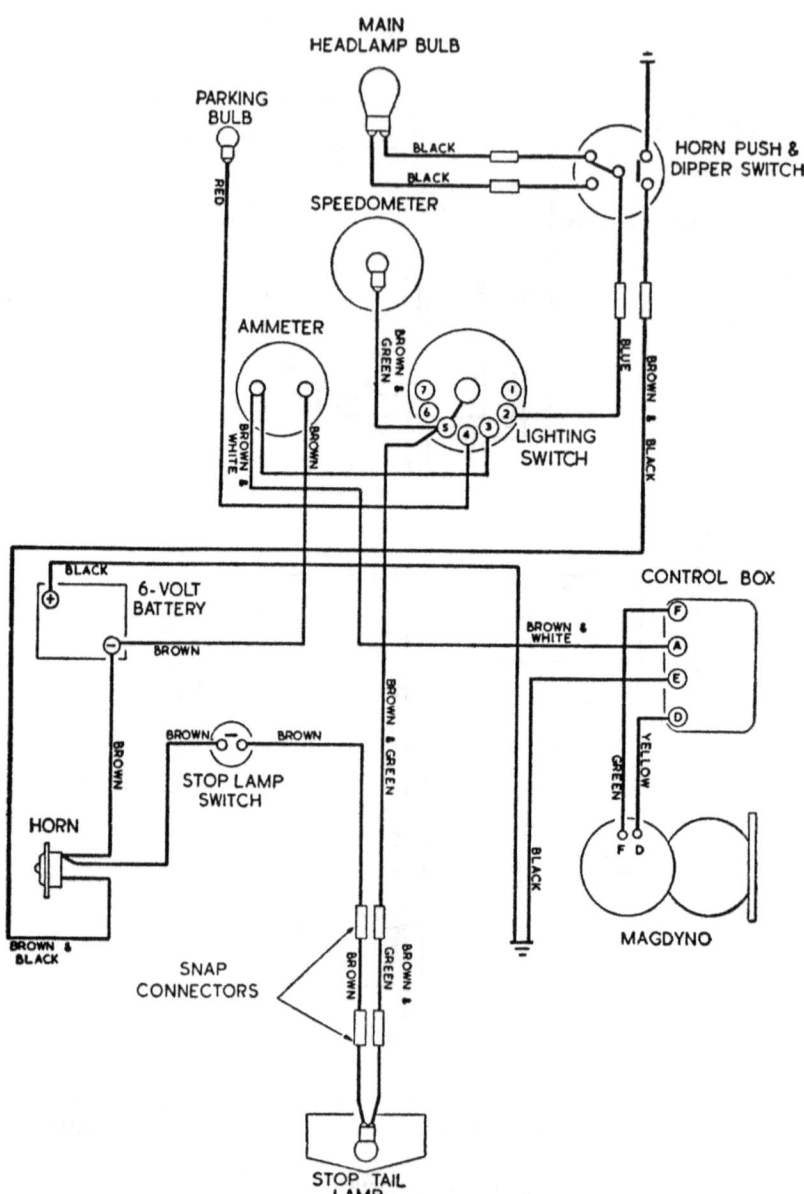

Fig. 28. Wiring Diagram for Lucas "Magdyno" Lighting Equipment with Compensated Voltage Control (1956-8, S.V., 1956-7 O.H.V. Models)

This (positive earth) diagram applies to machines with cowled SS700P headlamp and combined horn and dipper switch. Note that on the "swinging arm" O.H.V. models the horn lead is connected to the ammeter as shown in Fig. 27.

(B.S.A. Motor Cycles, Ltd.)

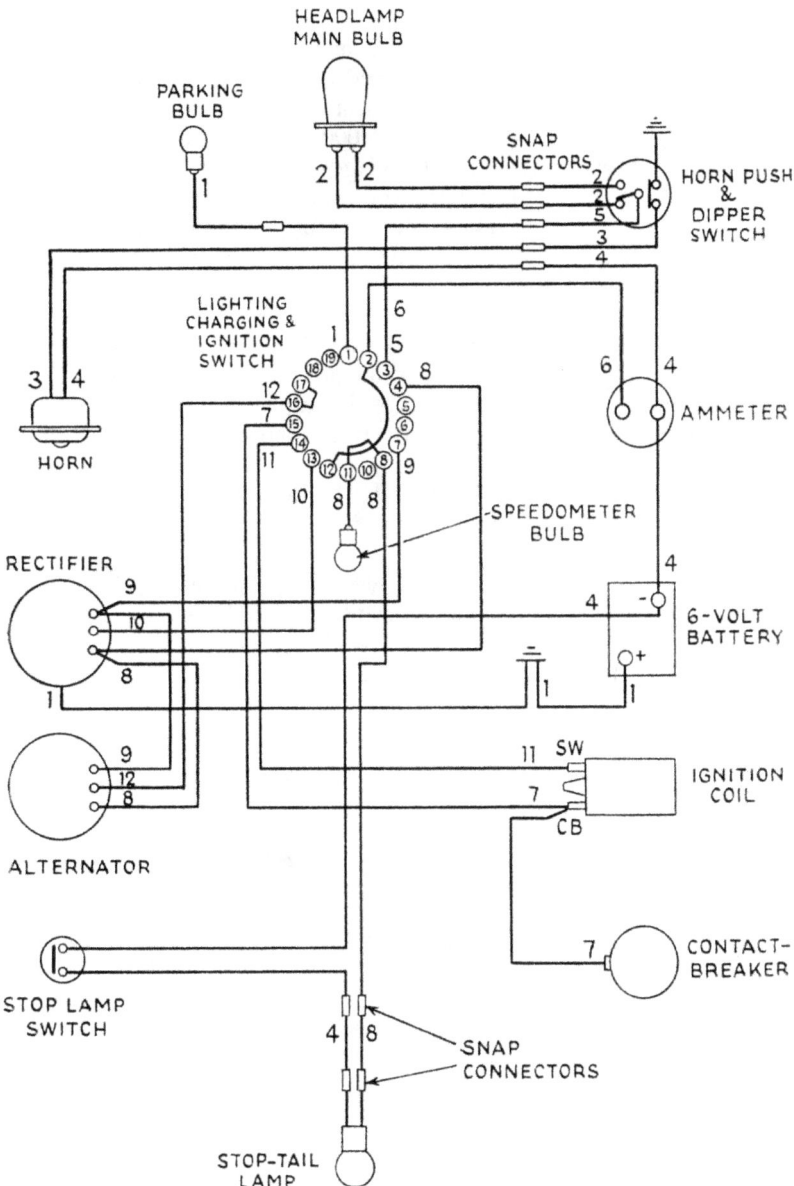

FIG. 29. WIRING DIAGRAM FOR LUCAS ALTERNATOR AND RECTIFIER EQUIPMENT

This (positive earth) diagram applies to all 1958-9 O.H.V. "swinging arm" models. There is, of course, no dynamo or C.V.C. unit. For key to sleeve colours, *see* page 48.
(B.S.A. Motor Cycles, Ltd.)

"**Factory Exchange" Units.** If the harness leads are kept properly clipped or taped to prevent chafing, and the leads are kept free from oil and grease, the wiring harness should last for years without attention. It is desirable, however, about every 15,000 miles (or during a complete overhaul) to remove a dynamo or "Magdyno" and submit it to a Lucas service depot for overhaul, lubrication, and an endurance test for condition. If its general condition has deteriorated, you can exchange the faulty unit for a factory-reconditioned unit. The same applies to the compensated-voltage-control unit.

The Electric Horn. Failure to function properly may be caused by a short-circuit in the wiring, a loose connexion, or a discharged battery. If none of these faults exists, try turning the adjuster screw (at the back of the horn) clockwise or anti-clockwise while depressing the horn button.

SLEEVE COLOURS, Fig. 29

1. Red	5. Blue	9. Dark green
2. Black	6. Brown and white	10. Purple
3. Black and brown	7. Black and white	11. White
4. Brown and blue	8. Brown and green	12. Green and yellow

CHAPTER IV

B.S.A. LUBRICATION

THE dry sump lubrication system provided on the 1945-59 250 c.c., 350 c.c., 500 c.c., 600 c.c. side-valve and overhead-valve single-cylinder engines is an improved form of the 1939 system. Instructions contained in this chapter are fully comprehensive for all machines having the improved and later D.S. system.

Five Points to Remember. Whatever B.S.A. model you have, there are five essential points to observe. They are—
1. A new engine must be run-in with great care.
2. Sufficient oil must be kept in circulation.
3. The oil must be of good quality.
4. The oil must be kept clean.
5. Oil dilution must not occur.

Running-in. General advice on running-in the engine during the first 1,000-1,500 miles is given on page 11, and the author would again emphasize the importance of these instructions. With regard to lubrication during the running-in period, the makers recommend the use of some upper-cylinder lubricant (*see* page 12), and it is important to keep the level of oil in the tank high and to change the oil regularly (*see* page 54).

Inspect Oil Level Every 300 Miles. The oil level in the tank of all 1945 and later models should be inspected regularly and the oil replenished if necessary. The tank holds $3\frac{1}{4}$-$5\frac{1}{2}$ pints. The level of oil in a tank should *never be allowed to fall below the oil level mark on the outside of the tank.* When replenishing, do not fill the tank more than about one inch below the top of the tank, otherwise oil will seep from the filler cap. It would also not be possible to observe properly the oil returning from the engine into the tank.

Suitable Engine Oils. To obtain maximum performance from your B.S.A. engine, with the minimum amount of wear, the manufacturers recommend the use of one of the following high-grade engine oils (not tabulated in any special order)—
1. Castrol Grand Prix (XL during winter).
2. Mobiloil D (A during winter).
3. Shell X 100-50 (X 100-30 during winter).

4. B.P. Energol SAE 50 (SAE 30 during winter).
5. Esso Extra 40/50 (29W/30 during winter).

DRY SUMP LUBRICATION

Models C10, C11, B31-B34, M20, M21, M33. With slight variations due to differences in valve gear and tank filters, the same lubrication system is used for all the single-cylinder models. As may be seen in Figs. 31, 32, the lubricating oil is circulated by a double gear-pump located in the bottom of the crankcase towards the off-side. Except for the supply and return pipes from the oil tank, all oilways are internal. On the B31-B34, M33 engines, however, there is also an external feed from the return pipe (*see* Figs. 30, 33) to the overhead rockers. On the C11, O.H.V. engine the rockers are lubricated by oil mist passing up the tunnel which encloses the push-rods.

Engine oil flows from the tank, after permeating its filter (excluding "M" engines), to the top pair of gears comprising the supply pump. It is then pumped past the pressure valve A along the hollow timing-side mainshaft to the big-end roller bearing, and also, on all except the 250 c.c. coil ignition O.H.V. engine, to the oilways feeding the cam spindles (*see* Fig. 31).

Having lubricated the big-end bearing and circulated throughout the engine, in the form of oil mist, the oil drains down through a filter in the base of the crankcase. From there it is scavenged by the lower pair of gears comprising the return pump, is passed through the ball valve C, and is delivered through the return pipe to the tank. On the M20, M21, M33, 500, 600 c.c. engines the returning oil passes through a star-shaped filter element in the oil tank. On all other engines the cylindrical gauze filter is on the supply side.

On M33, B31-B34 O.H.V. engines, some of the returning oil is by-passed up the oil feed pipe to the enclosed rockers and valves, the feed pipe being connected by three unions as shown in Figs. 30 and 33. Surplus oil is returned to the crankcase on 1945-57 engines through the rocker-box oil return pipe which is connected by a union to the base of the inlet valve spring housing. On 1958-9 engines surplus oil flows back through the vertical push-rod cover.

Checking the Oil Circulation. To check the oil circulation on all S.V. and O.H.V. engines, remove the filler cap from the oil tank with the engine ticking over. Then note whether oil issues steadily from the orifice of the oil return pipe. If it does not do so, investigate the reason immediately. Begin by checking the level of oil in the tank (*see* page 49).

Rectifying Lubrication Trouble. Leakage of oil at the filler cap sometimes occurs. This is generally due to excessive pressure inside the oil tank caused by an obstruction in the pressure-release pipe. The remedy is to insert a length of flexible wire right up the pipe so as to clear it. The wire should be introduced into the lower end close to the mudguard, except on 1954-9 "swinging arm" models. On these machines make sure that the short horizontal pipe on the oil-breather tower (*see* Fig. 33) below the dual seat is unobstructed.

Gradual draining of the oil in the tank to the crankcase is another

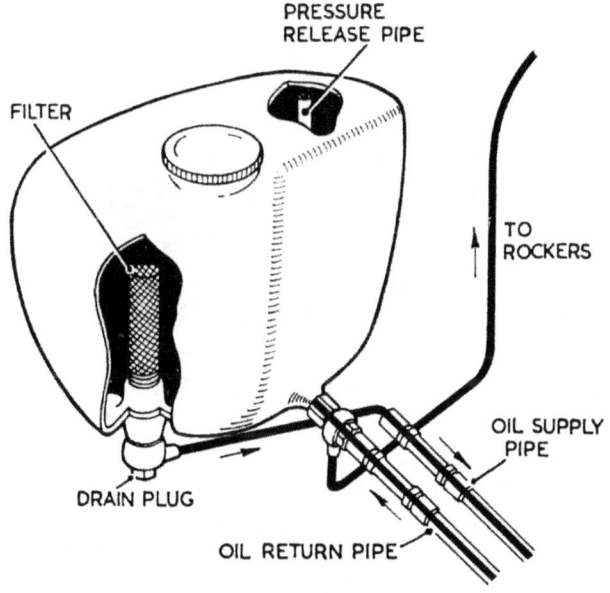

Fig. 30. Oil Tank and Associated Pipes on the 1945-53 O.H.V. B.S.A. Models, B31, B32, B33, B34

The arrangement is identical on the 250 c.c. models C10, C11, except that on both these two coil-ignition machines the oil-feed pipe to the rockers is omitted. All 1948-53 oil tanks have two drain plugs.

trouble which is occasionally met. It takes place with the engine not running and is caused through poor seating of the ball valve shown at A in Figs. 31, 32. To rectify the trouble, remove the plug over the valve, and detach both the ball and its spring. Clean the ball and its seating, replace the ball, deliver a sharp tap (with a hammer and copper drift) fit the spring, plug, and washer, and then test for oil leakage.

Yet another lubrication trouble is failure of the oil to return to the oil tank due to sticking of the ball valve shown in C in Figs. 31, 32. To restore the oil return, remove the cover plate from beneath the oil pump, insert some wire into the valve orifice, and free the valve by lifting the ball off its seating.

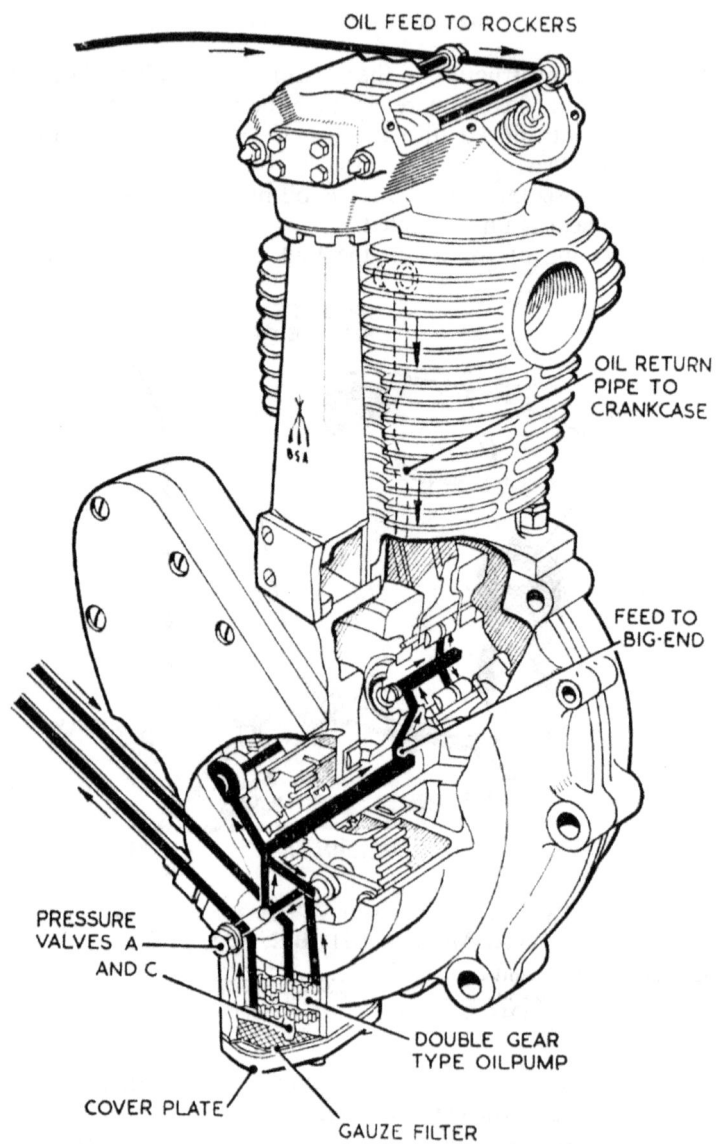

Fig. 31. How Oil Circulates in the 350 c.c., 500 c.c., O.H.V. B.S.A. Engine (Models B31, B32, B33, B34 and M33)

This diagram applies also to the 500, 600 c.c. S.V. models M20, M21, but these machines have, of course, no overhead rockers to be lubricated. The double-gear type pump is mounted independently of the gauze filter and should not be disturbed when the filter is removed for cleaning. On 1958-9 engines the oil return pipe to the crankcase is omitted, the surplus oil from the rocker-box draining down the push-rod cover tube.

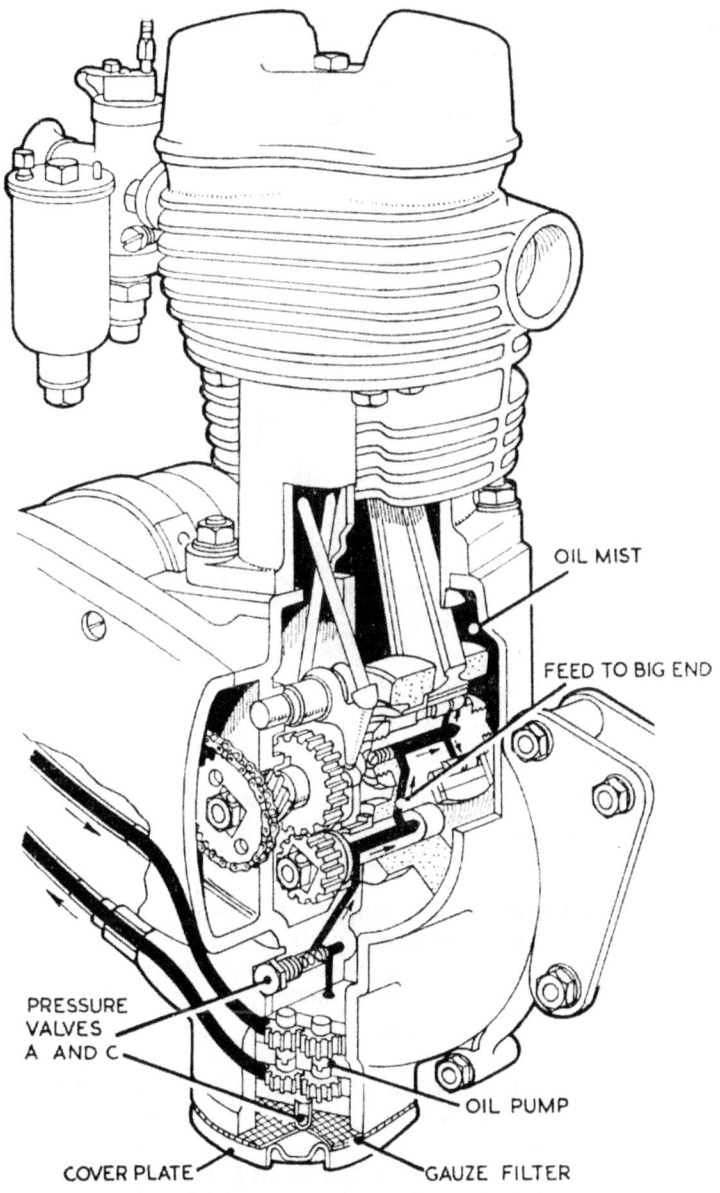

Fig. 32. Oil Circulation in the 240 c.c. O.H.V. Model C11 B.S.A. Engine

Oil circulation is identical in the S.V. Model C10 engine.

Oil Loss from Timing Case Breather. Check pressure valves *A* and *C* (*see* Fig. 31). If leakage *persists* past valve *A*, lightly grind-in a standard size ball on the seating, using a ball soldered to the end of a 3 in. nail or thin rod. Use only a trace of grinding paste and be sure *all* is afterwards removed. See that the breather diaphragm (a tiny fibre disc) is free and that its polished surface is *uppermost*. Test the breather with the mouth,

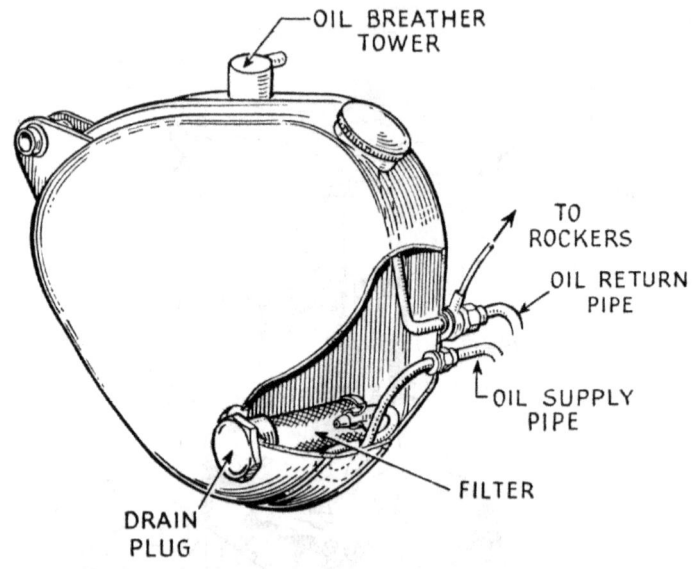

Fig. 33. The Oil Tank and Filter (1954-9 Swinging Arm Models)
Note the oil breather-tower on top of the 5½ pint tank, used instead of a long pressure-release pipe (*see* Fig. 30).

and adjust the thickness of the washer so that the hole near the top of the pipe faces towards the cover and slightly to the rear. Bad oil loss (experienced by the author) may be caused by oil flooding into the timing case because of worn or perished rubber oil-seals for the camwheel spindles. Renew these (and the spindle bushes also) if necessary.

Change the Oil and Drain the Crankcase Every 2,000 Miles. About every 2,000 miles, preferably with the engine warm after running, drain off the whole of the oil in the tank. To do this on 1945-7 O.H.V. engines it is necessary to remove the combined drain plug and vertical filter (*see* Fig. 30), but on 1948-53 O.H.V. engines and 1945-58 S.V. engines a separate drain plug is provided. On all 1954-9 "swinging arm" models remove the large chromium-plated drain plug to which the horizontal filter is attached (*see* Fig. 33). Then wash the tank out with suitable flushing oil or thin machine oil. Do not employ petrol or paraffin for the purpose. Remove the filter in the oil tank for thorough cleaning; also drain the crankcase and clean the pump filter. Having cleaned the tank and both filters, replenish the oil tank with the correct grade and brand of engine oil (*see* page 49). On new machines the oil tank should be drained after the first 250 miles and again at 1,000 miles. Thereafter draining every 2,000 miles is sufficient.

Before draining the oil tank place a fairly large funnel beneath the drain plug and allow the oil to drain off into a receptacle large enough to hold

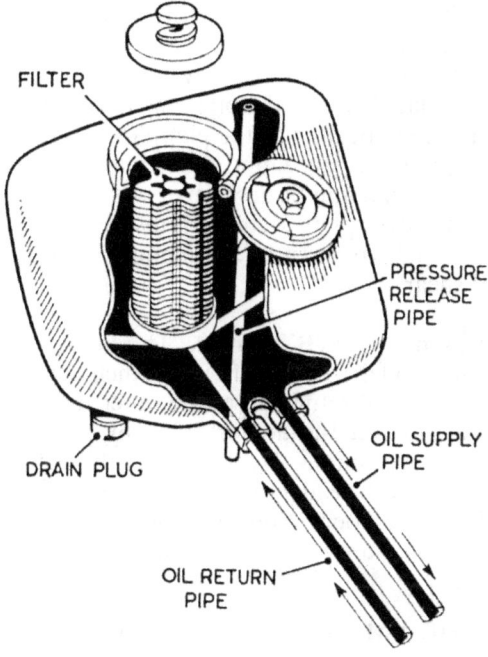

FIG. 34. DETAILS OF THE B.S.A. OIL TANK ON 1945-58 S.V., O.H.V. MODELS M20, M21, M33

On these engines the star-shaped filter element is on the return side of the lubrication system instead of the delivery side as on the "B" and "C" models. (*See* Fig. 30.)

about half a gallon. When replacing the drain plug, be sure to replace the fibre washer.

Cleaning the Tank and Pump Filters. Both filters should be thoroughly washed in petrol or paraffin and dried properly before replacement. No attempt should be made to remove the oil pump itself, unless this is essential for some particular reason. When cleaning the oil tank filter, place the filter in a receptacle of sufficient size to enable it to be completely submerged and never use a rag on it, in case fluff gets caught in the mesh.

To remove the filter from the oil tank on S.V., O.H.V. models M20, M21, M33, release the tank filler-cap and the spring-loaded cap is thereby exposed. The star-shaped filter (Fig. 34) can then be lifted out for cleaning.

To remove the oil tank filter on S.V. and O.H.V. models C10, C11, B31–B34, remove the oil pipe banjo-union plug at the base of the oil tank and withdraw the cylindrical filter attached to the plug. This should be done after draining the oil tank, where a separate drain plug is provided. Be very careful not to bend the gauze when withdrawing the filter and plug unit. First disconnect the speedometer drive from the gearbox by removing the union nut. On 1945-53 B31–B34 O.H.V. engines it is desirable to remove the tool box also.

To remove the pump filter it is only necessary to remove the nuts securing the cover plate beneath the oil pump and withdraw the flat gauze filter for cleaning. Do not disturb the pump (held by two bolts).

When replacing the flat gauze, and cover plate, see that the sump and plate faces are quite clean and fit new paper washers above and below the gauze. Tighten the cover-plate securing nuts evenly and firmly to ensure an oil-tight joint. Tighten again after running. *Avoid excessive leverage*, or the studs will shear.

To Remove the Oil Tank ("B" Series). To remove the oil tank (except on "swinging arm" models), first drain it and then unscrew the union nuts from both ends of the oil-return pipe (the outer main pipe) and remove the pipe. Also disconnect the delivery pipe by removing the filter and plug securing the banjo-union. Next take off the battery (being careful to cover the ends of both leads) and remove the four bolts securing the oil tank to the battery carrier. You can now withdraw the tank from the off side, pulling the pressure-release pipe away from its socket on the near side of the machine.

THE "MAGDYNO," DYNAMO, ETC.

"Magdyno" Lubrication. Every Lucas "Magdyno" during assembly has the bearings and gear-wheels packed with grease, and for this reason no lubricators are provided on the instrument. After many thousands of miles' running, when a general overhaul is required, the "Magdyno" should be returned to a Lucas service depot (*see* page 48) for dismantling, cleaning, and repacking with grease.

The ignition portion has a face-cam type contact-breaker (Fig. 44) and the cam is lubricated by a wick in the base of the contact-breaker. A few drops of thin machine oil should be added every 3,000-4,000 miles. By removing the spring arm carrying the moving contact the small wick-screw can be unscrewed and withdrawn. At the same time remove the contact-breaker securing screw and contact-breaker; withdraw the tappet operating the spring arm, and lightly smear it with a little *thin* machine oil. Replace the tappet, contact-breaker, and also the wick-screw. When replacing the spring arm, see that the small backing spring is located correctly on the *outside* of the spring arm, with the curved portion facing *outwards*. Replace the spring washer and securing screw, and tighten the latter securely. On certain earlier "Magdynos" a lubricator is provided on the commutator driving-end bracket (*see* Fig. 13) of the E3HM dynamo, and a few drops of *thin* oil should be added every 2,000-3,000 miles.

Oil Leakage from the "Magdyno" Drive. To cure oil leakage from the "Magdyno" drive on 1945-57 "B" and "M" models, slacken the strap and pull the instrument towards the nearside. This ensures the maintenance of a perfect oil seal between the rubber washer and the "Magdyno" pinion. Hold the instrument in this position and re-tighten the securing strap bolt firmly.

Dynamo Lubrication (Coil Ignition Models). The armature ball bearings of the Lucas type dynamo fitted on the coil-ignition Models C10, C11 are packed with grease on assembly, and this should suffice until your B.S.A. is stripped down for a general overhaul, when the dynamo should be taken or sent to a Lucas service depot for dismantling, cleaning, adjustment, and re-greasing (H.M.P. grease is required for the bearings).

Where a lubricator is provided (E3H dynamo) on the commutator driving-end bracket (*see* Fig. 13), inject a few drops of *thin* oil every 2,000-3,000 miles. Smear lightly with a little grease the surface of the steel cam (*see* Fig. 35) of the contact-breaker (*see* page 81) about every 3,000 miles. If grease is not available, use a little engine oil, but be most careful not to allow any lubricant to get on to the contacts, which would cause burning and pitting. Every 3,000 miles lift the contact-breaker lever off its pivot (*see* page 79) and smear the pivot with a small quantity of grease or engine oil.

Automatic Ignition Advance. This is provided instead of manual control on the coil ignition Models C10, C11, the centrifugal type mechanism being located beneath the contact-breaker. About every 3,000 miles remove the cover from the contact-breaker, and then add a few drops of clean engine oil (*see* page 49) into (Fig. 35) the hole in the contact-breaker base through which the cam shaft passes. Be very careful not to allow any oil to get on the contacts.

To obtain access to the automatic-advance mechanism, remove both screws shown at *A* in Fig. 46 and withdraw the contact-breaker unit. Unless some trouble is experienced, it should not be necessary to expose the automatic ignition-advance mechanism.

About every 3,000 miles remove the lubricator (*see* Fig. 35) provided for lubricating the cam shaft, and add to it a few drops of *thin* machine oil.

Lubrication of the Dynamo Chain. This is completely enclosed (Models C10, C11) in the engine chain-case and automatically lubricated from the timing case. On the "Magdyno" models the gears driving the dynamo armature are similarly enclosed and automatically lubricated.

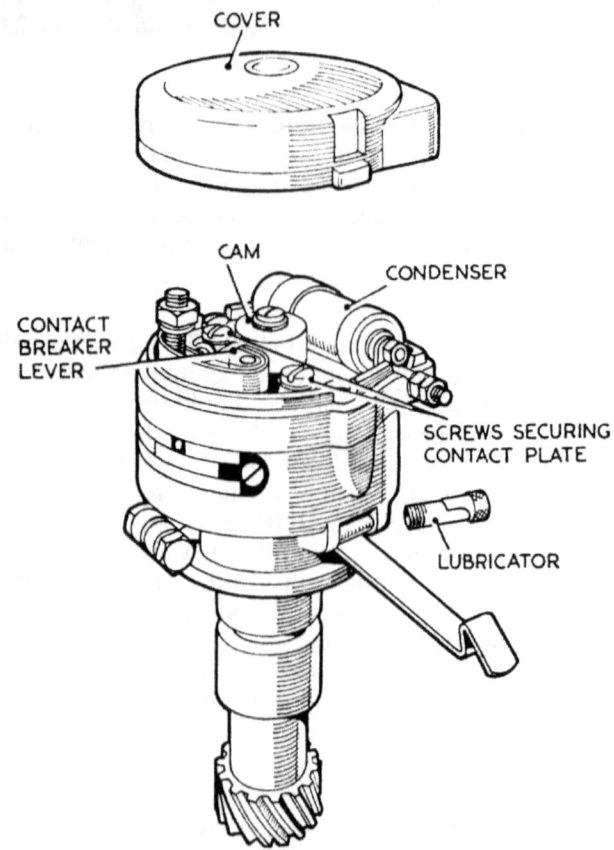

FIG. 35. LUCAS CONTACT-BREAKER ON COIL IGNITION MODELS C10 AND C11

Note the lubricator for the shaft. A plan view of the contact-breaker is shown in Fig. 46.

Air Filters (Oil-dip Type). Appropriate instructions for dealing with the Vokes or C. & W. oil-dip type air filters fitted to the air-intakes of the carburettors on many 1945-59 models are given on pages 25-6.

THE MOTOR-CYCLE PARTS

Although engine lubrication is obviously of major importance, correct lubrication of motor-cycle parts should not be neglected, otherwise waste of power and undue wear and tear of the transmission and machine will be caused. A lubrication chart for side-valve and overhead-valve models is shown in Fig. 36.

Suitable Greases. Grease nipples are provided for motor-cycle parts which need regular greasing, and a Tecalemit grease-gun for grease injection is included in the tool kit. Certain parts require to be lubricated with engine oil (*see* page 49) and oil caps or oil holes with protective spring covers are fitted for this purpose. Always use a high quality grease. Suitable greases, recommended by B.S.A. Motor Cycles, Ltd., are as follows—
1. Mobilgrease MP.
2. Shell Retinax A or CD.
3. Castrolease Heavy.
4. Esso High Temperature Grease.
5. B.P. Energrease C3.

Grease containers designed for quick filling of the grease-gun are available and obviate the messy job of filling the gun by hand. For winter use, Castrolease Medium is suitable as an alternative to Castrolease Heavy (except for the wheel hubs), and the author finds it can often be more readily injected. After a long run in very rainy weather it is a good plan to apply the grease-gun to all grease nipples, as this will force out any water which may have penetrated into the moving parts.

Lubrication of the Gearbox. On all 1945 and subsequent models B.S.A. gearboxes are specified. These are designed to run on *engine oil only*. Suitable brands of oil are given on page 49. The filler cap on the off side of the gearbox should be removed and the oil level checked every 300 miles; top-up with some engine oil. The correct oil level on all "Magdyno" models, except 1954-9 "swinging arm" models, is the level of the filler-cap orifice.

In the case of the 1945 and later 250 c.c. S.V. and O.H.V. coil-ignition Models C10, C11, however, a separate level plug (shown at E in Fig. 72) is provided, and after removing *both* plugs oil should be poured in through the filler-plug orifice until it begins to flow from the level-plug hole. When replenishing a B.S.A. gearbox, first see that the machine is upright and on level ground. For filling it is advisable to use a small funnel. Complete filling is assisted by slowly operating the kick-starter several times. After replenishment tighten up securely the filler cap, and on Models C10, C11, the level plug also.

On the 1954-9 "swinging arm" models an improved type of four-speed gearbox is fitted, and this also has a separate level plug (shown at (K) in Fig. 81). To top up the gearbox remove the oval cover-plate on the off-side of the gearbox; it is secured by two screws. Then pour in suitable engine oil (*see* page 49) until it begins to trickle from the level-plug orifice. Afterwards make sure that the level plug and the oval cover plate are both screwed home firmly.

Draining the Gearbox. On a brand new machine, after the first 500 miles and thereafter about every 2,000 miles place an oil tray beneath the gearbox, remove the drain plug and allow all the oil to drain off. On "B"

FIG. 36. WHEN AND WHERE TO LUBRICATE (1945 ONWARDS)

The above chart (showing a 1953 Model B33 "springer") applies to all 1945 and subsequent B.S.A. singles, but note the following: S.V. Models M20, M21 have a rear stand instead of a central stand (page 68); the plunger springing shown is superseded by "swinging arm" type (page 68); Models C10, C11 have coil ignition (page 57) instead of a "Magdyno." For instructions concerning the speedometer drive, and oil-dip type air filter (where fitted), *see* text.

engines, for accessibility remove the exhaust (not necessary on "swinging arm" models). Swill out thoroughly with flushing oil and after replacing the drain plug, replenish with fresh engine oil.

On "swinging arm" models (1954 onwards) remove the drain plug (shown at (*L*) in Fig. 81), completely drain the gearbox, flush it out with flushing oil, again drain the gearbox, replace the drain plug, and then top-up with suitable engine oil to the level of the hole exposed by removing the level plug (*K*).

The Clutch Control. On 1952-8 "Magdyno" and 1958-9 alternator models a grease nipple is provided (as shown at *F* in Figs. 74, 81); it is desirable about every 1,000 miles to inject some grease (*see* page 59) through the nipple to ensure free movement of the clutch operating-arm. On pre-1952 "Magdyno" models and 250 c.c. coil-ignition models apply weekly a few drops of engine oil with the oil-can to the end of the control arm farthest from the exposed portion of the operating cable which (on all models) should also be oiled weekly. On 1945-8 side-valve "M" models about every 1,000 miles it is advisable to add a few drops of engine oil to the clutch control-arm ball (*see* Fig. 75).

Key to Fig. 36

Item No.	Description	Lubrication, etc., Required	Page Ref.
1	Oil tank	Every 300 miles inspect oil level and top-up as required. Every 2,000 miles change the oil and clean the tank filter	49, 54
2	Engine crankcase	Every 2,000 miles drain the crankcase and clean the pump filter	54
3	Lucas "Magdyno"	Every 3,000 miles add a few drops of thin oil to the contact-breaker wick and tappet. Every 2,000-3,000 miles similarly oil the dynamo lubricator (where fitted)	56
4	Gearbox filler cap	Every 300 miles remove the cap and inspect the oil level. Top-up to the level of the cap orifice or separate level plug (Models C10, C11, "swinging arm")	61
5	Gearbox drain plug	Every 2,000 miles drain the gearbox and replenish with new engine oil	61
6	Clutch control	Every 1,000 miles apply the grease-gun to the nipple (where provided), or oil the arm weekly	61
7	Primary chain	Every 2,000 miles drain the oil bath and replenish with new engine oil to the level of the level plug orifice. Every 300 miles inspect level in the oil-bath	62
8	Secondary chain	About every 500 miles smear some grease or engine oil on the chain. Every 2,000 miles remove, clean, and grease the chain	62
9	Front forks { telescopic type / girder type }	Top-up (1945-7) or replenish (1948-59) with a little special oil if movement of the legs becomes excessive. Every 500 miles grease the fork spindles with the grease-gun	64-6 / 54
10	Steering head	Every 1,000 miles grease the lower bearing with the grease-gun	64
11	Handlebar controls	Weekly apply a few drops of oil to the control levers and exposed cables	66
12	Front and rear hubs	Every 1,000 miles apply the grease-gun to the hub nipples (1945-57 models)	64
13	Brake cam spindles	Every 1,000 miles apply a few drops of oil, or grease (where nipple provided)	67
14	Front brake cable	Weekly oil the ends of exposed portion	67
15	Rear brake pedal	Weekly apply a few drops of oil	67
16	Central stand	Every 1,000 miles apply the grease-gun to the nipple	68
17	Saddle-nose bolt	Weekly grease the nipple with the grease-gun	67
18	Spring frame (Plunger type)	Every 500 miles apply the grease-gun to the nipple on each rear fork leg	67

On the 1954 and later "swinging arm" models about every 1,000 miles with the grease gun inject a little grease (*see* page 59) through the nipple shown at (*F*) in Fig. 81. The clutch control-arm needs this occasional attention.

Lubrication of the Primary Chain. Except on "swinging arm" models the primary chain runs in a pressed-steel oil-bath chain case. Every 2,000 miles drain the case and (with the level plug removed) replenish with

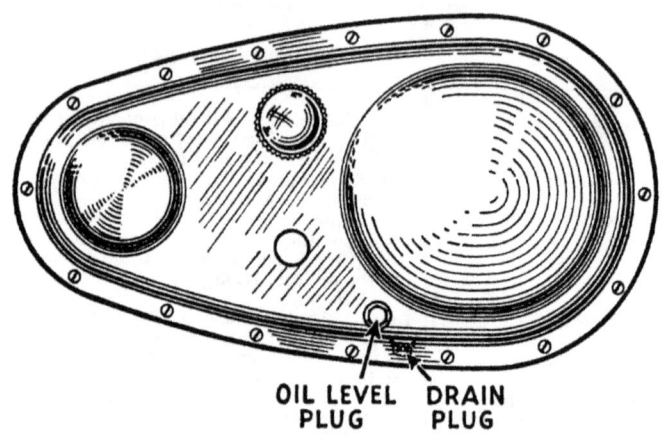

OIL LEVEL   DRAIN
    PLUG   PLUG

Fig. 37. The Pressed-steel Oil-bath Chain Case

Its capacity is 2 fluid ounces. An aluminium oil-bath chain case is fitted to all "swinging arm" models.

new engine oil (*see* page 49) to the level of the plug orifice on the side of the chain case (*see* Fig. 37). Avoid over-filling the case, otherwise the clutch may slip. When checking the level of oil, make certain that the machine is perfectly upright. Periodically (about every 5,000 miles) it is a good plan to remove the primary chain and clean it in paraffin. Every 300 miles inspect the oil-level and top up.

On 1954 and later "swinging arm" models the primary chain runs in an aluminium oil-bath chain case (*see* Fig. 38). It should be drained and replenished with fresh engine oil (*see* page 49) every 2,000 miles. Remove the *red-painted* cover fixing screw (*A*) and allow all oil to drain out. Then replace the screw (*A*), remove the cap (*C*), and pour in engine oil to the level of the *red-painted* cover fixing screw (*B*) which must be temporarily removed. Note that when the oil-bath is replenished the motor-cycle should be on level ground, with the stand up. It is desirable to inspect the oil level about every 300 miles.

Lubrication of the Secondary Chain. Where an oil-bath primary chain case is fitted to some "C" series models, the secondary chain is automatically lubricated by an adjustable feed at the rear of the primary-chain case. Where no automatic lubrication is provided it is desirable to smear grease with a brush on to the chain about every 500 miles, or whenever the chain seems dry.

Engine oil can be used for the rear chain, and the best method of oiling is to rotate the chain with the wheel and apply an oil-can to the top of the lower chain run. See that the oil is falling upon the rollers, not on the ground, and make a practice of oiling regularly. If the chain is neglected,

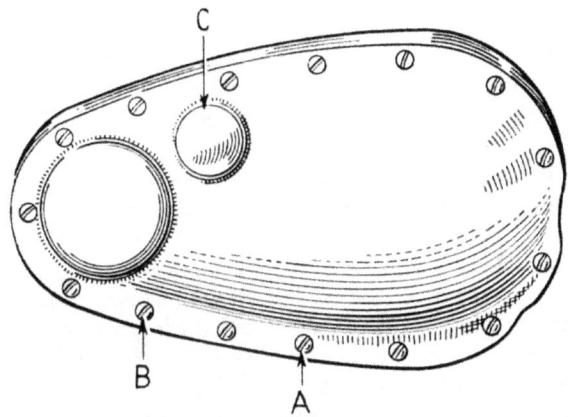

FIG. 38. THE ALUMINIUM OIL-BATH CHAIN CASE

On alternator models use ½ pint of grade S.A.E. 20 engine oil during the summer and winter. Note the outer cover is secured to the chain case (capacity: 8 fluid ounces) by three (larger diameter) short bolts at the front, six long bolts at the rear, and six intermediate size bolts between.

undue wear of both chain and sprockets will ensue, and the transmission will be harsh. From time to time (say once every 2,000 miles) take off the chain and give it a bath in paraffin. If allowed to soak well, the whole of the dirt will be extracted, and the chain may be hung up to dry before refitting. Cleaning is unnecessary if the chain is fully enclosed.

Before refitting the chain the wisest course is to immerse it in a receptacle containing a mixture of warm graphite and grease, such as Mobilgrease No. 2, which will then permeate all the roller bearings. There is no better treatment for a main driving chain, although plain engine oil or regular greasing will answer satisfactorily. After it has cooled, wipe off the excess lubricant. As the lubricant will be gradually squeezed out under load, the process should therefore be repeated about every 2,000 miles. Clean the sprockets and, on replacing the chain, see that the split end of the spring link faces opposite to the direction of the chain travel.

The foregoing instructions are applicable to 1954 and later "swinging arm" models. On 1956-9 "B" models, however, the secondary chain runs in a pressed-steel chain case (where specified). Where total enclosure is provided, remove the front rubber-plug and afterwards apply an oil-can through the inspection hole. When removing the chain for cleaning and greasing (rarely necessary) first remove the rear section of the chain case, and then the upper and lower middle-sections.

The Transmission Shock-Absorber. No lubrication of the engine shaft shock-absorber is needed, as this, being enclosed in the chain case, is adequately lubricated by oil thrown off the primary chain. On alternator models (1958-9) there is no engine-shaft shock-absorber.

The Hub Bearings. About every 1,000 miles apply a grease-gun to the nipples, except on full-width light-alloy hubs. Here it is only necessary to repack the bearings with grease during a complete overhaul. If a sidecar outfit is concerned, do not overlook the hub of the sidecar wheel. Three to four strokes of the gun should be ample. If excessive grease is injected, some of it may get on the brake linings and cause reduced braking power.

The Steering Head Lock. On 1955-9 models having a steering-head lock it is important to note that oil should *not* be inserted into the keyhole. Specially prepared lubricant is introduced during assembly and the subsequent insertion of oil is likely to clog the wards and wash away the special lubricant. It is permissible, however, after a big mileage or under adverse weather conditions to apply a few drops of thin machine-oil to the periphery of the moving drum.

The Steering Head. Lubricate the (lower) thrust ball-bearings in the steering head every 1,000 miles by applying the grease-gun to the nipple. Two to three strokes should suffice.

Girder Type Front Forks. Where girder-type front forks are fitted (earlier 250 c.c., and 500, 600 c.c. S.V. models), about every 500 miles a little grease or heavy oil should be injected through the nipples provided until it begins to exude at the fork-link ends.

The Telescopic Forks (1945-7). Top-up both fork legs as required with suitable lubricant as soon as excessive up-and-down fork movement occurs. The total quantity of lubricant for each fork leg when fully topped-up is approximately *five fluid ounces* (142 *c.c.*).* The oil content must never greatly exceed this amount. When topping-up, use engine oil (*see* page 49) or on Models B32, B34: Castrolite, Mobiloil Arctic, Shell X 100-20, Esso Extra 20W/30, or B.P. Energol SAE 20.

To Check the Oil Content of the Forks (1945-7). Place your B.S.A. on its central or rear stand, and remove the large hexagon-headed cap (and

* *See* footnote on page 66.

B.S.A. LUBRICATION

washer) shown at *A* in Fig. 94 from the top of each fork leg. Then, referring to Fig. 39, compress or extend the forks until the distance from the lower edge of the top dust-cover to the groove *B* on each fork leg is as indicated in Fig. 39. Normal friction in the fork-leg assembly should

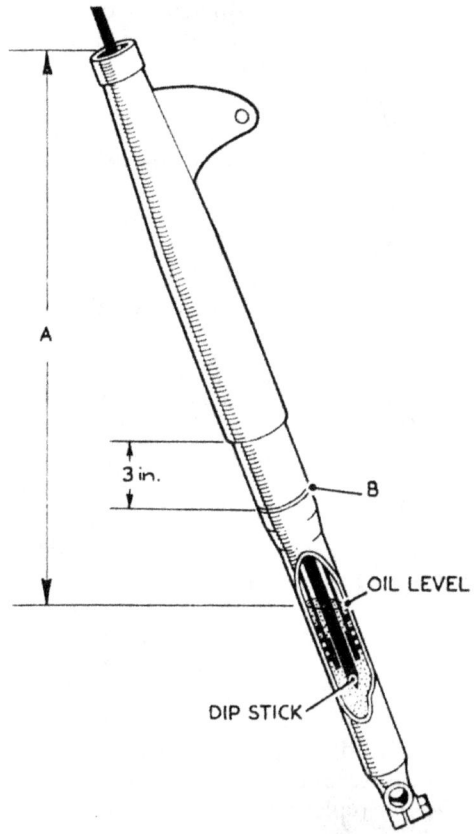

FIG. 39. USING DIP-STICK TO CHECK OIL CONTENT OF TELESCOPIC FRONT FORK LEG

Not necessary on 1948 and subsequent models.

enable this position to be maintained when checking the oil content, which should be done as described below.

Obtain a length of $\frac{5}{8}$-$\frac{1}{2}$ in. rod and use this as a dip-stick. The lower end must be pointed. Insert the dip-stick through the inner leg of the fork until it contacts the oil inside. Mark the upper end of the dip-stick where it emerges from the top of the fork leg, and withdraw the dip-stick. Distance *A* on the dip-stick (Fig. 39) is an indication of the existing oil level. On "B," "C," and "M" models, it should be 22-4 in., 20-2 in., and 23-5 in. respectively.

Should the oil content be found excessive, employ a syringe and rubber tube to remove the surplus. If the content is found to be insufficient, add oil through the top of the fork leg until distance A is correct, according to the series of machine concerned. It is advisable to check the oil content every 10,000 miles.

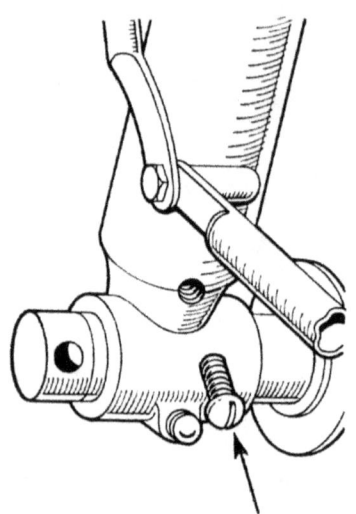

FIG. 40. DRAIN PLUG ON 1948 AND LATER TYPE B.S.A. FORK LEG

The arrow shows the plug removed from the fork leg.

Replenishing the Telescopic Forks (1948 Onwards). All 1948 and later type forks have drain plugs fitted, and it is simpler to replenish entirely each fork leg rather than to top-it up. If excessive up-and-down movement of the forks occurs, replenishment should be effected as described in the following two paragraphs.

First remove the large hexagon-headed cap (and washer) shown at A in Fig. 94 from the top of the fork leg. Also with a screwdriver remove the small drain plug (indicated by an arrow in Fig. 40) from the base of the fork leg, replace the drain plug, and replenish with *five fluid ounces* (142 c.c.)* of new oil. Suitable oils are given on page 64. Although no ill effects will follow replenishing with slightly more than the stipulated amount, it is essential not to exceed the amount by a large extent. If each leg is filled right up it will cease to provide good suspension. A suitable glass measure and small funnel can be obtained from a hardware store. Do *not* replenish with engine oil.

Draining the Telescopic Front Forks. A tip to remember when draining 1948 and later telescopic-type front forks is that *complete* draining is facilitated by standing astride the machine, grasping the handlebars, and working the forks up and down. Drain every 10,000 miles.

Exposed Cables, Control Levers, and Joints. To prevent corrosion and to ensure smooth action, apply a few drops of oil weekly.

The Speedometer Drive. Every 1,000 miles apply the grease-gun to the drive nipple (where provided). Give only a few strokes. It is a good plan

* On Models B32, B34 Comp., and all "swinging arm" models, the total amount of oil should be $7\frac{1}{2}$ fluid ounces (213 c.c.) of an SAE 20 oil.

occasionally to unscrew the knurled ring nut attaching the drive to the speedometer, carefully pull the drive clear, and then squirt some oil down between the drive and the outer casing. When reconnecting the drive, see that the connexion goes properly home without force before the ring nut is tightened.

The Saddle-nose Bolt. A grease nipple apt to be overlooked is that for the saddle-nose bolt. Give one or two strokes of the grease-gun weekly. No grease nipple is provided where a dual seat is fitted.

The Spring Frame (Plunger Type). A single nipple is provided for each rear fork leg (*see* Figs. 82, 85) and about every 500 miles apply the grease-gun. Give several strokes with the gun. It should always be possible to feel a thin film of grease on the upper part of the chromium-plated telescopic member. Wear and rusting will otherwise occur.

The Rear Brake Pedal. Each week apply a few drops of oil to the lubrication hole for the brake-pedal shaft. Apply a little thin oil to the stop-light switch mechanism occasionally.

Lubrication of Brake Cross-over Shaft. The cross-over shaft for the rear brake on 1956-9 "swingers" is well smeared with grease during assembly. After a considerable mileage it is advisable to remove the shaft, wipe it clean, and smear it with fresh grease prior to replacing it.

To remove the cross-over shaft, it is necessary first to disconnect the rear-brake pedal and the cross-over shaft lever. Loosen the pinch-bolts and pull the levers away from the shaft, noting their exact positions to ensure correct re-assembly. *This is most important.* Then pull the cross-over shaft out of the swinging-arm member.

The Brake Cam Spindles. Every 1,000 miles approximately, apply a few drops of oil to the holes provided for lubricating the brake cam spindles. Afterwards do not forget to re-position the spring-clip cover over each hole. The 8-in. front brake, and all 1956-9 light-alloy hubs have a grease nipple; one shot of grease is sufficient.

The Front Brake. Besides oiling the handlebar controls each week (along with the other lever controls), do not omit to oil lightly both ends of the exposed portion of the cable running parallel with the front fork legs.

The Sidecar Chassis. When greasing the hubs of the motor-cycle wheels about every 1,000 miles, or at a complete overhaul (light-alloy hubs), remember to lubricate the hub of the sidecar. Also about every 250 miles apply the grease gun to the rear spring and shackle-link bolts. If special instructions are issued by the sidecar makers, follow these closely.

The Central or Rear Stand. Central spring-up stands are fitted to all except rigid-frame models, and a grease nipple is provided for the grease-gun which should be applied every 1,000 miles. Where a rear stand is fitted, oil the fulcrum points.

The Dipper Switch. Every 5,000 miles lubricate the moving parts of the dipper switch with a little *thin* oil. Be careful, or you may cause a short.

"Swinging Arm" Rear Suspension. The hydraulic dampers (1954-9 "B" series models) require no lubrication or other maintenance. It is, however, possible to obtain stiffer springing by turning the adjuster cams with a Cee spanner to the second or third alternative positions (*see* page 144).

CHAPTER V

GENERAL MAINTENANCE

IN this chapter the author has included *all* essential information about the maintenance, dismantling, and assembling of 1945 and later models. Detailed reference to carburation, lubrication, and the lighting system has, however, been omitted, since these subjects have already been fully discussed. To assist the reader in finding what he needs quickly, the chapter has been sub-divided into a number of main sections.

Spares and Repairs. When you have to forward or deliver parts to the makers (B.S.A. Motor Cycles, Ltd., Service Dept., Waverly Works, Birmingham, 10) or to an appointed B.S.A. dealer, remember to attach to each part a label bearing clearly your *full name and address*. Correspondence concerning technical advice and repairs should always be written on separate sheets to ensure prompt attention. To assist identification, also always quote the year and model of machine, and the engine or frame number (see footnote on page 1), according to which is applicable

A useful spares list is obtainable from B.S.A. Motor Cycles, Ltd., or from an appointed spares stockist. Throughout the U.K. there are over 170 of these stockists who maintain a comprehensive stock of B.S.A. spares. Among those in the London area may be mentioned: Whitbys of Acton, Ltd.; Kays of Ealing, Ltd.; Godfreys, Ltd.; Eleanor Motors; F. Parks & Son, Ltd.; Lovett's, Ltd.; Glanfield Lawrence, Ltd.; Owen Bros.; Naylor & Root; Cleares, Ltd.; Harry Nash Motors, Ltd.; Slocombes, Ltd.; West End Motors, Ltd.; and also the firms below marked with an asterisk.

Some Large Accessory Firms. Eight large accessory firms (some of which have branches throughout the U.K.) handling motor-cycle accessories, equipment, proprietary spares, tools, clothing, etc. are: Marble Arch Motor Supplies, Ltd.; The Halford Cycle Co., Ltd.; James Grose, Ltd.*; Turner's Stores*; George Grose, Ltd.*; Claude Rye, Ltd.*; Pride & Clarke, Ltd.; and Whitbys of Acton, Ltd.*

Items Required for Maintenance. Some items besides the standard tool kit you *must* have handy in the lock-up or garage. These include: a can of paraffin for cleaning purposes; a stiff brush for scouring dirt off the crankcase and underneath the motor-cycle; a tin of suitable engine oil for the engine and gearbox (*see* page 49); a small funnel for topping-up the gearbox; a canister of grease (*see* page 59); a receptacle for oil when draining the oil tank and crankcase; some dishes or jars for washing parts in; some non-fluffy rags; valve-grinding paste such as Richford's (coarse and fine); some fine emery cloth; a set of engine gaskets. You should also have: a pair of new gudgeon-pin circlips; a good valve-spring compressor (*see* page 100) for removing valves. A gudgeon-pin extractor (*see* page 102) is useful, and it is desirable to obtain a wire brush.

Other very desirable items which the author strongly recommends be bought are shown in Fig. 41. Items 1, 4, 5, 6, 8, 10 are really essential, and the remainder form very useful additions to the standard B.S.A. tool kit. The whole of these items do not cost very much, and the author has found them to be worth-while additions. You are also likely to need a "Magdyno" pinion extractor (*see* page 108) and an extractor for the clutch centre (*see* page 120).

For the maintenance of the motor-cycle parts you should obtain: a box of spare chain links and a chain rivet extractor; a Lucas battery filler (*see* page 34) for topping-up the battery; a hydrometer for checking the specific gravity of the battery electrolyte (*see* page 35); a chamois leather; a sponge and pail (if a hose is not available); some soft dusters (preferably of the Selvyt type); a tin of good wax or other polish for the enamelled parts; and a tin of hand cleanser.

Tools for Repair Work. If you decide to undertake as much repair work as possible besides routine maintenance, stripping-down, and assembly, it is desirable to rig up a suitable bench, complete with vice, and to purchase some extra tools.

To begin, it is a good plan to buy a medium-weight hammer, a hand-drill and an assortment of twist-drills, a hacksaw, some large and small (smooth and rough) files, and a good soldering outfit for the repair of control cables. Repair work is beyond the scope of this handbook, and you need fair technical knowledge and skill in handling tools.

If rebushing of the engine and other components is undertaken, this will necessitate the use of suitable extractors, punches, etc. A number of B.S.A. special service tools may also be obtained if required.

Keep Your B.S.A. Clean. Keep your mount nice and clean. Doubtless it cost quite a sum, and it is well worth careful looking after. With regular and proper cleaning it will function better, will last longer, maintain its good looks, and retain a good market value. A dirty motor-cycle is an eyesore, and remember that dirt hides defects, encourages rusting, and is a menace when stripping down. Never leave your B.S.A. soaking wet overnight. If you have no time for cleaning in wet weather, grease the machine all over *before* use.

Cleaning the Engine and Gearbox. See that the cylinder barrel and cylinder-head fins are kept clean and black. If the enamel has worn away, paint the fins with some proprietary cylinder black after thorough cleaning with a stiff brush dipped in paraffin. Note that rusted fins, besides looking shabby, cause an appreciable loss in heat dispersion.

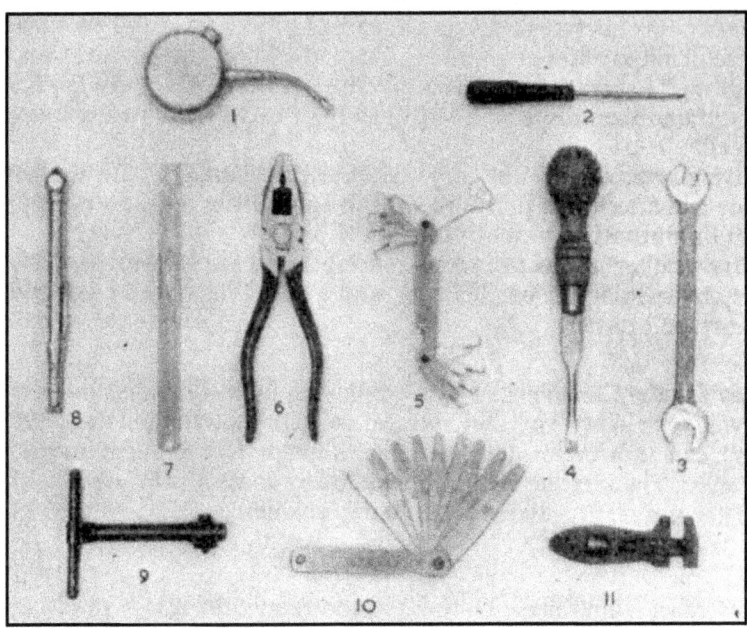

FIG. 41. SOME USEFUL ADDITIONS TO THE STANDARD TOOL KIT

Various items added by the author to his own Model B31 tool kit.
1. Oil can (for engine oil)
2. Small screwdriver
3. Garrington double-ended spanner ($\frac{3}{16}$ in. and $\frac{1}{8}$ in. W.). Fits acorn nuts at base of push-rod cover tube, rocker-box cover nuts, secondary chain adjusters, sump filter cover-plate nuts (*see* page 56), and battery strap securing-bolt
4. Medium-size screwdriver
5. Sparking plug re-gapping tool and plug point gauges. Champion and Lodge tools are available
6. Pliers (with wire cutter)
7. Six-inch steel rule
8. Tyre pressure gauge (6-50 lb per sq in.)*
9. Valve-grinding tool (not required if suction tool is provided)
10. A good set of feeler gauges
11. Small adjustable spanner

* The tyre pressure gauge illustrated is a Dunlop pencil type No. 6. Other suitable gauges are the Schrader No. 7750, the Holdtite, and the Romac.

Scour off all filth from the lower part of the engine and gearbox with stiff brushes and paraffin. Clean all aluminium alloy and bright surfaces first with a rag damped in paraffin, assisted by brushes where necessary, and then with a dry rag.

Cleaning the Enamel. Never attempt to remove mud from the enamelled parts when dry and caked, as this is likely to damage the surfaces. Soak the mud off with a hose if available. In the case of a very dirty machine it may be advisable to paint the surfaces over with a cleaning compound such as "Gunk" before directing a stream of water on to the dirty surfaces. Be careful not to allow any water to get on the wheel hub-bearings, and the "Magdyno" (where fitted) and carburettor. If a hose is not available, soak the mud and then disperse it with plenty of clean water, using a sponge and pail.

Having removed all dirt, dry the enamelled surfaces with a chamois leather and afterwards polish them with soft dusters and some good wax polish or a proprietary polish such as "Karpol."

"Dry weather" riders can keep a machine in almost showroom condition merely by rubbing the enamel over with a paraffin-damped rag, followed by a dry, soft duster.

Cleaning the Chromium. Never employ liquid metal polish or paste, as this will wear down the thin surface. A good chromium-cleaning compound can, however, safely be used, though too frequent use is not desirable. The normal method of removing tarnish (salt deposits) is to clean the surfaces regularly with a damp chamois leather and then polish them with soft dusters.

To Reduce Tarnishing. During the winter months it is a good plan to wipe over occasionally all surfaces with a soft cloth soaked in a proprietary anti-tarnish preparation. An example is "Tekall," obtainable in $\frac{1}{2}$-pint and 1-pint tins.

Petrol-tank Enamel. Occasionally a B.S.A. owner may have the misfortune to scratch or damage a small portion of the tank enamel. Matching up colours is notoriously difficult, and it is worth noting that B.S.A. Motor Cycles, Ltd. supply their spares stockists with small tins of quick-drying cellulose paint of the *exact* colour required (also "Tipon pencils" for general touching-up).

Regularly Check Nuts for Tightness. This is particularly important during running-in (*see* page 11), as some "bedding down" of parts occurs. Regularly apply spanners to the various external nuts to ensure tightness, paying special attention to the engine bolts and nuts, the engine mounting nuts, and the pipe unions. After running-in check them about every 2,000 miles, but after decarbonizing and running for about 250 miles, check the cylinder-head bolts for tightness, tightening diagonally. Do not use spanners of greater length than the standard ones when tightening nuts, especially those on the crankcase studs.

GENERAL MAINTENANCE 73

Carburettor Maintenance and Tuning. For detailed instructions, *see* Chapter II.

B.S.A. Lubrication. Detailed instructions for the lubrication of 1945 and later models are given in Chapter IV, and the lubrication chart on page 59 shows when and where the application of grease or oil is required.

CARE OF THE IGNITION SYSTEM

All 1945-57 B.S.A. S.V. and O.H.V. models except Models C10, C11, have Lucas "Magdyno" lighting and ignition equipment provided. For all practical purposes the magneto and E3HM or E3LM dynamo portion (used for lighting only) of the "Magdyno" are separate units. They are united only by a strap and can be separated (*see* page 29).

All 1958-9 O.H.V. models have coil instead of magneto ignition, with a Lucas alternator and rectifier (*see* page 30) supplying current to a battery (below the dual seat) which delivers current for both lighting and ignition. A separate contact-breaker is provided on the off side of the machine instead of on the near side where it was formerly located on the magneto. The rectifier and coil are fitted above the tool compartment.

On 1945-53 models C10, C11, coil ignition and lighting equipment is included. An E3H Lucas dynamo supplies current to the battery which passes on the current to the ignition and lighting systems.

The maintenance of the E3H and E3L dynamos, the alternator, the rectifier, and the battery, has already been dealt with in Chapter III. It remains to cover those components concerned solely with ignition.

Suitable Sparking Plugs. To obtain easy starting and maximum performance throughout the throttle range, it is essential always to run on a suitable sparking plug. Three reliable makes of sparking plugs are the Champion, the Lodge, and the K.L.G. All 1945 and subsequent engines require 14 mm size plugs, and suitable types are—

S.V. ENGINES. Where a side-valve engine has an aluminium-alloy cylinder head, use a Champion type N-8B or NB, a Lodge type HLN, or a K.L.G. type FE50 sparking plug. If a cast-iron cylinder head is fitted (earlier models), use a Champion type L-10, a Lodge type C14, or a K.L.G. type F50.

O.H.V. ENGINES. On all overhead-valve engines, use a Champion type L-10S or L7, a Lodge type H14, or a K.L.G. type F70 or the watertight equivalent. For competition models such as Models B32 and B34 the Champion NA-8 plug is recommended.

In the author's opinion single-point and three-point plugs are equally good. With both types the gap can be adjusted readily, safely, and precisely. All of the above-mentioned plugs provide cool and efficient running.

"Ignition Suppression" Plugs. To meet recent legislation concerning sparking plugs fitted to new machines (*see* page 2), various plugs incorporating a resistor are available. While it is not compulsory to fit a "suppressor" type plug to a machine registered prior to 2nd July, 1953, it is recommended that this be done, as "suppressor" plugs, besides causing no annoyance to "viewers" and "listeners," also have longer wearing electrodes. An alternative to fitting a plug with a built-in ignition suppressor is to fit to the existing plug a terminal cover embodying a resistor.

Weatherproof Sparking Plugs. All-weather riders usually find it advantageous to fit a weatherproof plug terminal cover or (in the event of

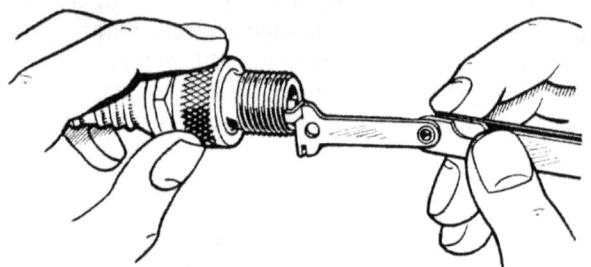

FIG. 42. THE BEST WAY TO RE-GAP A PLUG
Using the metal tool shown at (5) in Fig. 41.

plug renewal being required) to fit a watertight sparking plug such as the well-known K.L.G. type.

Keep the Plug Gap Correct. This is extremely important. It is advisable to check the plug gap about every 1,000 miles and to adjust the gap if burning of the points has caused the gap to exceed 0·020 in. B.S.A. Motor Cycles, Ltd. recommend a gap of 0·018-0·020 in. For obvious reasons, when re-gapping it is best to set the gap at the *bottom* limit. Check the gap with a wire or feeler gauge such as those shown at (5) and (10) respectively in Fig. 41. The gauge should just enter without springing the points.

When adjusting the plug gap, never attempt to bend or tap the centre electrode. Use a pair of snipe-nose pliers, or a Champion or Lodge re-gapping tool (Fig. 42), to bend the outside (earth) electrode. Tapping the earth electrode is not a good method. When the plug has to be thoroughly cleaned, this should be done as described below, and the plug re-gapped *afterwards*.

Cleaning the Sparking Plug. If carburation is correct and excessive oil is not entering the combustion chamber, it should not be necessary to inspect and clean the sparking plug thoroughly more often than about

GENERAL MAINTENANCE 75

once every 1,000 miles. When running-in a new or rebored engine, however, it is advisable to remove and check the plug for cleanliness at intervals of about 500 miles.

Quick cleaning of a plug can be done by brushing the points and lightly rubbing their firing sides with some smooth emery cloth. Alternatively the plug can be cleaned with a proprietary gadget, comprising a metal reservoir, containing steel wires and petrol, into which the plug is screwed and then shaken. Thorough cleaning (internal and external), however, is not possible without dismantling the plug.

Cleaning Lodge and K.L.G. Plugs. Fig. 43 shows a typical detachable type (K.L.G.) sparking plug dismantled for thorough cleaning. To dismantle a detachable-type sparking plug, grip the hexagon of the gland nut in a vice or with a box spanner. If you use a vice, be most careful not to exert any pressure on the hexagon faces. Then with a suitable spanner (preferably a box or ring spanner), unscrew the large hexagon E, being careful not to distort the integral metal body. The centre electrode F with its insulation (comprising the insulated electrode assembly A) can now be detached from the gland nut. Take care not to lose the internal sealing-washer H.

To clean the "Sintox" or "Corundite" insulation, used on Lodge and K.L.G. plugs respectively, wipe it clean with a cloth soaked in petrol or paraffin. If the insulation is coated with hard carbon deposits, remove these with some fine emery cloth, but make no attempt to scrape off the deposits. The internal sealing-washer H and the surfaces on the insulator and in the metal body on which this washer rests are very important, as they prevent gas leakage through the plug. Therefore wipe them only with a rag soaked in petrol or paraffin. Any damage caused while dismantling will render the plug unserviceable.

To clean the metal parts (plug body and gland nut), wipe them clean with petrol, or, if necessary, scrape off the deposits with a small knife, or use a wire brush. Afterwards rinse the parts in petrol. The gland nut seldom gets very fouled, but the inside of the plug body may be very dirty, and the same may apply to the external threads of the plug. Clean and polish the points of the centre and outside (earth) electrodes F and G (Fig. 43) with some fine emery cloth.

See that there is no dirt or grit lodged between the body of the plug and the insulation, and particularly on the internal sealing-washer and the contacting faces. Smear a little thin oil on the internal washer and make sure that it seats properly. When assembling the sparking plug, see that the centre electrode and insulation are positioned centrally in the body bore. If not, remove, re-position by rotating the centre a quarter of a turn, and reassemble. Do not attempt to force or bend them into position.

Tighten the gland nut into the plug body only with a single-handed normal pressure applied to the tommy-bar of the box spanner or ring spanner. It is not advisable to use an open type spanner; this may exert excessive pressure, which will result in distortion of the gland nut and possible damage to the insulation. Finally, it should be verified that the plug gap is correct.

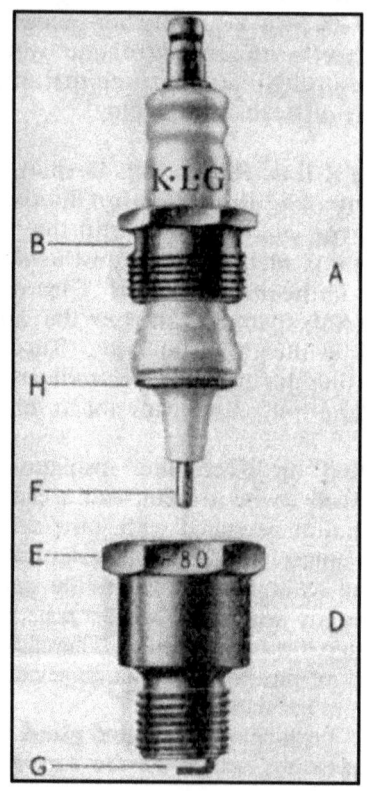

Fig. 43. Detachable Type Sparking Plug (K.L.G.) Dismantled for thorough Cleaning

The gland nut *B* and the internal washer *H* are shown still in position on the insulation.

Cleaning Champion Plugs. A Champion non-detachable plug such as the L-10S can not be dismantled and cleaned like the detachable Lodge and K.L.G. plugs. Quick cleaning is, of course, done in the same manner (*see* page 75). The best method of cleaning a Champion plug thoroughly is to take it to a nearby garage having an "air-blast" unit. In a matter of a few minutes the plug can be thoroughly cleaned of all deposits, washed, subjected to a high-pressure air line, and subsequently tested for sparking at a pressure exceeding 100 lb per sq in.

Keep the tip and outside of the insulation thoroughly clean. After

GENERAL MAINTENANCE

removing all carbon, polish the electrodes with some *fine* emery cloth. Finally check the plug gap (0.018-0.020 in.).

Replacing the Sparking Plug. Before replacing the plug, renew the copper washer if it is worn or flattened, and clean the plug threads. Screw the plug home by hand as far as possible, and always use the box spanner for final

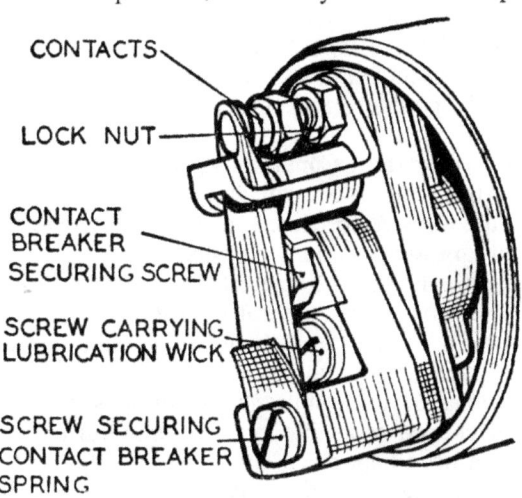

FIG. 44. THE FACE-CAM TYPE CONTACT-BREAKER USED ON LUCAS "MAGDYNOS" (1945 ONWARDS)

tightening. An adjustable spanner should not be used, as this may cause distortion.

Keep the "Magdyno" Contact-breaker Gap Correct. Little attention to the ignition portion of the Lucas "Magdyno" is needed, other than occasional lubrication (*see* page 56) and attention to the face-cam type contact-breaker, shown in Fig. 44. Any serious internal trouble should be dealt with by a Lucas service depot.

The contacts of the contact-breaker (Fig. 44) should be examined on a new machine after the first 100 miles, again after 500 miles and subsequently about every 3,000 miles. If the "break," with the contacts full open is appreciably more, or less, than will just take a 0.012-0.015 in. blade of a feeler gauge, the contacts should be adjusted (*after* cleaning, if necessary). Too great a gap will advance the timing. The magneto spanner gauge or the blade of a proprietary set of feelers can be useful for checking the "break," the procedure for which is as follows—

1. Remove the contact-breaker cover and rotate the engine slowly forwards until the contacts of the contact-breaker are wide open (near T.D.C. on the firing stroke).

2. Insert the blade of the feeler gauge between the contacts.

3. If the feeler gauge *just* slides in without friction, the gap is correct and no adjustment is needed. If the gauge is a slack fit or the contacts have to be sprung to enable it to enter, adjust the gap as follows.

4. With the magneto spanner loosen the lock-nut which secures the stationary-contact screw (*see* Fig. 44) and then adjust this screw by means of its hexagon head until the correct gap is obtained between the fixed (outer) and adjustable (inner) contacts.

5. Re-tighten the contact screw lock-nut and again check the gap. If correct, replace the contact-breaker cover.

Cleaning the "Magdyno" Contacts. At intervals of about 3,000 miles, when checking the contact-breaker gap, scrutinize the contacts closely. If the contacts are allowed to become dirty or oily, rapid burning, pitting, and consequent ignition trouble will ensue.

If inspection reveals that the contacts have a *grey, frosted* appearance, with no blackening or pitting, do not interfere with them (assuming that the gap is correct). If the contacts are only slightly discoloured, clean them with a rag moistened with petrol.

On examination after a big mileage the contacts may be found to have irregular and blackened areas due to pitting and burning (especially if the contacts have not been kept clean and correctly adjusted). In this case it is essential to clean them up, otherwise misfiring and rapid deterioration of the contacts will follow.

To clean the contacts, use a *fine* carborundum slip or a piece of *fine* emery cloth (do not use a nail file), and with the contact-breaker spring arm (*see* Fig. 44) removed, clean and polish the contacts until all pitting disappears and the contact surfaces are smooth all over. Be careful to keep the contact faces "square" as well as uniform. *This is most important.** If pitting is not serious, it is perhaps best not to remove the spring arm, but to insert the emery cloth between the two contacts, while both are in position. If pitting is serious, or if it is necessary to examine contacts effectively, the spring arm must be removed.

To remove the spring arm (carrying the moving contact) on a face-cam type contact-breaker (*see* Fig. 44), it is only necessary to remove the securing screw and spring washer. When replacing the spring arm, make certain that the small backing spring is replaced immediately under the securing screw and spring washer, with the curved portion facing *outwards* as shown in Fig. 44. See that the contacts are perfectly aligned before tightening the securing screw firmly.

Where very deep pitting is present, it may be necessary to remove the complete contact-breaker after detaching the spring arm. To do this,

---

* Note that the later type Lucas contacts have slightly convex (not flat) faces, which must be cleaned with fine emery cloth only.

GENERAL MAINTENANCE

unlock the tab-washer and remove the contact-breaker securing screw, when the complete contact-breaker can be withdrawn, and dealt with on a bench or table if desired. When replacing the contact-breaker, see that a new tab-washer is fitted and locked over the securing screw. It is not advisable to remove much metal from the contacts, and if a reasonable amount of facing-up fails to restore the surfaces to normal, fit a new pair of contacts (including, of course, a new spring arm). After dealing with the contacts as described, wipe away any metal dust with a petrol-dampened cloth and check the gap.

The "Magdyno" Slip-ring. Moisture, oil, or dirt accumulating on the slip-ring is liable to cause difficult starting and misfiring. About every 4,000 miles (when cleaning both filters) remove the h.t. pick-up from the "Magdyno" and thoroughly clean the flanges and track of the slip-ring. Do this by holding a soft, dry cloth, wrapped round a pencil, through the pick-up hole, and, with the cloth lightly pressed against the slip-ring, slowly turn the engine. The h.t. pick-up is secured to the body of the "Magdyno" by two small screws. The near-side screw is rather inaccessible on some models, and to remove and tighten both screws it is necessary first to remove the oil tank (*see* page 56).

The H.T. Pick-up. When cleaning the slip-ring, also clean the surface of the pick-up moulding with a cloth moistened with petrol, and polish with a fine, dry cloth. Examine the pick-up moulding for cracks, and closely inspect the spring and carbon brush. The brush must move freely in its holder, but be careful not to stretch the spring. Renew the spring at once if it has weakened, and always renew a badly worn brush. When replacing the h.t. pick-up moulding, do not forget to replace the small gasket. Examine the earth brush (held by a cheese-head screw).

Renewing the H.T. Cable. When renewing a cracked or perished h.t. cable, utilize 7 mm plastic-covered ignition cable. Bare the end of the cable (*see* Fig. 45) for about $\frac{1}{4}$ in. and thread the cable through the moulded terminal nut. Pass the wire through the bronze washer and then bend back the cable strands as illustrated. Finally screw the moulded terminal-nut into the pick-up connexion.

Cleaning the Contacts (Coil Ignition). At 6,000 miles on 1945-53 Models C10, C11, remove the moulded cover and inspect the contact-breaker, shown in Figs. 35, 46. The contacts must be kept quite clean and free from grease and oil. If burned or blackened, clean the contacts as in the case of the "Magdyno" with a fine carborundum slip or fine emery cloth and afterwards wipe quite clean with a petrol-moistened rag. If much attention is necessary to the contacts it is best to remove the contact-breaker lever (carrying the moving contact) as follows: unscrew the nut securing the end of the contact-breaker spring and remove the nut together with the spring washer. Remove the metal bush and lift the contact-breaker lever off its bearings. Finally, after polishing and cleaning the contacts, refit the rocker arm, contact-breaker lever, metal bush, and spring washer. Afterwards replace and tighten up the nut.

The Contact-breaker Gap (Models C10, C11). The gap should be maintained at 0·010-0·012 in., and to test the gap, which requires adjustment only at very long intervals, slowly rotate the engine by hand until the contacts are wide open. Then insert between the contacts a feeler gauge

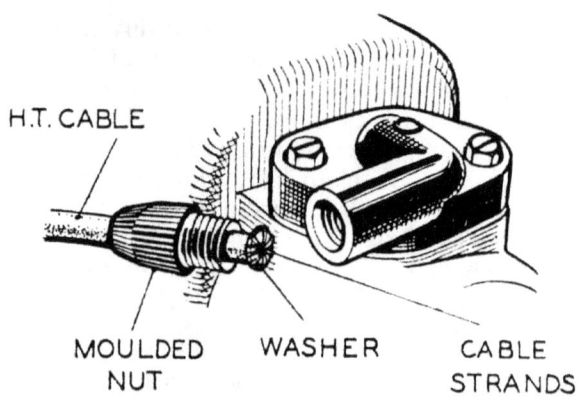

Fig. 45. Renewing H.T. Cable on Lucas "Magdyno"

or the gauge provided on the contact-breaker spanner, which should just slide in. If the gap is considerably too large or too small, adjust by opening the contacts fully and then slackening the locking screws B (Fig. 46) until the plate C, carrying the stationary contact, can just be moved. Now adjust the position of the plate until the correct gap at the contacts is obtained. Afterwards the locking screws B must be firmly re-tightened and the gap again checked.

The Contact-breaker Gap (1958-9 Models B31, B33). The contact-breaker assembly on the 1958-9 350 c.c. and 500 c.c. coil-ignition models is shown in Fig. 68. Always maintain the gap between the contacts at 0·012-0·015 in. An adjustment is normally necessary only at long intervals (about every 3,000 miles), but during the running-in period the gap should be checked after the first few hundred miles.

Referring to Fig. 68, to make a contact-breaker adjustment, rotate the engine until the contacts are wide open and insert the appropriate blades of a set of feeler gauges between the contacts. Should the gap be found incorrect, loosen the screw E and move the plate F gently with a screwdriver until the gap is as stated above. Afterwards firmly tighten screw E and again check the contact-breaker gap.

GENERAL MAINTENANCE 81

Cleaning the Contacts (1958-9 Models B31, B33). Cleaning is necessary only at long intervals, but when checking the contact-breaker gap it is desirable to inspect the contacts to see that they are clean and not blackened or pitted (*see* page 78). Slightly discoloured contacts can be cleaned with a rag moistened with petrol, but thorough cleaning should be effected by

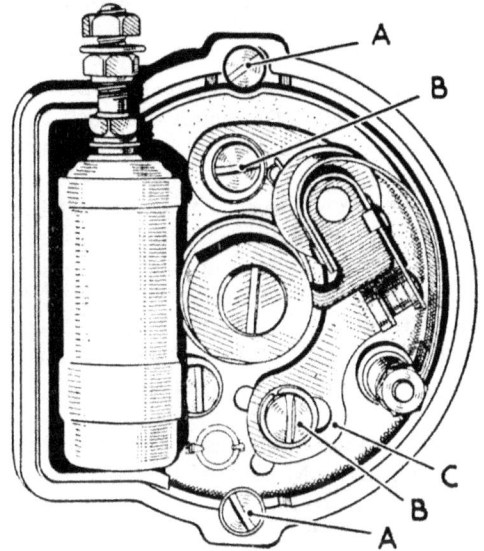

FIG. 46. LUCAS CONTACT-BREAKER (MODELS C10, C11)

Another view is shown in Fig. 35. To obtain access to the automatic ignition-advance mechanism remove screws *A* and withdraw the complete contact-breaker. It is necessary to lubricate the cam occasionally as described on page 57.

withdrawing the moving contact and cleaning both contacts with a fine carborundum slip or some fine emery cloth.

The Battery. On all the coil-ignition models it is important to keep the battery in good condition owing to the dual demands made upon it for lighting and ignition (*see* page 31).

Attention to the Coil. The Lucas coil used on coil-ignition models requires no attention whatever other than occasional cleaning of the exterior, especially the space between the terminals. See that the connexions at the terminals are kept tight, and the wiring is in good condition. On 1958-9 models the coil is well protected in the tool box.

Ignition Warning Lamp (Models C10, C11). The ignition warning lamp, which is combined with the ammeter on the headlamp on the coil-ignition models, gives a red light when the engine is stationary and the ignition is switched on. This red light warns the rider that he should switch off the ignition to prevent current discharging from the battery in the event of the contacts at the contact-breaker being closed. The warning lamp goes out immediately the engine runs fast enough to cause the dynamo to charge, but it may continue to show when the engine is idling slowly. Should the bulb burn out, running of the engine will not be affected, but the bulb should be replaced as soon as possible. Always fit a Lucas 2·5-volt (0·2 amp) bulb on 1945-53 models.

The ignition key (which is detachable) is incorporated in the centre of the headlamp lighting switch. To switch on, push the key in and turn *clockwise*. Coil-ignition wiring diagrams are given on pages 41 and 42.

Symptoms of a Faulty Condenser. The condenser (which is connected in parallel with the contact-breaker circuit) is primarily designed to prevent arcing between the contacts at the moment of the "break." It rarely develops a defect and the symptoms of condenser trouble are unmistakable — a pronounced tendency for the contacts to become rapidly burnt and pitted, in spite of their being kept clean and correctly adjusted. If such trouble occurs, inspect the condenser immediately.

Automatic Ignition-advance Mechanism. No adjustment of the A.I.A. mechanism on coil-ignition Models C10, C11 is provided, but very occasionally it may be advisable to remove the contact-breaker (*see* Fig. 46) and check that the bob-weights move freely. Turn the A.I.A. unit to the full advance position (bob-weights fully extended outwards) and then release it. The springs should automatically withdraw the bob-weights to the inner position (fully retarded). If necessary lubricate the mechanism thoroughly with some thin oil (*see* page 57).

To Adjust the Dynamo Chain (Coil-Ignition Models). On Models C10, C11, do not allow a total whip of less or more than ½ in. To adjust the dynamo chain tension, slacken off the clip bolt and rotate the eccentrically-mounted dynamo gently. To ensure a proper oil seal, it is essential to keep the dynamo pressed against the chain case when re-tightening the clip bolt. On all "Magdyno" models the "Magdyno" is gear-driven.

TAPPET ADJUSTMENT

It is very important to maintain the correct valve clearances on all B.S.A. engines and the clearances should be checked about every 1,000 miles when the engine is *quite cold*; after 250 miles in the case of new engines where considerable "bedding down" of the parts occurs; after grinding-in the valves. It should be noted that incorrect valve clearances interfere with both the lift of the valves and also the valve timing.

Excessive clearances result in reduced valve lift and late opening of the valves, which causes undue noise and loss of efficiency, but this is not likely

GENERAL MAINTENANCE

to damage the valves. Insufficient valve clearances, besides resulting in loss of compression, flexibility, and power, may cause distortion and perhaps burning of the exhaust valve due to gas leakage past it during the power strokes. Experienced riders can usually tell by the sound and "feel" of an engine whether the valve clearances are correct. Before checking the valve clearances it is essential to set the piston at top dead centre and then check that there is sufficient clearance at the exhaust-valve lifter (*see* page 86).

Model C10. On this 250 c.c. S.V. engine, first put the piston at true T.D.C. on the compression stroke. To do this, turn the engine over until the piston is near the top of the compression stroke, and locate T.D.C. by inserting a piece of slim rod into the compression-plug hole (in middle of the head) so that the piston crown can be felt. Proceed to check the valve clearances when the piston is at true T.D.C. with inlet and exhaust valves closed, and when slight backward or forward turning of the engine does not open or close either valve.

Unscrew the four retaining screws and remove the tappet cover, being careful not to damage the gasket. Then check the clearance between the base of each valve and the tappet head, using the appropriate feeler gauge. Referring to Fig. 47, if either tappet clearance is incorrect (*see* Table IV),

TABLE IV
CORRECT 1945-59 VALVE CLEARANCES (ENGINE COLD)

Model	C10 1945-53	C11 1945-53	B31-B34, M33*	M20* 1945-55	M21* 1945-58
Inlet	0·004 in.	0·003 in.	0·003 in.	0·010 in.	0·010 in.
Exhaust	0·006 in.	0·003 in.	0·003 in.	0·012 in.	0·012 in.

hold the tappet head *A* with a tappet spanner and loosen the lock-nut *B*. Then with another tappet spanner (see Fig. 47) hold the flat *C* and turn the tappet head as required, clockwise or anti-clockwise to reduce or increase the valve clearance respectively. Holding head *A* in this position, firmly tighten lock-nut *B* against *A*, and again check the tappet clearance with a feeler gauge in case the adjustment has moved. Renew the cover gasket if damaged, and replace the compression plug.

Model C11. This has direct-acting push-rods with no tappets. The valve-clearance adjustment comprises an adjuster screw on the push-rod end of each overhead rocker, as may be seen in Fig. 48. Check the valve

* The inlet and exhaust valve clearances quoted above should be regarded as being the minimum permissible, especially for the exhaust valve.

clearances, with the engine *quite cold*, in this manner. Remove the rocker-box cover which is held by one central bolt. Be careful not to damage the gasket, or the oil will leak. Remove the sparking plug to enable the engine to be turned readily by hand, and then position the piston so that it is

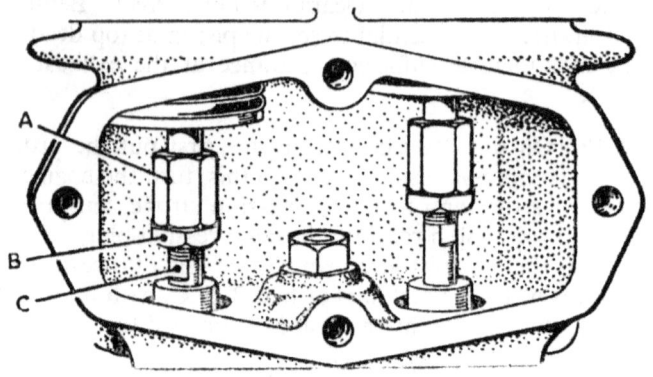

Fig. 47. Tappet Adjustment on 250 c.c. S.V. (Model C10)

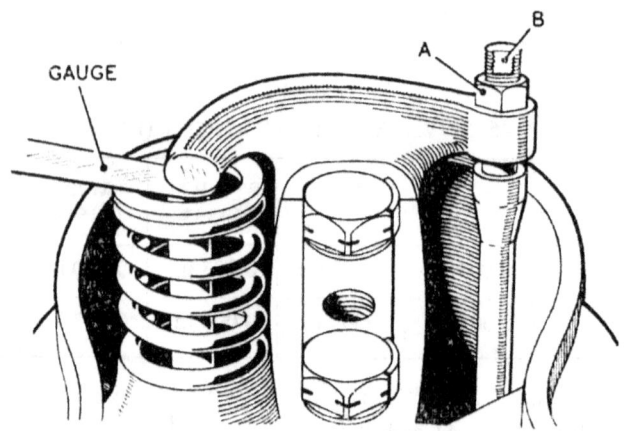

Fig. 48. O.H. Rocker Adjustment on the 250 c.c. O.H.V. Model C11

All other models have a tappet adjustment.

exactly at top dead-centre, with both valves closed. Insert a piece of slim rod into the plug hole to find the precise position of the piston. Now insert a feeler gauge of the correct size (0.003 in.) between each overhead rocker arm and the top of the valve stem as shown in Fig. 48. The gauge should just enter without binding.

Referring to Fig. 48, if an overhead rocker adjustment is needed, slacken the lock-nut *A* with the appropriate spanner, while holding the

GENERAL MAINTENANCE

adjuster screw stationary with another spanner applied to the flats *B* on each side of the adjuster screw. Turn the adjuster screw clockwise or anti-clockwise as required until the correct valve clearance is obtained. Then while holding the adjuster stationary, with a spanner applied to the adjuster-screw flats, re-tighten the lock-nut *A* against the rocker arm, and again check the valve clearance, in case it should have altered during the tightening of the lock-nut. Finally replace the sparking plug and the rocker-box cover, renewing the cover gasket if necessary.

Models B31-B34, M20, M21, M33. A similar method of checking and adjusting valve clearances is used for 350 c.c., 500 c.c. O.H.V. engines

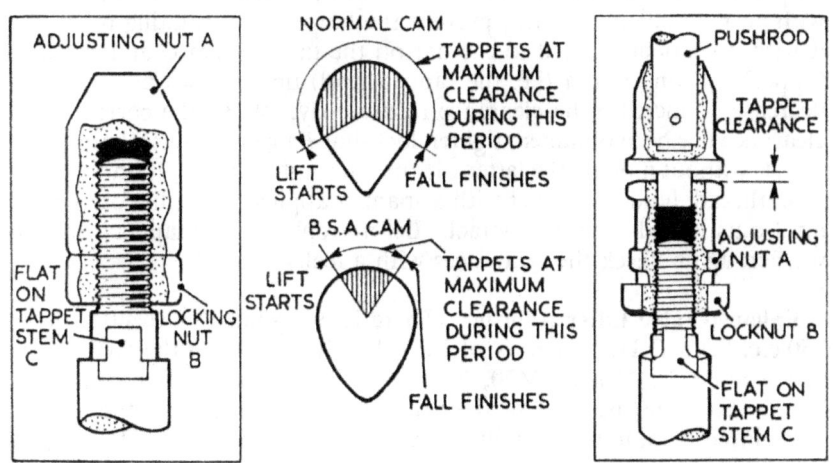

Fig. 49. S.V. (Left) and O.H.V. (Right) Tappet Adjustment
(Applies to all except 250 c.c. models.)

and 500 c.c., 600 c.c. S.V. engines. On all these engines (which have twin camwheels instead of a single one as used on the 250 c.c. models) the design of the inlet and exhaust cams is such that the foot of each tappet rests on the "neutral" portion of the cam for a comparatively short period (*see* Fig. 49). It is therefore absolutely imperative to make certain that the cams are correctly positioned prior to adjusting the tappets, and to verify that there is sufficient clearance at the exhaust-valve lifter (*see* page 86). To ensure correct cam positioning, the following procedure must be observed—

Remove the tappet cover and slowly rotate the engine in its normal direction of rotation until the *inlet* valve has just closed (remember by "I see" (I.C.)), the tappet being just free to rotate. Then check the *exhaust* tappet clearance with a suitable feeler gauge inserted between the tappet head and valve stem (S.V.) or push-rod (O.H.V.). For the correct valve clearances, see Table IV on page 83. If necessary, adjust the exhaust-valve clearance.

Further rotate the engine in its normal direction of rotation until the exhaust tappet clearance is reduced to *nil* without causing the exhaust valve to lift. Then check and if necessary adjust the *inlet* tappet clearance (*see* Table IV), using the same procedure as for the exhaust tappet.

On O.H.V.s (B31–B34, M33) it is best, when checking the tappet clearance with a feeler gauge, to take the weight of the push-rod off the tappet by lifting the push-rod with the fingers. This facilitates proper entry of the feeler gauge and accurate checking of the valve clearance.

Referring to Fig. 49, to adjust the tappet clearance, with the appropriate tappet spanner, loosen the lock-nut B while holding the tappet head A with another spanner. Then prevent the tappet from rotating by holding it with a spanner applied to the flat on the tappet stem C and screw the tappet adjusting nut A (i.e. the tappet head) up or down as required to decrease or increase the clearance respectively. When the correct tappet clearance has been obtained, tighten lock-nut B firmly against the adjusting nut A, without moving the latter. If the lock-nut is at all stiff on the tappet stem thread, hold the tappet with a spanner applied to the flat on the stem until nuts A and B are in contact. Before replacing the tappet cover and washer, again check the clearances with a feeler gauge.

Exhaust-Valve Lifter Adjuster. There is no exhaust-valve lifter on the 250 c.c. S.V., O.H.V. engines of Models C10, C11. On the 500, 600 c.c. S.V. engines of Models M20, M21, the exhaust-valve lifter cam in the tappet chest must be clear of the exhaust-tappet collar when the exhaust-valve lifter is not in use. Similarly on the 350 c.c., 500 c.c. O.H.V. engines (B31–B34, M33) the exhaust-valve lifter cam (Fig. 50) must be kept well clear of the rocker arm inside the exhaust rocker-box. Failure to maintain adequate exhaust-valve lifter clearance upsets tappet clearance, occasions mechanical noise, and worse still, causes a tendency for the exhaust valve to burn up. On the S.V. engines adjust the exhaust-valve lifter by means of the cable adjuster provided on the side of the tappet chest. On the 350 c.c., 500 c.c. O.H.V. engines, effect exhaust-valve lifter adjustment by the cable adjuster screwed into the exhaust rocker-box cover. An additional adjustment on these engines can be made by removing and altering the position of the actuating lever on the serrated cam spindle.

DECARBONIZING AND VALVE GRINDING

Generally speaking, the removal of carbon deposits is necessary only when the engine displays a tendency to run hot, and when certain characteristic symptoms (*see* below) become manifest. Under normal running conditions decarbonizing should only be undertaken at periods exceeding 4,000 miles, and not till the engine *really needs it*. Valve grinding can be conveniently done when decarbonizing, and the valves and their seats

GENERAL MAINTENANCE 87

should be inspected. Certain items required for the complete maintenance operation are mentioned on page 70.

The cylinder barrel should also be removed, if it is felt that the piston rings should be inspected. An inspection of the piston rings is advisable where engine compression is poor (in spite of valve condition being good), and where there is a tendency for blue smoke to issue from the exhaust. Decarbonizing is very simple, especially on S.V. engines, and it is not necessary to remove the cylinder barrel during each "top overhaul" because most of the carbon deposits form on the piston crown, which is

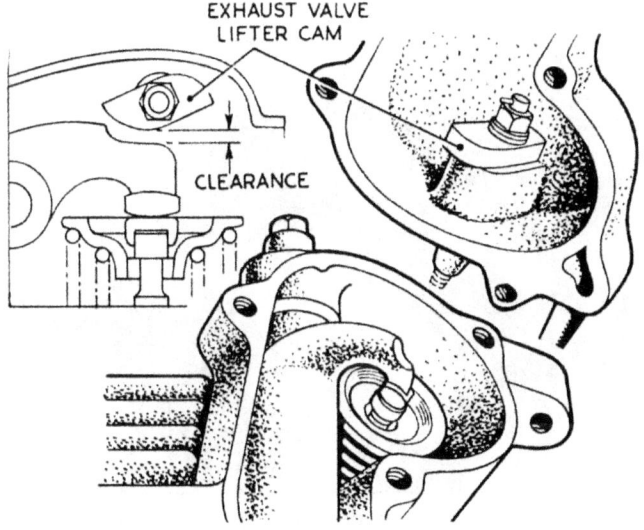

FIG. 50. EXHAUST-VALVE LIFTER ADJUSTMENT ON B.S.A. 350 C.C., 500 C.C. O.H.V. ENGINES (B31-B34, M33)

Position cam correctly on fitting rocker cover. Check split-pin.

accessible on removing the cylinder head. The necessity for decarbonizing is indicated by a gradual falling off in power (especially on hills), a tendency for "pinking" (injurious to the engine) under slight provocation, and a "woolly" exhaust. The sparking plug also tends to become dirty very quickly.

Removal of the Petrol Tank (1945-53). This is necessary except on the 250 c.c. S.V. Model C10. First turn off the petrol tap and remove the petrol pipe from the tank to the carburettor. Then on the 1945-7 Models B31, B33, disconnect the drive for the tank-mounted speedometer by releasing the strainer bolt beneath the tank. Raise the speedometer itself clear of the petrol tank and unscrew the knurled ring-nut which connects the drive to the speedometer. The petrol tank itself is fastened to the frame by two bolts which pass through the special lug at the rear of the frame top-tube, and by one bolt which passes through the steering head lug. Break the wire locking of the two rear vertical bolts. Remove all three bolts and carefully lift the petrol tank off the machine. Note the correct order of the rubber pads and washers on which the tank is mounted at the rear, to ensure correct replacement (*see* page 106).

Removal of the Petrol Tank (1954-9 "Swinging Arm" Models). Turn off the petrol and detach the petrol pipe. Then remove the two nuts and detach the strap positioned beneath the front end of the tank. Pull off the

FIG. 51. REMOVING QUICKLY-DETACHABLE PETROL TANK
On "swinging-arm" machines the tank (which holds 2 or 4 gal) can be removed very quickly and safely.

rubber grommet which conceals the tank central securing-bolt, and with a box spanner and tommy-bar remove the bolt. The petrol tank can then be withdrawn as shown in Fig. 51.

1. Preliminary Dismantling (Model C10). On this 250 c.c. S.V. model, if the cylinder head only is to be removed, disconnect the h.t. lead at the sparking plug and remove the plug. Where the cylinder barrel also is to be removed, detach the exhaust pipe (a push fit in the cylinder) by slackening the clip bolts which secure it to the frame and pulling the pipe clear. Also remove the petrol pipe between the petrol tank and the carburettor, and remove the Amal carburettor. Unscrew the ring nut at the top of the mixing chamber and withdraw the throttle and air slides. Then unscrew the carburettor attachment-flange nuts and remove the complete carburettor assembly. Tie the carburettor slides to the top-tube out of the way. Remove the tappet cover and paper washer which must be intact.

GENERAL MAINTENANCE

2. Preliminary Dismantling (Model C11). On the 250 c.c. O.H.V. model it is assumed that the petrol tank has been removed (*see* page 87). Then proceed as described in Section 1 for Model C10, following all the removal instructions irrespective of whether the cylinder barrel is to be removed or not. Also remove the rocker-box cover and gasket by undoing the central bolt. See that the gasket is undamaged and not causing oil leakage.

3. Preliminary Dismantling (Models B31-B34, M20, M21, M33). On 350 c.c., 500 c.c. O.H.V. and 500, 600 c.c. S.V. models it is assumed the petrol tank has already been removed. Next detach the h.t. lead at the plug and remove the latter. Also disconnect the steady-stay (a plate, 1954-9) from the frame to the rear of the cylinder head. On O.H.V. engines in any case, and on the S.V. engines *where barrel removal is intended*, unscrew the ring nut on top of the carburettor mixing chamber and withdraw the carburettor slides and place them out of the way. Then remove the Amal carburettor as a unit, after removing the two flange securing-nuts. Be careful not to damage the flange washer (two washers and distance-piece, M20, M21). Also remove the exhaust system after removing the nuts securing the pipe and silencer clips to the frame. The pipe is a push fit in the exhaust port. It may be necessary to tap it carefully (avoid denting) with a mallet.

The engine is now in exactly the condition shown in Fig. 52. On 1958-9 models there is, of course, no "Magdyno" fitted.

Removing the Cylinder Head (Model C10). After preliminary dismantling has been effected as described in Section 1, loosen the cylinder head securing-bolts, in the reverse order to that shown in Fig. 62, and remove all eight bolts. If the cylinder head is reluctant to come off, tap it carefully *low down on the vertical fins*, using a wooden mallet, until it is freed. Avoid using excessive force, otherwise the fins may become cracked. If the cylinder head gasket has black areas, it is "blowing" and requires renewal.

Removal of the cylinder head exposes the piston and the valves. Position the piston at T.D.C. and scrape off carbon deposits with a blunt screwdriver or other suitable scraper, being careful not to scratch the metal deeply. Also remove all carbon deposits from the combustion chamber (*see* notes on page 97).

Turn the engine over until the valves are opened in turn and inspect the valves and their seatings. If a good and unbroken contact area is observed, do not disturb the valves, but if pitting and/or corrosion marks are detected, the valves must be ground-in (*see* page 99). In order to grind-in the valves, it is always advisable to remove the cylinder barrel.

Removing the Cylinder Barrel (Model C10). With a suitable spanner remove the five nuts which secure the flanged base of the barrel to the crankcase. One of these five nuts is located inside the tappet chest (*see* Fig. 47), the remainder being external.

Set the piston at B.D.C. and lift the cylinder barrel upward and forward as far as is practicable until the piston emerges. Steady the piston as it

FIG. 52. DISMANTLING O.H.V. ENGINE FOR DECARBONIZING—STAGE 1
A 1952 B31 engine is shown, but the general dismantling procedure applies to all 1945-59 350 c.c. and 500 c.c. O.H.V. engines.

KEY
1. Support for tank (1945-53)
2. Plug terminal cover and h.t. lead (detached)
3. Hole for plug (removed)
4. Engine steady-stay (disconnected). Plate fitted, 1954-9
5. Mixing chamber ring nut (removed from carburettor)
6. Carburettor slides (tucked away)
7. Flange for carburettor (removed)
8. Exhaust port (pipe and silencer removed altogether)
9. Unions for rocker-spindle oil feed pipe. Central feed, 1954-9
10. Union for rocker-box oil return pipe (omitted, 1958-9)

leaves the cylinder mouth. Wrap a clean rag around it to prevent damage, and cover up the crankcase hole.

Removing the Cylinder Head (Model C11). After completing preliminary dismantling as described in Section 2, set the piston at T.D.C. on the compression stroke (valves closed). Then remove the cylinder-head securing nuts which are located between the cylinder fins at the side of the cylinder barrel (*see* Fig. 53). Free the cylinder head by tapping it lightly with a wooden mallet just beneath the exhaust port. Then lift the head

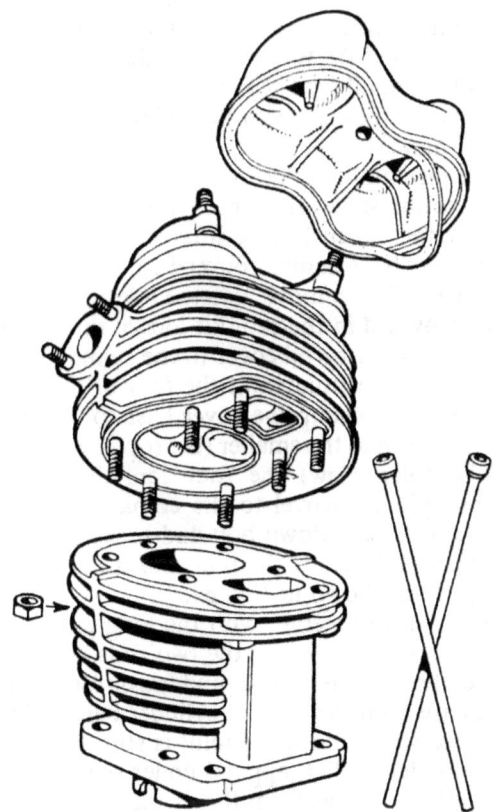

Fig. 53. Details of Cylinder Barrel, Cylinder Head, and Rocker Box on 250 c.c. Model C11 O.H.V. Engine

An unusual feature of the Model C11 engine is that the inlet and exhaust push-rods are crossed.

(*From "The Motor Cycle," London*)

sufficiently to enable the crossed push-rods to be freed from the ball-ended pins of the overhead rockers. Withdraw both push-rods and then lift the cylinder head and gasket (renew if damaged) off the cylinder barrel. *Note:* Always loosen the cylinder-head nuts in the reverse order to that shown in Fig. 64.

Removing Cylinder Head (Models M20, M21). It is assumed that preliminary dismantling has been effected as described in Section 3. Proceed to loosen the cylinder head securing-bolts in the reverse order to that shown in Fig. 63 and remove all ten bolts. Then proceed to remove the head in the same manner as described for Model C10 (*see* page 90).

FIG. 55. REMOVING CYLINDER HEAD AND PUSH-ROD COVER TOGETHER

When doing this, first lower the push-rods (not shown) on to the crank-case face. It is possible to remove the head and the cover separately, but this is not advised because it is likely to damage the rubber oil seal between the head and the cover.

Removing the Cylinder Barrel (Models M20, M21). Disconnect the exhaust lifter from the lever at the front of the valve chest. Then proceed exactly as described (page 89) for Model C10.

Piston Removal. The piston (removal seldom needed) is of aluminium alloy with two compression rings and one slotted scraper ring (Fig. 57). It is held to the small end of the connecting-rod by a fully floating gudgeon-pin, secured to the piston by circlips (*see* Fig. 56). The gudgeon-pin is a close fit in the piston when the latter is cold. To remove it safely, *first warm the piston* by laying an electric iron on its crown, or by applying a rag immersed in boiling water and wrung out. Then press out the pin after circlip removal.

GENERAL MAINTENANCE 95

The gudgeon-pin may be pressed out with a gudgeon-pin extractor tool (*see* Fig. 61), or tapped out with a light hammer and soft-nosed punch. Where a piston has had considerable service, it may be possible to push the pin out by hand, provided that the piston is reasonably warm.

Remove the circlips with a small screwdriver or pointed instrument such as the tang end of a ground file. Then press or tap the gudgeon-pin out from one side, supporting the piston if tapping the pin out. A circlip must fit snugly into its groove in the piston boss because if it works loose, it may ruin the cylinder. Whatever the condition of a circlip, renew it with

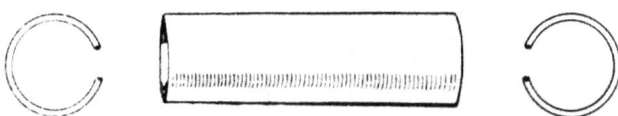

FIG. 56. GUDGEON-PIN AND CIRCLIPS
Note that the circlips have plain ends.

a genuine B.S.A. one. On removing the gudgeon-pin, make a slight nick on one end to ensure correct replacement.

Marking the Piston. A piston laps out the cylinder in a certain manner depending upon piston thrust, lubrication and other factors, and it is most vital not to replace it in any except its original position on the connecting-rod; it should not be replaced back to front. Therefore, unless the piston has some distinguishing characteristic it is always advisable to mark it to ensure its correct replacement. Perhaps the best plan is to scratch an "F" on the inside to indicate which is the front. Always remember that a piston should be handled with great care, as it is readily distorted or cracked. Test the connecting-rod for vertical play. None should exist, but a little side play is normal.

TABLE V
SOME USEFUL DATA

Model	C10	C11	B31,* B32	B33,* B34	M20	M21	M33
Comp. Ratio	5/1	6·5/1	6·5/1	6·5/1	4·9/1	5/1	6·5/1
Bore (mm)	63	63	71	85	82	82	85
Stroke (mm)	80	80	88	88	94	112	88
c.c.	249	249	348	499	496	591	499
Fuel (gal)	$2\frac{1}{2}$	$2\frac{1}{2}$	3	3	3	3	3
Oil (pt)	4	4	$4\frac{1}{2}, 3\frac{1}{4}$	$4\frac{1}{2}$	5	5	5

* On "swinging arm" models the fuel and oil tank capacities are 2 or 4 gal and $5\frac{1}{2}$ pints respectively.

Examining and Removing the Piston Rings. The piston rings are the main-guard of the compression. They must, therefore, be full of spring, free in their grooves, and set with their slots opposite to each other (i.e. at 120° in the case of a three-ring piston). If all three rings have a smooth metallic surface, they are satisfactorily contacting the cylinder walls, and are perfect, and should be left alone. If, on the other hand, they are shiny or stained at some points, they are not in good contact with the walls of the cylinder. Perhaps they are stuck in their grooves with burnt oil, but will function properly if the grooves are cleaned. If the rings are scored,

 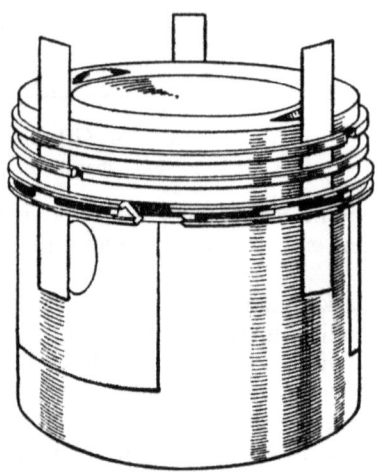

FIG. 57. PISTON AND SAFE METHOD OF REMOVING RINGS

This method (see text) should also be used for refitting rings. Note the slotted scraper ring below the two compression rings. On all later type engines a split-skirt type piston is fitted. The piston shown on the left is worn, scored and blackened (rebore and oversize piston needed).

or have lost their tension (minimum free gap: $\frac{3}{16}$ in.), or are vertically loose in their grooves or have brown patches, the rings must be renewed.

Piston rings are of cast-iron and, being of very small section, must be handled very, very carefully. If not, they will certainly be broken. Scraper rings are particularly vulnerable; they cannot safely be opened out wider than will allow them to slip over the crown of the piston. Therefore, to put them on or remove them requires the insertion of small strips of sheet-metal, about $\frac{1}{2}$ in. wide by 2 in. long, which are placed in the manner shown in Fig. 57. Be most careful to note the order in which the rings are removed so as to ensure proper replacement. When fitting piston rings, thoroughly clean the grooves into which they fit, as any deposit left at the back of new rings forces them out and makes them too tight a fit. Paraffin usually loosens stuck piston rings.

Piston rings are made to very accurate dimensions, and it is very bad practice to attempt to "fit" oversize or undersize rings unless you know exactly what you are doing. Lapping-in oversize piston rings is a skilful job, and unless the slot sizes are exactly right, the rings will not function well, and may even produce an engine seizure. Therefore, always use piston rings supplied by B.S.A. Motor Cycles, Ltd. The gap for all new rings should not be less than 0·008 in. or exceed 0·012 in. (all engines). Test the gap occasionally with feeler gauges and if it exceeds 0·025 in. fit a new ring (if barrel wear is not excessive). Check its gap. When testing the ring gap, insert the ring into the least worn part of cylinder bore and slide up the piston so that its top locates the ring squarely.

Keep an eye on the ends of the three rings. If they are bright, this indicates that the gap is insufficient; if, on the other hand, they are thick with carbon the gap is probably excessive. If the gap of a new ring is less than 0·008 in. clamp the ring between two wood blocks in a vice and file one of the diagonal ends slightly. If a new ring is found to be a tight fit in its groove, rub down one side of the ring on a piece of carborundum paper laid on a sheet of plate glass. A slotted scraper ring is fitted on B.S.A. pistons (Fig. 57) and this can usually be fitted either way up.* All three rings should be assembled in the manner shown in Fig. 57. A final word of advice: if the piston is doing its job well, leave the rings alone. Good compression indicates that all is well.

Removing the Carbon. Thoroughness in decarbonizing well repays the labour expended. To clean the cylinder head, the best tool is a proprietary scraper, blunt knife, or screwdriver, with which the carbon can be scraped and chipped from the head, great care being taken to see that the combustion chamber is not deeply scratched. The author finds that a small electrical screwdriver is excellent for decarbonizing the curved walls of the combustion chamber. To avoid damaging the valve seats, always first insert the valves in their guides if these have been removed.

Remove all traces of carbon from the interior surfaces and do not forget the sparking plug hole and the exhaust port. Carbon forms less readily on a smooth surface and therefore it is a good plan to polish a cast-iron type head with fine emery cloth, but do this *before* removing the valves, and afterwards clear all abrasive particles away with paraffin. Also scrape all carbon from the valve heads. Be very careful with an aluminium-alloy head and do not use emery cloth on it.

In the case of an O.H.V. head with metal-to-metal joint, care should be taken that the ground joint of the head is not damaged. A good method of holding the head whilst decarbonizing is to fit a hexagon steel bar, turned and threaded at one end into the plug hole. The cylinder head may then be held in a vice by means of the steel bar. If such a bar is not available, an old sparking plug makes a useful substitute.

* With a stepped or chamfered scraper ring, fit the ring with the step or chamfer uppermost.

With a soft aluminium-alloy piston (moved to T.D.C.) be careful when removing the carbon. *Do not use emery cloth;* the carbon can be removed by means of a proprietary scraper, a blunt knife, or blunt screwdriver, and the surface afterwards can be wiped with a rag damped in paraffin. Never attempt to remove carbon from the skirt or the lands between the rings. A little carbon is usually deposited on the *inside* of the piston. When the piston is removed, this should be removed. The screwdriver, or other scraper can be used for this until all carbon is scraped off. If the piston is not removed, do not disturb the carbon on its circumference, which forms a good oil seal. It is a good plan to place an old piston ring on top of the piston. Examine all ring grooves for carbon. Should

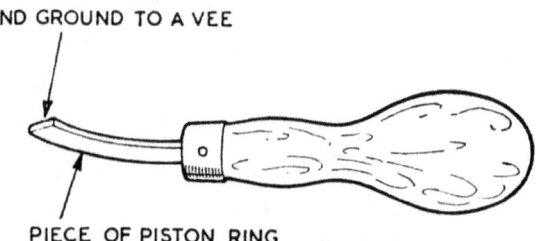

FIG. 58. A USEFUL TOOL FOR CLEANING PISTON RING GROOVES

any be present, scrape out with a tool such as that shown in Fig. 58. The rings should also be scraped at the back. Wash the piston and rings thoroughly in clean paraffin. Refit the rings by slipping them over the piston, using, if necessary, the method shown in Fig. 57.

Stripping the Cylinder Head (B31, B32, B33, B64, M33). It is not necessary when removing valves for grinding-in, to detach the overhead rockers, but if a complete strip is decided upon, proceed in the following manner. With a suitable spanner remove the acorn nuts on the rocker spindles. Then tap the spindles out, using a small centre-punch to prevent damaging the threads on the spindle ends. When dismantling, note the correct order of assembly for future attention. This is: (*a*) spring; (*b*) steel washer; (*c*) aluminium oil-seal washer.

To Remove the Valves. As has already been mentioned (page 86) the valves should be removed and inspected when you are decarbonizing, and *if necessary* ground-in. On S.V. engines it is possible to remove the valves with the cylinder in position, but it is preferable to take off the barrel. On O.H.V. engines the valves are, of course, housed in the detachable head. Split collets are used for valve-spring anchorage on all B.S.A. engines. To remove them, it is desirable to use a good valve-spring compressor (which may be purchased from any B.S.A. dealer). This particularly applies to O.H.V. engines where the outer valve spring

GENERAL MAINTENANCE

collars are awkwardly placed. Split collets often become stuck, and after turning the tommy-bar or wing nut of the compressor a few turns, loosen the split collet by delivering a sharp tap with a hammer on the forked end of the compressor. Be careful not to lose the valve-stem end caps (B31 and B32 engines). *Do not mix up inlet and exhaust collets.*

Should no valve-spring compressor be available, the following method can be employed for compressing the valve springs on S.V. or O.H.V. engines. Place some hard packing under the valve heads (O.H.V.); place the cylinder or cylinder head so that the valves or packing are flush with the bench. Then press down on the valve spring outer collar with a spanner or other suitable tool until the spring is compressed enough to enable the split collet to be removed. The valve can then be drawn out, and the duplex spring and collars removed. The valve springs are powerful and the author strongly advises the use of a compressor (*see* Fig. 60) for valve removal. For Model C10, use compressor Part No. 61-3340.

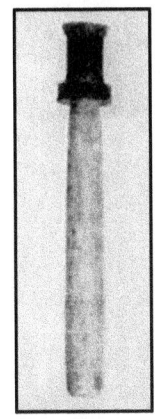

FIG. 59.
VALVE-
GRINDING
TOOL (O.H.V.)

How to Grind-in Valves. Use a screwdriver for S.V. engines and the valve grinding tool* shown in Fig. 59 for O.H.V. engines. To grind-in a valve (see that it is the correct one), holding the cylinder or cylinder head firmly on a bench or in a vice (*see* page 97), clean both the valve seat and valve; smear, with a piece of rag or the finger tip, a thin film of fine grinding paste (coarse at first if dealing with a valve and seat in poor condition) on the valve face; replace the valve in its guide minus the valve spring. Before replacing it, however, it is a good plan to insert a light spring between the valve head and valve guide. This avoids the necessity of frequently lifting the valve off its seat, by hand, when turning it round to avoid the formation of grooves or rings on the valve face. Never interchange the inlet and exhaust valves (marked "IN" and "EX" respectively). On many O.H.V. engines the valves cannot be interchanged because the diameter of the exhaust-valve stem is greater than that of the inlet-valve stem.

When grinding-in, a light pressure on the grinding tool is required and care must be taken not to rock the valve, particularly if the valve guide is somewhat worn. Rotate the valve about *a third of a turn* in one direction and then an equal amount in the opposite direction, pausing every few oscillations to raise the valve from its seat and turn it one-third to a quarter of a revolution. Cease grinding-in when no "cut" can be felt (and the valve begins to "sing") and put some more paste on the bevelled

* To secure good adhesion, the rubber end should be moistened before use.

edge of the valve face if, after cleaning the valve in paraffin, some pitting is still visible.

Continue grinding-in until both the valve face and seat have a matt metallic surface uniformly over an appreciable width (line contact is not sufficient) and there are no pit marks left after wiping the paste off. Excessive grinding-in after a good seating has been effected eventually leads to the valves becoming "pocketed," which causes a considerable decline in power output. Take badly pitted valves or seats to a B.S.A. dealer for re-grinding and re-facing (at 45 deg.) respectively.

After grinding-in the inlet and exhaust valves, wipe both the valves and their seats thoroughly clean with a paraffin- or petrol-soaked rag to ensure that there is absolutely no trace of any abrasive left. Examine the valve guides for wear and renew if much play exists, otherwise slow-running will become difficult. Often a valve stem wears more than its guide does, and a distinct shoulder is felt near the neck of the valve. In this case fitting a new valve (which must be ground-in) will probably remedy slackness without fitting a new valve guide. Also renew the valve springs if weak. If rough, smooth the ports with a riffler.

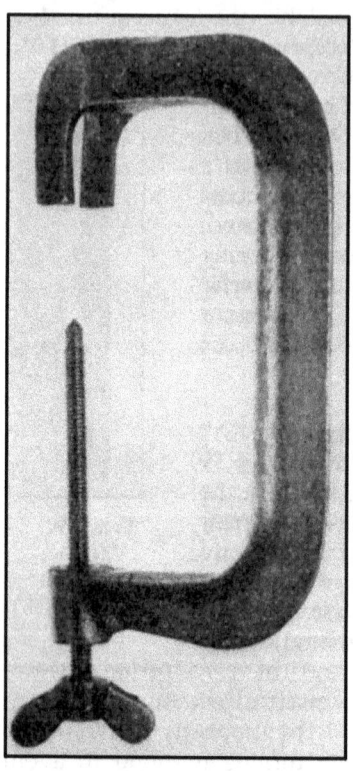

Fig. 60. The B.S.A. Valve-spring Compressor for O.H.V. Engines

Fitting New Valve Guides. If the valve guides on a S.V. engine are worn badly enough to require renewal, the old guides can be driven out with a single punch applied through the lower end of the cylinder barrel. New valve guides can be driven in through the top of the cylinder barrel. Because the guides have no locating step, they must be positioned so that the top of the inlet guide is $1\frac{1}{8}$ in., and the top of the exhaust guide $\frac{15}{16}$ in., below the top of the cylinder barrel.

On an O.H.V. engine the old guides may be driven out with a single punch applied from inside the cylinder head. New guides must be driven in from the top as far as they can go. Note that when new valve guides are fitted on a S.V. or O.H.V. engine it is essential to have the valve seats refaced with a proper valve seat cutter. This ensures that each seat is concentric with the bore of the corresponding valve guide.

Refitting the Valves. After grinding-in the valves you should reassemble them in the correct positions in the cylinder head.

On B31, B32 engines, do not forget to replace the hardened valve stem end-caps. Before replacing the valve springs, check that they have not lost their tension by comparing them with a new spring. Loss of tension, due mainly to heat, sometimes occurs after several thousand miles, and the free length of the valve springs is reduced. This necessitates renewal and where such renewal is, or soon will be, required, it is obviously wise to effect valve spring renewal during decarbonizing procedure.

Smear the valve stems with oil and replace them in their guides. Then refit the valve springs and collars, being careful not to mix up the upper and lower collars. Next compress each valve spring and refit the split collet, making certain that it "beds down" properly. On O.H.V. engines the application of a little grease to the inside of a split-collet enables it to stick on the valve stem until the duplex spring is released, and thereby facilitates reassembly. *Note*: the exhaust collet is *thinner* than the inlet. Wrong replacement can cause a valve to drop into the cylinder!

Valve Spring Renewal. Valve springs are cheap and, if shortened, may damage the valves. The correct free lengths for *new* (O.H.V.) inner and outer springs are $1\frac{13}{16}$ in. and $2\frac{5}{32}$ in. respectively. S.V. springs: 2 in.

Fitting Overhead Rockers. To fit each rocker, tap in the spindle and fit spring, steel washer, rocker, and aluminium washer; tap the spindle hard home and tighten the acorn nuts. *The oil groove should be uppermost.*

Grinding-in the Cylinder Head and Barrel Faces. If either face on an O.H.V. engine (with metal-to-metal joint) has been damaged in removal of the head, it will be necessary to regrind them in, in the same manner as one would a valve. The holes from which the bolts have been taken should first be filled with grease, so that the grinding compound is kept out of the threads. The head and barrel should then be ground-in.

Rebores and Oversize Pistons. Inspect the bore of the cylinder barrel closely for wear when the barrel is removed. Should a deep ridge be felt at the top end, it may be desirable to have the cylinder rebored. Take the cylinder barrel to the nearest B.S.A. dealer to get an expert opinion. The cylinder barrel will also need to be rebored if there are any deep score marks causing loss of compression and excessive oil consumption. Shiny marks on the bore surface indicate that a seizure has occurred, and the piston should be closely examined.

Note that pistons $\frac{1}{2}$ mm and 1 mm oversize are obtainable for rebore purposes. In the U.K. there is also an Exchange Replacement system enabling a rebored cylinder barrel with piston to match to be obtained from a local B.S.A. spares stockist.

Refitting the Piston and Cylinder Barrel. This should be done in the reverse order of dismantling. Smear the piston and inside of the cylinder barrel with engine oil and refit the piston on the connecting-rod the correct way round (page 95), pressing or tapping home the oiled gudgeon-pin, from one side after fitting a new circlip on the other. If the gudgeon-pin

Fig. 61. Pressing the Gudgeon-pin Home into the Piston with a Terry Tool

On the stripped machine illustrated (the author's 1952 Model B31) the gudgeon-pin has been pressed nearly home into the 0·02-in. over-size Hepolite piston, after fitting a new circlip on the near side. Note the three alternative pressure pads on the ends of the tommy-bar and pressure screw. A new exhaust tappet and guide have just been fitted, and the guide is shown partly screwed home. To remove the exhaust tappet, by the way, it is necessary to remove the exhaust camwheel-spindle and also the main-shaft pinion, using B.S.A. extractors, Part Nos. 61-691 and 61-1735 respectively. The outrigger plate (*see* Fig. 65) has not yet been bolted on. If a "Magdyno" is removed, be sure to replace the original base shims.

refuses to go home, warm the piston (see page 94), and do not forget to support it when using a hammer and soft-nosed drift.

Fit a second new circlip (even if the old one seems perfect) and see that it beds down properly in the piston-boss slot and is fully expanded. Remember that if a circlip fails while the engine is running you may have to put your hand in your pocket for a new piston and cylinder. Also see that the cylinder-barrel spigot and mouth of the crankcase are scrupulously clean and that the base washer is intact and replaced. Smear it lightly with some jointing compound (*see* page 106).

GENERAL MAINTENANCE 103

To replace the cylinder barrel, put the crank slightly past B.D.C. with tappets or push-rods (C11) right down, position the ring gaps (*see* page 96), hold the cylinder barrel with both hands (or suspend it from the top-tube) over the piston; with help (or unaided), offer up the piston. The rings must be squeezed together (by hand or with a proprietary metal strap), and the barrel slid over the piston until the complete piston enters the cylinder. Avoid putting any side strain on the piston or connecting-rod.

After seeing that the barrel spigot "beds down" on the crankcase squarely and closely, tighten up the cylinder-base nuts (C10, C11, M20, M21), finger-tight at first, and then securely with a spanner, giving *a quarter* of a turn at a time, diagonally, on the external nuts. Even tightening is important, otherwise there is some risk of distorting the cylinder flange and preventing it "bedding down" properly on the crankcase. On S.V. engines do not forget the nut inside the valve chest, which should be tightened last of all, and that if a new cylinder-base washer is fitted, the barrel securing nuts should be checked for tightness after 250 miles. On B31-B34, M33 engines the long bolts which secure the cylinder barrel and head are not, of course, raised and tightened until *after* the cylinder head has been replaced. Put piston at T.D.C.

Final Reassembly (Models C10, M20, M21). Clean the faces of the cylinder barrel and cylinder head and then replace the cylinder-head gasket; if it shows signs of leakage (indicated by black patches), fit a new one. Now carefully lower the cylinder head on to the barrel, insert the cylinder-head bolts and tighten them down evenly *a quarter of a turn* at a time in the correct order (*see* Figs. 62, 63). On Models M20, M21, replace the engine steady-stay. The bolts will require re-tightening after about 250 miles, particularly if a new gasket has been fitted. Check the tappet clearances carefully, re-connect the exhaust-valve lifter, and replace the tappet cover. Now fit the exhaust system and carburettor. When replacing the latter, be careful not to damage the jet-needle while replacing the throttle slide. See that the carburettor is firmly bolted to the cylinder, also that the flange is not distorted. Finally replace the sparking plug and h.t. lead. If the petrol tank has been removed (necessary except on Model C10) replace it, and fit the petrol pipe.

Final Reassembly (Model C11). Verify that the condition of the cylinder-head gasket is sound, with no evidence of "blowing." Then replace and fit loosely in position the cylinder head. Fit the push-rods before bolting the head down. As may be seen in Fig. 53, the push-rods must be fitted so that the inlet and exhaust rods cross. First fit the exhaust push-rod so that the plain end fits into the cup formed on the cam rocker (bottom left), and the cupped end fits over the ball end of the exhaust rocker screw (top right). Now bolt the cylinder head firmly down, using the order shown in Fig. 64.

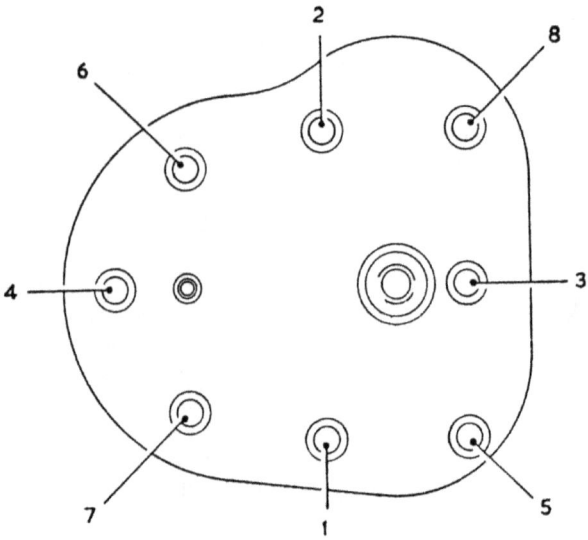

Fig. 62. Sequence for Tightening Cylinder-head Bolts on B.S.A. Model C10

Check for tightness after 250 miles subsequent to decarbonizing and on a new machine. This applies also to Models C11, M20, and M21.

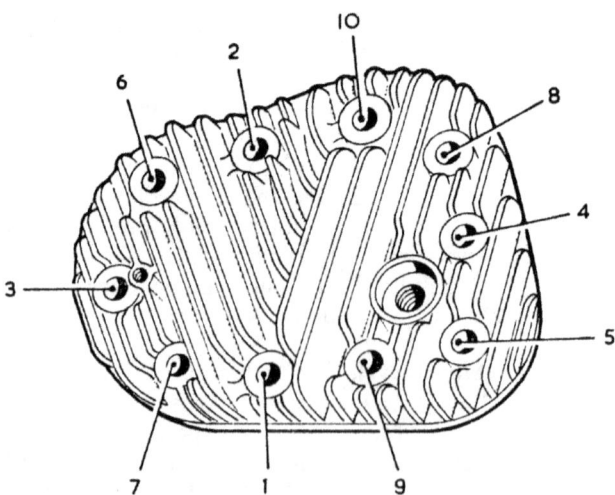

Fig. 63. Sequence for Tightening Cylinder-head Bolts on B.S.A. Models M20, M21

Check the valve clearances (page 83) before replacing the rocker-box cover and gasket (which must be undamaged) and make whatever adjustment is necessary. After covering 250 miles, check the cylinder head securing-nuts for tightness. If tightening is required, check the valve clearance and, if necessary, effect an adjustment.

Replace the Amal carburettor, taking care not to damage the jet-needle when inserting the throttle slide. See that the washer for the carburettor

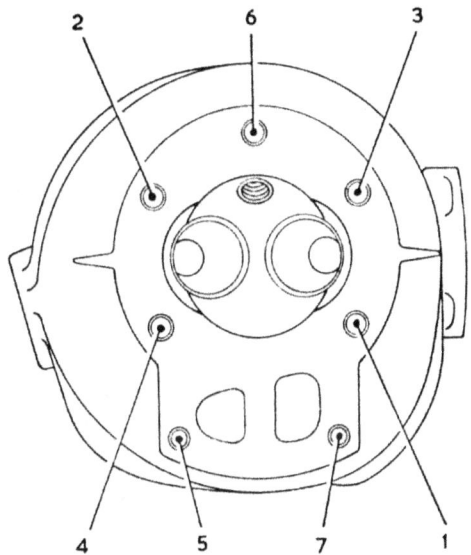

FIG. 64. ORDER OF TIGHTENING CYLINDER-HEAD NUTS ON B.S.A. MODEL C11

flange is sound, otherwise air leaks will cause poor starting. Replace and firmly secure the exhaust system. Dismantle and clean the plug, replace this, and finally fit the petrol tank and fuel pipe. Wire-lock the two rear tank bolts.

Final Reassembly (Models B31, B32, B33, B34, M33). Place the cover for the push-rods into position in the cylinder head; do not tighten up the gland nut. Fit the push-rods into the long cover and offer up the cylinder head (with rocker inspection-cover removed). Keep the cylinder head slightly raised while positioning the lower ends of the push-rods (not crossed) on the tappets. Then locate the upper ends of the push-rods on the overhead rockers.

Lower the cylinder head into position, replace and tighten firmly the two acorn nuts which secure the push-rod cover base and fit and screw up diagonally the four long cylinder-barrel and head securing-bolts. These bolts must be tightened firmly and evenly. Tighten securely the gland nut of the long push-rod cover, using the "C" spanner in the tool kit.

Check the tappet clearances (*see* page 85) prior to fitting the tappet and rocker inspection-covers, and adjust the clearances if necessary. Replace the cylinder head steady-stay and connect up the oil feed and return pipe to the rockers and head (test for oil flow). Tighten firmly the union screws (9) and (10) (Fig. 52).

Fit both rocker-box covers, the Amal carburettor unit, the exhaust system, and the petrol tank and pipe. When replacing the petrol tank on 1945-53 models, lay a round rubber pad above each tank rear-support lug, and on its underside place a rectangular rubber pad and steel washer (next to the bolt head). First fit both rear bolts; wire-lock with some 22-gauge wire. Also connect the speedometer drive to the instrument on 1945-7 tanks.

On 1954-9 "swinging arm" models after positioning the quickly-detachable petrol tank (*see* Fig. 51) replace the strap at the front end of the tank and tighten evenly the two fixing nuts. Then with the box spanner and tommy-bar provided, tighten down the single bolt which secures the petrol tank to the frame top tube. Afterwards replace the rubber grommet and connect up the petrol pipe. Replace the sparking plug, which is assumed to have been dismantled, cleaned, and if necessary re-gapped.

Note Concerning Gaskets. The 350 c.c. and 500 c.c. O.H.V. engines have a metal-to-metal cylinder-head joint and no gasket or jointing compound is necessary. Paper washers are required elsewhere (rocker-box covers, tappet and rocker inspection-covers, sump filter cover-plate, timing-case cover, cylinder base, etc.). To prevent oil leaks it is essential that all joint faces are absolutely clean. For cleaning up joint faces the author finds a carpenter's scraper plate very suitable.

The author advocates using jointing compound (except for the rocker and tappet inspection-cover washers, which should be greased). If a home-made timing-case cover washer is used, see that the small oil-hole is included at its base.

IGNITION AND VALVE TIMING

Ignition Timing. Accurate ignition timing is extremely important. Many riders imagine that by advancing their timing they will necessarily get more speed. This is a fallacy, and it only throws unfair loads on the engine, spoiling its flexibility, and eventually damaging it throughout. For all normal road uses, the spark settings given in Table VI should be closely adhered to. Only for genuine racing purposes is it advisable to increase the spark advance beyond these limits, and even then undue spark advance should be avoided. It should always be remembered that should the timing be so far advanced that maximum combustion pressures are reached with the crank in true T.D.C. position, the big-end comes in for

GENERAL MAINTENANCE

a terrific hammering for which it is not designed. If a "Magdyno" has been removed for any purpose, or the drive disturbed, it will be necessary to re-time the ignition.

It is a rare occurrence on "Magdyno" models for the "Magdyno" sprocket to slacken off, and normally the ignition timing is best not interfered with.

Adjusting the Ignition Timing (Models C10, C11). If for any reason the contact-breaker unit (Figs. 35, 46) is removed, the ignition timing should be checked after the unit has been replaced. The correct procedure for the 250 c.c. S.V. and O.H.V. engines is described below.

First check that the contact-breaker gap is correct. Set the piston at T.D.C., on the compression stroke, with both valves closed, and then, using a slim rod marked to indicate T.D.C. (*see* page 108), rotate the engine *backwards* (turn rear wheel with top gear engaged) until it has descended a distance equal to the ignition advance given in Table VI. Position the cam follower correctly and rotate the spindle until there is about $\frac{3}{8}$ in. between the opening position of the cam and the cam follower. Next insert the contact-breaker unit in its housing with the flat side of the body towards the *rear* of the motor-cycle. Push the unit down on to its seating and observe that, as the spindle gear meshes with the driving pinion, the contact-breaker shaft turns slightly, so that the cam takes up a new position. Then rotate the body slightly until the contact-breaker points are commencing to "break."* In this position finally tighten the clip bolt on the locking plate just below the housing. Afterwards check the ignition timing again and also the contact-breaker gap (*see* page 80).

TABLE VI
1945-59 B.S.A. IGNITION TIMINGS

Model . .	C10	C11	B31-4, M33	M20	M21
Maximum advance . (*see* Fig. 65)	$\frac{1}{32}$ in. before T.D.C.	$\frac{1}{32}$ in. before T.D.C.	$\frac{7}{16}$ in.† before T.D.C.	$\frac{7}{16}$ in. before T.D.C.	$\frac{7}{16}$ in. before T.D.C.

Adjusting the Ignition Timing ("Magdyno" Models B31, B32, B33, B34, M20, M21, M33). If adjustment is necessary, first verify that the gap between the contacts of the contact-breaker, fully open, is 0·012–0·015 in. (page 77). Next detach the timing cover. When doing this, be

---

* Note that when the engine is stationary the timing is automatically *fully retarded*, the normal position for timing the ignition.

† On the 1949-57 O.H.V. Model M33 and the 1956-9 O.H.V. Model B33, the contacts should begin to open with the piston $\frac{3}{8}$ in. before T.D.C.

particularly careful not to damage the small nozzle inside, which delivers pressure oil to the hollow timing-side mainshaft. As a precaution it is advisable while actually breaking the timing-cover joint to leave three equally spaced timing-cover screws in position. Half unscrew them.

Having removed the timing cover, remove the locking nut which secures the "Magdyno" pinion to its armature shaft. Engage a gear and lock the rear wheel to prevent the engine turning, and then use the special

FIG. 65. TIMING COVER REMOVED, SHOWING "MAGDYNO" DRIVING GEAR (TOP LEFT) AND OUTRIGGER PLATE SUPPORTING INTERMEDIATE GEAR AND BOTH CAMWHEELS

Applies to all 1945 and later models except C10, C11. An extractor (61/1903) and spanner are in position ready for "Magdyno" pinion withdrawal.

B.S.A. "Magdyno" pinion extractor; screw the externally-threaded body of the extractor (Part No. 61/1903) into the pinion boss, and then turn the extractor screw *clockwise*. A few turns should immediately free the "Magdyno" pinion from the armature-shaft taper. Renew the rubber oil-seal behind the pinion, if worn.

To adjust the ignition timing, first turn the engine in the normal direction of rotation until the piston is at true T.D.C. on the compression stroke. Check the piston position with a piece of slim rod inserted through the plug hole or compression-plug hole ("M" engines). Mark the rod to show true T.D.C. Scratch another mark $\frac{7}{16}$ in. (*see* Table VI) above the first mark. Now turn the engine slowly *backwards* (by engaging top gear and turning the rear wheel backwards) until the rod has descended in the cylinder a distance equal to a little more than the ignition-marking advance (page 107). Come *forward* to the exact point of maximum ignition-advance (taking up backlash in the process). Then move the contact-breaker in its normal direction of rotation until the contacts are just opening (*see* Fig. 66), with the ignition lever *fully advanced.*

FIG. 66. AN ACCURATE METHOD OF CHECKING THE IGNITION TIMING WHEN THE CYLINDER HEAD IS REMOVED

A steel scraper plate 1 (useful for cleaning joint faces) has been laid across the barrel top face, and a vertical measurement of the piston position before T.D.C. (compression stroke) is being taken with the steel rule 2. The ignition lever is in the full-advance position, and the contacts are beginning to break as indicated by the thin celophane slip 3 being just released (by a gentle pull) from the contacts. The oil bath chain-case cover need not, of course, be removed.

With the Lucas "Magdyno" armature and engine in this position, with a box spanner and hammer, lightly tap the "Magdyno" pinion on to its plain taper. Now moderately tighten the locking nut and proceed to check the exact ignition timing, with the ignition lever fully advanced. Make quite sure that the ignition lever *is* in the *full advance position*, otherwise you will have to retime again. Frankly, the author prefers to time the ignition by the method shown in Fig. 66. A steel rule cannot lie, whereas a piece of rod inserted through the plug hole can do so in certain circumstances. If the timing is correct, firmly tighten the "Magdyno" pinion nut, again check the timing and finally replace the timing cover. Renew the rubber oil-seals and cover washer if damaged.

Adjusting the Ignition Timing (1958-9 Models B31, B33). On the coil ignition models with an alternator instead of a dynamo it is rarely necessary to check or re-adjust the ignition timing. Before checking the timing first verify that the gap between the contacts is 0·012-0·015 in. with the contacts fully open. Adjust the gap if necessary (*see* page 80).

To check the ignition timing, first remove the contact-breaker cover and also the sparking plug. Turn the engine in its normal direction of rotation until the piston is at true T.D.C. on the compression stroke (i.e. with both valves closed). Insert a piece of slim rod through the sparking-plug hole to feel the crown of the piston, and mark the T.D.C. position on the rod when slight backward and forward movement of the engine (by means of the rear wheel with top gear engaged) causes no piston movement. Keep the rod as vertical as possible. Scratch another mark on the rod $\frac{7}{16}$ in. (B31) or $\frac{3}{8}$ in. (B33) above the T.D.C. mark.

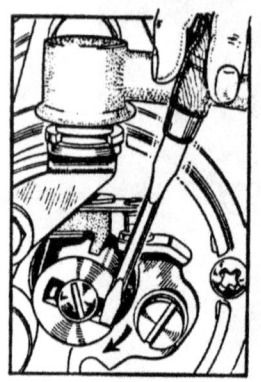

Fig. 67. Moving Cam to Full Advance
(Applicable to 1958-9 O.H.V. Models.)

Now turn the engine *backwards* through about 45 degrees and bring it forward again until the contacts of the contact-breaker are just beginning to open with the *ignition fully advanced*. To obtain the fully advanced position, move the cam as indicated in Fig. 67. The position of the contacts at the moment of opening is best determined by inserting a thin cellophane slip or a piece of fine paper between them and exerting a gentle pull. If the ignition timing is correct, the $\frac{7}{16}$ in. or $\frac{3}{8}$ in. mark on the rod should exactly replace the position of the T.D.C. mark with the piston at T.D.C.

Referring to Fig. 68, if the ignition timing is found to be *slightly* incorrect, loosen bolt *A* and rotate the contact-breaker a few degrees backwards or forwards as required (with the piston position correct) until the contacts are on the point of opening. Afterwards re-tighten bolt *A*.

If the ignition timing is found to be *considerably* wrong, remove the contact-breaker, complete with housing, by withdrawing the three top timing-cover screws (that at the top of the timing cover and one on each side). These three screws are longer than the other timing-cover screws which need not be removed and have nuts *B* at the back. Having withdrawn the three screws, draw out the contact-breaker, with housing, as a complete unit, together with the driving pinion which is still in position. Disconnect the l.t. cable *C* from its terminal.

GENERAL MAINTENANCE

Turn the engine until the piston is in the correct ignition timing position (*see* Table VI). Hold the contact-breaker unit, remove its cover, and turn the driving pinion until the contacts are about to open with the cam held fully advanced. Release the cam and hold the unit (*see* Fig. 68) in such a position that the nut *A* and terminal *C* are vertical. If they are not in alignment, loosen the pinch bolt *D* and turn the housing until *A* comes into line with *C*. Afterwards re-tighten the pinch bolt *D*. With the unit held in this position, gently insert it into its register at the back of the

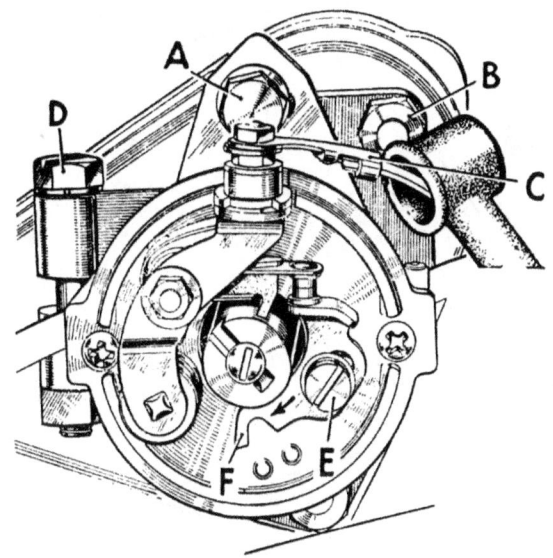

Fig. 68. The 1958-9 Contact-breaker Assembly
(Not applicable to 1958 S.V. Model M21)

timing cover. Should it fail to go right home, withdraw the unit and turn the pinion the fraction of a tooth (to permit it to mesh with the idler pinion) and position it. Replace the three timing-cover securing screws and check the ignition timing. Make any necessary adjustment by means of bolt *A*.

Valve Timing. The correct valve timing (*see* Fig. 69) for the various B.S.A. engines has been determined by the manufacturers after much experiment and calculation, and B.S.A. owners are advised not to alter the original timings. All B.S.A. timing gears are marked for assembly.

Valve Timing (Models C10, C11). Do not dismantle the timing gears unless this is *really* necessary. When removing the timing-case cover, note the positions of the timing-case cover securing-screws, which have different lengths. To remove the timing case itself it may be advisable to loosen the dynamo securing-strap and turn the dynamo slightly.

The dynamo driving-chain is of the "endless" type and to remove it, it is therefore necessary to remove the nut and locking washer, and then extract the large sprocket from its shaft by screwing two ¼-in. B.S.F. screws into the extractor holes. Now lift the dynamo chain off the sprocket.

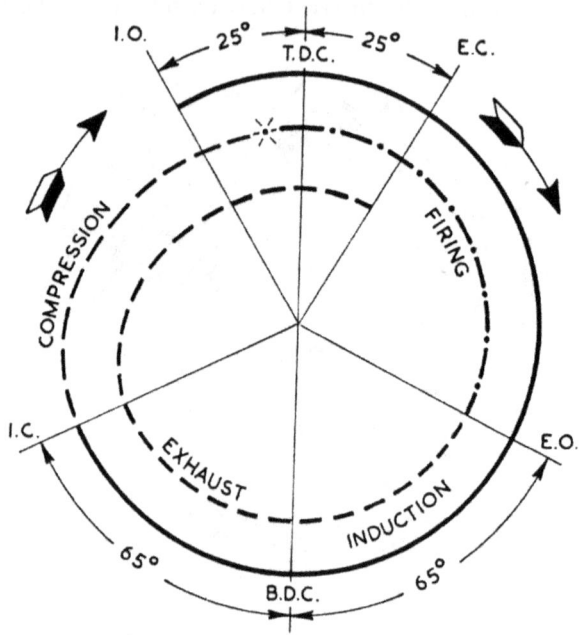

Fig. 69. Valve Timing Diagram for all B.S.A. Models (Except Models C10, C11)

The diagram shown applies to the engines of the two coil-ignition models (C10, C11) except that on these engines the inlet valve closes 70 degrees after B.D.C. and the exhaust valve opens 70 degrees before B.D.C.

Observe that the timing cover is secured to the crankcase by six screws and two dowels. As you draw off the timing case, see that the camshaft and rocker spindle do not come away with it. As a precaution it is advisable to raise the contact-breaker unit. When removing the timing-case cover the two paper gaskets usually require to be renewed.

The simple arrangement of the valve-timing gears on the 250 c.c. coil ignition models is shown in Fig. 70. As may be seen, a single camwheel is used. If for any reason it is necessary to withdraw the camwheel and spindle, it is essential first to raise the contact-breaker unit, otherwise its driving pinion may become damaged. To withdraw the contact-breaker

GENERAL MAINTENANCE 113

unit, first loosen the clip bolt on the locking plate under the body; then raise the contact-breaker unit about ½ in.

When the contact-breaker unit or camwheel has been withdrawn it will be necessary to re-time the ignition (*see* page 107).

Removal of the camwheel necessitates re-timing the valves. As regards valve timing, one tooth-space of the camwheel and one tooth of the crankshaft pinion are each etched with a dash. To ensure that the valve timing is correct, it is only necessary to position the piston at T.D.C. on

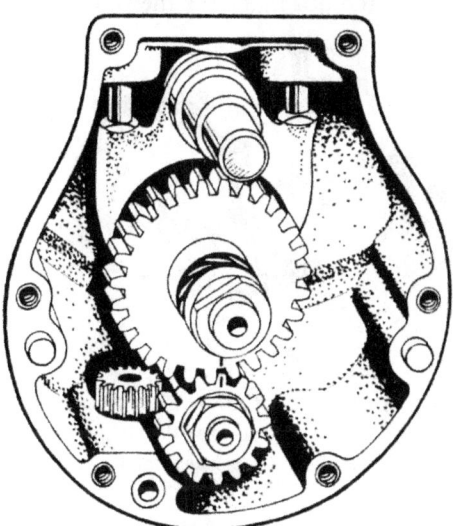

FIG. 70. TIMING-CASE COVER REMOVED (1945-53 COIL-IGNITION MODELS)

The valve timing is correct when the dash marks are aligned as shown.

the compression stroke and then to engage the camwheel with the crankshaft pinion so that the dash marks register as shown in Fig. 70. The marks should, of course, register at every second crankshaft revolution.

After checking that the valve timing is correct, replace the timing-case cover. Make quite sure that the paper washers on both sides of the cover are sound, and renew them if necessary, otherwise oil will leak. Fit the dynamo sprocket and driving chain, and adjust the chain by rotating the eccentrically-mounted dynamo (*see* page 82). Afterwards re-tighten the dynamo strap and replace the dynamo-chain cover.

Valve Timing (Models B31, B32, B33, B34, M20, M21, M33). On the 1945-59 350 c.c., 500 c.c., 600 c.c. B.S.A. models, removal of the timing cover cannot cause the two camwheels to be withdrawn, as these are supported by an outrigger plate (*see* Fig. 65) bolted to bosses inside the timing case. If this outrigger plate is removed and the camwheels are withdrawn, re-time in the following manner. Position the engine pinion keyway uppermost. Replace the inlet camwheel so that the dash mark etched between two teeth of the camwheel registers with the dash mark etched on the crankshaft pinion. Similarly replace the exhaust camwheel so that the dot between two teeth of the camwheel registers with the dot on the crankshaft pinion. The timing *must* then be correct.

Note that the timing marks are duplicated on both camwheels, because the cams are interchangeable. The dash mark must be used only for the inlet valve timing, and the dot mark for the timing of the exhaust valve.

FIG. 71. TIMING-CASE COVER AND OUTRIGGER PLATE REMOVED (B.S.A. "MAGDYNO" MODELS)

Showing dash (inlet) and dot (exhaust) marks aligned for correct valve timing. *See also* Fig. 65.

Absolutely correct valve timing is essential, and it is even more important than precise ignition timing. The timing diagram (Fig. 69) shows (in crankshaft degrees before T.D.C.) the exact moments when the inlet and exhaust valves open and close on the "Magdyno" models. The valve timing can, if desired, be checked by attaching a degree disc to the crankshaft and noting the exact valve openings and closings, but this should ordinarily be quite unnecessary if the timing gears are always replaced so that their timing dash or dot marks register.

CARE OF TRANSMISSION

Clutch Adjustment (Models C10, C11, B31, B32, B33, B34). To prevent clutch slip or drag, it is essential to keep the clutch properly adjusted. Check the adjustment about every 1,000 miles. The same instructions apply to "B" and "C" series B.S.A. models without "swinging arm" rear suspension. Referring to Figs. 72, 73, 74, it will be noted that the main clutch adjustment is completely enclosed in the outer cover of the gearbox. In order to make an adjustment it is therefore necessary first to unscrew the gearbox knurled filler-plug (secured by two screws on C10, C11 four-speed gearbox).

GENERAL MAINTENANCE 115

To effect a main adjustment of the clutch, slacken the lock-nut *A* and then, with a suitable screwdriver, turn the adjusting pin *B* until the external lever on the gearbox cover is *at right angles* to the clutch push-rod (with clutch fully disengaged). This ensures the minimum side-thrust being imposed. Afterwards tighten the lock-nut *A* and fit and tighten the filler plug. When tightening the locknut be careful not to turn the pin also.

Now make a clutch operating-cable adjustment, by means of the

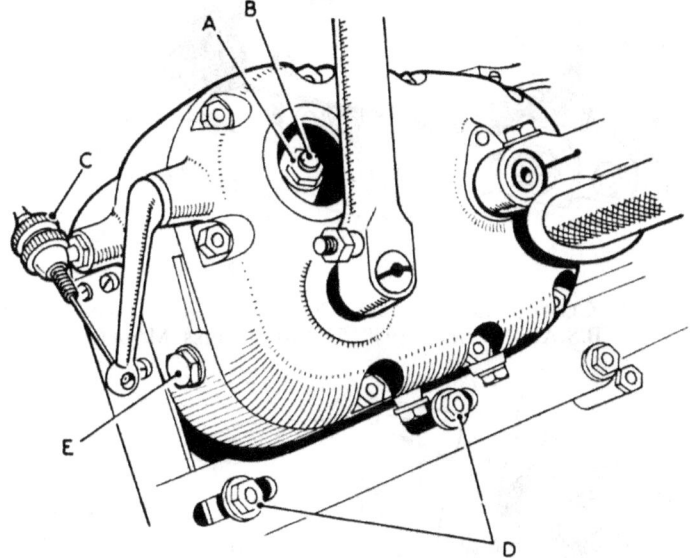

Fig. 72. Clutch and Primary Chain Adjustment on B.S.A. Models C10 and C11 (1945-53).

knurled thumb-nut *C* which is positioned on the gearbox as illustrated. Final adjustment of the clutch must always be made such that there is a little backlash in the clutch control cable. Absence of backlash causes the clutch to slip and subjects the plates to undue wear and tear. On the other hand, excessive backlash may give rise to clutch drag and general inefficiency. There should always be about $\frac{1}{8}$ in. free movement of the clutch control cable at the handlebar end. The clearance decreases as the friction inserts wear.

Clutch Adjustment (1945-8 Models M20, M21, M33). On these models also, two separate adjustments are provided for the clutch on the outer cover of the gearbox. As may be seen in Fig. 75, the effective length of the clutch actuating-rod can be adjusted by means of a grub-screw and

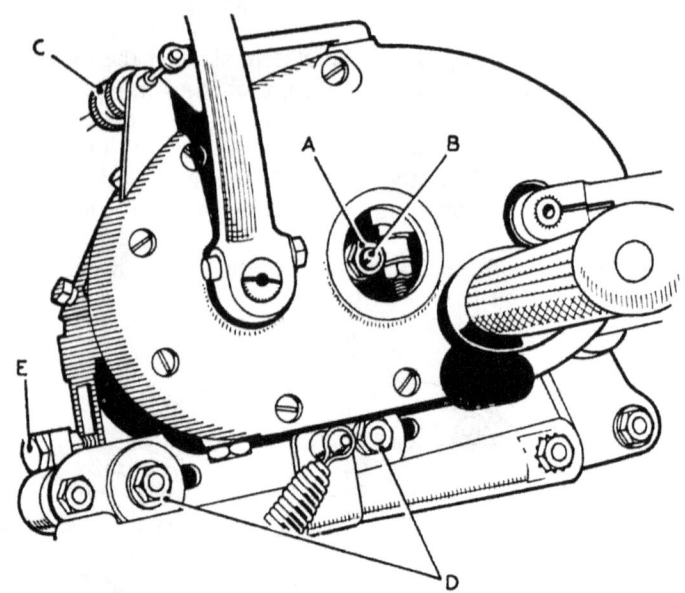

Fig. 73. Clutch and Primary Chain Adjustment on 1945-51 B.S.A. "B" and 1949-51 "M" Series Models

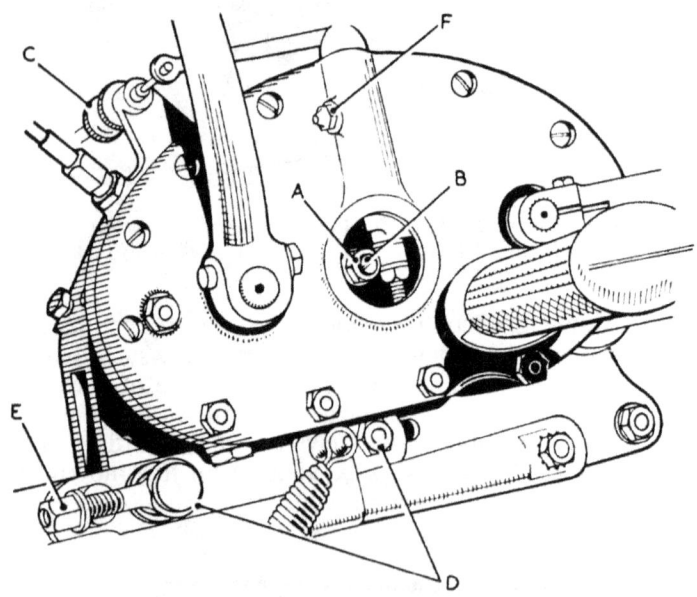

Fig. 74. Clutch and Primary Chain Adjustment on 1952-3 B.S.A. "B" and 1952-8 "M" Series Models

lock-nut. A steel ball is interposed between the grub-screw and the actuating rod. When making an adjustment, see that the control arm is as vertical as possible with the clutch not in operation, and turn the grub-screw until there is slight clearance between the grub-screw and actuating rod. Afterwards tighten the lock-nut.

The second adjustment comprises altering the effective length of the Bowden cable. When the clutch control arm has been set to a new position,

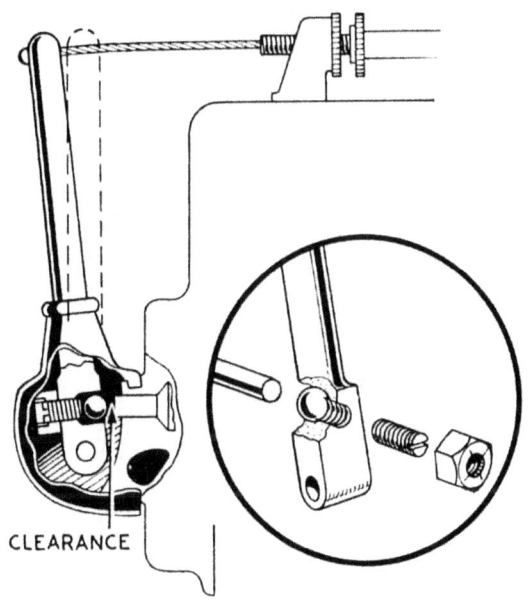

Fig. 75. Clutch Adjustment on B.S.A. Models M20, M21, M33 (1945-8)

adjust the cable length to suit by means of the thumb nut on the cable stop on top of the gearbox. Maintain $\frac{1}{16}$-$\frac{1}{8}$ in. backlash at the control arm.

Clutch Adjustment (1949-57 Models M20, M21, M33). On these models the dual clutch adjustment is identical to that previously described for the "B" Series models (*see* Figs. 73, 74).

Clutch Adjustment ("Swinging Arm" Models). There must always be about $\frac{1}{8}$ in. free movement of the clutch control cable at the handlebar end (*see notes on* page 115) and the adjustment provided is shown in Fig. 81. To make an adjustment, remove the filler plug, loosen the lock-nut (*G*), and turn the small screw (*H*) until the long operating-lever is at right-angles to the clutch push-rod. Afterwards tighten the lock-nut securely.

A cable adjustment should then be made with the knurled thumb-nut (*E*). Instructions for adjusting the clutch spring pressure are on page 119.

Increasing the Clutch Spring Pressure (1945-57). After many miles have been covered, wear of the clutch inserts may necessitate an adjustment of the clutch-spring tension being made. To make this adjustment, first expose the plates by removing the near-side footrest and the primary chain-case cover (*see* Fig. 37). Note (*see* Fig. 76) that six springs

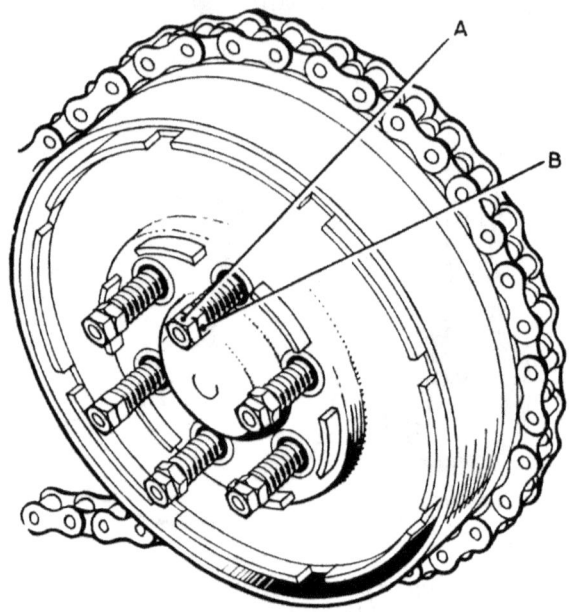

Fig. 76. Adjustment of B.S.A. Clutch Spring Tension
(1945-57 and 1958 "M" Models)

are provided to keep the clutch plates pressed together. Loosen with a box spanner each of the lock-nuts *A*, while holding the nuts *B* stationary with another spanner, and then, to increase the spring tension, tighten each of the adjusting nuts *B* (clockwise) 1-2 turns. To maintain true alignment of the clutch plates, and to prevent clutch drag, it is most important to tighten all six adjusting nuts *B*, *the same number of turns*. Having made the required adjustment, tighten the six lock-nuts *A* and replace the outer half of the chain case and the near-side footrest. Finally test the clutch by disengaging it and spinning the driving plates with the kick-starter. The outer plate must turn parallel with the other plates. Also test the pressure required to operate the handlebar clutch lever.

GENERAL MAINTENANCE

Clutch Spring Adjustment (1958-9 Models). A simplified type of clutch assembly is provided on 1958-9 models with coil ignition. If a clutch spring adjustment is required, first remove the outer cover from the oil-bath chain case. To do this it is necessary to remove the near-side footrest and the fifteen cover-securing screws. Then to increase the spring pressure slightly (only necessary after a considerable mileage), screw in the adjusters *A* (*see* Fig. 77) *one or two turns*. To make sure that

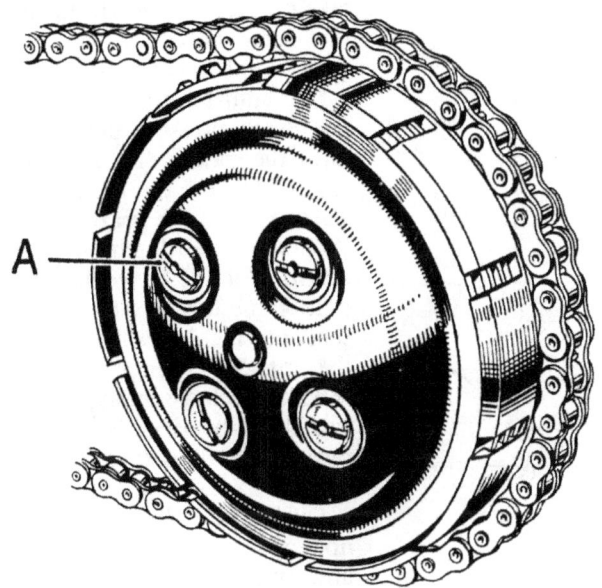

Fig. 77. Adjustment of B.S.A. Clutch Spring Tension
1958-9 "B" Models. The spring adjusters have no lock-nut as on the 1945-57 clutch.

the clutch end-plate does not tilt and that the clutch frees properly, operate the clutch by means of the handlebar lever. Should the end-plate tilt, the clutch will not free properly. The remedy is to re-adjust the nuts retaining the springs until the end-plate remains square when the clutch is disengaged.

To Dismantle the Clutch (1945-57). After a big mileage some oil may get on to the friction inserts of the clutch plates, or the inserts may be so worn that the clutch slips in spite of the adjustment of the clutch being correct. The remedy is to dismantle the clutch and clean the plates thoroughly with petrol, or get the friction plates relined, according to the state of affairs revealed when the plates are removed for inspection. Badly scored metal plates should be renewed, and the ball bearings for the clutch sprocket-plate must be in good condition.

It is desirable to inspect the central cage and the clutch-sprocket interior for burrs which can prevent the clutch plates sliding freely. Such burrs can generally be removed with a smooth file. On a machine which has done a big mileage the clutch-sprocket teeth should also be inspected. Worn teeth will cause rapid chain wear.

To dismantle the clutch (*see* Fig. 79), take off the near-side footrest and remove the outer cover of the oil-bath chain case. Next remove the six lock-nuts and spring adjuster-nuts (16) on the outside of the clutch pressure plate (13), and withdraw the springs (15) and the spring cups (14). Take off the clutch pressure-plate. This exposes the gearbox mainshaft nut (5) holding the clutch body (3) and clutch centre which is keyed to the main-shaft. Flatten the turned-over edge of the main-shaft-nut locking washer (4), and remove the nut (5). Then remove the complete B.S.A. clutch assembly, including the two caged ball-bearings (with one-piece inner races) from the keyed and splined clutch centre.*

During the dismantling, take careful note of the positions of the various plates and washers, to ensure correct reassembly. As may be seen in Figs. 78, 79, plain metal plates (with tongues on the inside diameter) and Ferodo-insert plates are fitted alternately. Note that the clutch-sprocket plate on Model B31 has cork inserts, instead of the Ferodo inserts fitted to the remaining friction plates. On all other "B" and "M" models *all* inserts are of Ferodo. On C10, C11 all inserts are of cork.

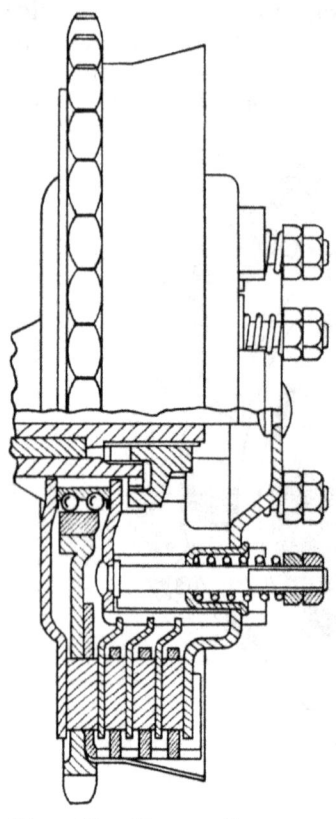

FIG. 78. PARTLY-SECTIONED VIEW OF B.S.A. CLUTCH ASSEMBLY (1945-57)

On certain models two extra plates are provided, but the general layout is the same for all 1945-57 models. It applies also to 1958 "M" Models.

When reassembling the clutch, fit the key to the mainshaft if this has been removed; tap home the clutch centre, complete with back plate, fit the two ball-bearings to the clutch centre (with unbroken cage-flanges wide apart), and replace the sprocket plate. Fit the studded clutch body, and then the locking washer and the mainshaft nut. Tighten this very firmly

* The splined clutch centre is a sleeve keyed to the mainshaft taper. To remove it, use an extractor (B.S.A. Part No. 61-3362). Do not forget to fit the key when replacing the sleeve.

with a box spanner. Afterwards with a stout screwdriver (a centre-punch is not suitable) and hammer, turn over the edge of the locking washer on to the face of the nut so as to lock it. *This is most important.* It will be observed at this stage that the clutch sprocket plate has some end movement and a "rock" of about one-sixteenth of an inch (bearing maximum

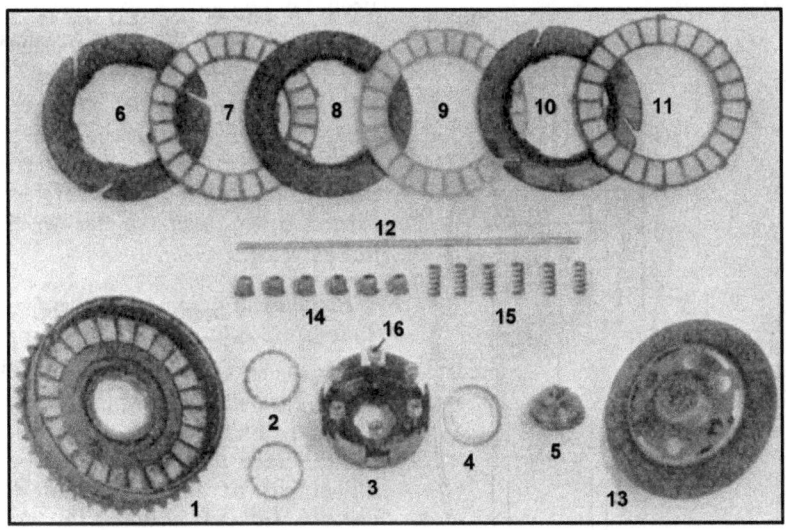

FIG. 79. THE B.S.A. CLUTCH DISMANTLED (1945-57)

The back plate on the keyed clutch centre is shown in position in Fig. 66. The remaining parts shown above are assembled in the sequence indicated by the numbers. Note particularly that the edge of the locking washer 4 must be hammered over the face of the retaining nut 5.

KEY TO FIG. 79

1. Clutch sprocket (B31) with cork inserts
2. Ball bearings for sprocket (inner races not shown)
3. Clutch body
4. Locking washer for nut 5
5. Nut securing sprocket and clutch centre
6, 8, 10. Steel (driven) plates

7, 9, 11. Friction plates (Ferodo inserts)
12. Clutch push-rod
13. Pressure plate carrying springs
14. Spring cups
15. Clutch springs (six)
16. Spring adjuster-nuts and lock-nuts

diametrical-play: 0·0015 in.). *This is quite normal.* Now fit the remaining plates (*see* Fig. 79).

When the pressure plate is replaced, smear a little grease on its centre against which the clutch push-rod bears, and see that the spring adjuster nuts are tightened evenly (*see* page 118).

To Dismantle Clutch (1958-9). On the 1958-9 "B" models it is quite simple to dismantle the clutch after removing the oil-bath chain case cover. Remove the four nuts *A* (Fig. 77) which retain the springs, and withdraw the clutch end-plate. Bend back the locking washer and unscrew the large central nut (*see* Fig. 80). Engage top gear and apply the rear brake to prevent the gearbox main-shaft from turning. The complete clutch assembly, with the exception of the central splined sleeve, can now be withdrawn.

The central splined sleeve engages on a taper on the gearbox main-shaft and to remove it a B.S.A. extractor (Part No. 61-3362) must be used. A key locates the sleeve and this must be correctly replaced. The large central nut must be tightened very securely after properly locating the locking washer on the splined sleeve. The washer must, of course, be afterwards turned down over the flat on the nut exterior.

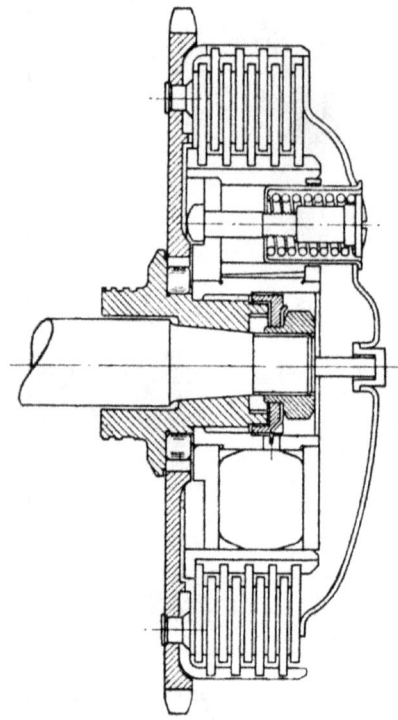

Fig. 80. Sectioned View of B.S.A. Clutch Assembly (1958-9)
Applies to the O.H.V. Models B31, B33.

Primary Chain Adjustment. At 2,000-mile intervals detach the inspection cover from the oil-bath chain case and check the tension of the primary chain. This chain should have a total up-and-down movement at the centre of the bottom run of about $\frac{1}{2}$ in., with the chain in its tightest position (obtained by slowly turning the engine). On all B.S.A. models re-tensioning is effected by drawing the gearbox backwards.

To adjust (except S.A. models), first slacken the two large nuts beneath the gearbox on the off-side. These nuts are shown at D in Figs. 72-74 for "B," "C," and "M" series models. On 1952-3 "B" and 1952-8 "M" models the large nut on the rear fixing bolt (to which the adjuster is attached) is located on the near-side and can be loosened with a set spanner. The large nut on the front fixing bolt, however, is in a somewhat inaccessible position on the off-side. To loosen it, you must employ a long $\frac{5}{16}$-in. W. box spanner and tommy-bar. Then move the gearbox to the rear as required; to do this tighten the adjuster (provided on all except the 250 c.c. machines). The adjuster on the "B" and "M" series models is shown at E in Figs. 73 and 74. After adjusting the primary-chain tension, be careful to re-tighten the two large gearbox securing-nuts. Also check the tension of the secondary chain which is certain to have been altered by the adjustment of the primary chain.

GENERAL MAINTENANCE 123

To make a primary chain adjustment on 1954-9 "swinging arm" (S.A.) models, first (see Fig. 81) loosen the large lock-nuts (*A*) and (*B*). Nut (*B*) also secures the adjuster in position. Then loosen the lock-nut (*C*) on the adjuster, and to tighten the primary chain turn the adjuster (*D*) *clockwise* as required to pivot the gearbox backwards the necessary amount. Finally

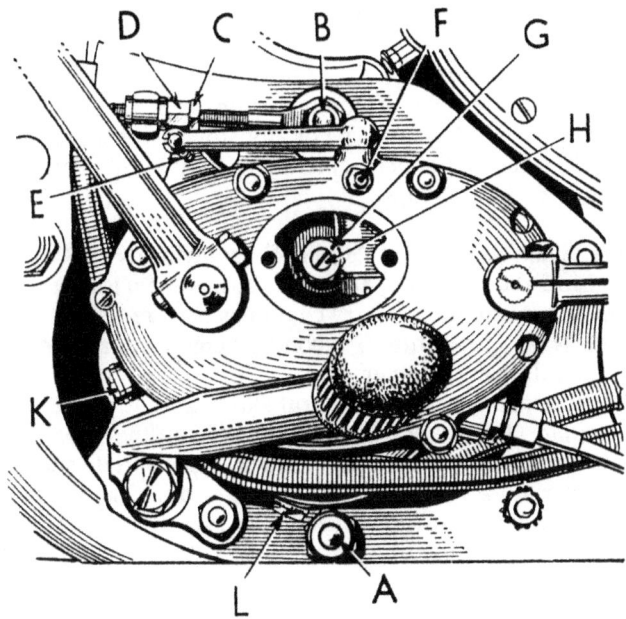

Fig. 81. Clutch and Primary Chain Adjustment on 1954-9 "Swinging Arm" Models

tighten the lock-nut (*C*) and nuts (*A*) and (*B*). Afterwards check the tension of the secondary chain.

Secondary Chain Adjustment (Rigid-Frame Models C10, C11). Adjustment of the secondary-chain tension (which should be checked about every 1,000 miles) is necessary whenever excessive slackness owing to chain stretch occurs, and is also generally necessary after the primary chain has been re-tensioned.

To re-tension the secondary chain, first slacken off the hand adjustment for the rear brake, in case a close adjustment should limit rear movement of the rear wheel. Loosen both spindle nuts sufficiently to enable the wheel to slide in the fork ends. Where a three-speed gearbox is fitted, release the speedometer drive lock-nut *C* in Fig. 92, so that the drive cable for the speedometer can assume a new position when the rear wheel is drawn rearwards.

Turn the rear-wheel spindle clockwise with a spanner applied to the square end of the spindle (*see* Fig. 92). This will rotate the rear-chain adjusting cams attached to the spindle and cause the rear wheel to move to the rear. Slowly rotate the wheel and check the secondary-chain tension with the chain in various positions. The tension is correct when there is about three-quarters of an inch total up-and-down movement at the centre of the bottom run, with the chain in its tightest position.

See that both cams are hard up against the stops in the fork ends, and re-tighten both spindle nuts. Tighten that on the near-side first, and then the off-side nut. With the cam type of adjustment, it should not be necessary to check wheel alignment, provided that both cams are pressed against the two fork-end stops.

Secondary Chain Adjustment (Spring-Frame Models C10, C11). Check the chain tension about every 1,000 miles. Adjustment is necessary because of slackness or because the primary chain has been re-tensioned. Where a spring frame (Fig. 82) is fitted, secondary-chain adjustment should be effected in the following manner.

First place the machine on its central stand so that the rear wheel is in its *lowest position*. Referring to Fig. 82, slacken off the brake-rod adjuster *D*, and also the two spindle nuts *E*. With the appropriate spanner tighten the two adjuster nuts *F equally* (to obtain correct alignment) until the rear wheel is drawn backwards sufficiently to give the correct chain tension (about $\frac{1}{2}$ in. at the centre of the bottom run with the chain in its tightest position).

When the chain is correctly tensioned, re-tighten the two wheel spindle nuts *E*, screw home the brake-rod adjuster *D* to give proper brake efficiency, and finally check the wheels for true alignment (*see* page 130).

Secondary Chain Adjustment (Rigid-Frame Models B31, B32, B33, B34). If the secondary chain has stretched (check tension about every 1,000 miles) or has become slack after re-tensioning of the primary chain, re-tension the chain by means of the two rear-chain adjusting cams on the wheel spindle. As may be seen in Fig. 83, these cams bear against stops on the rear fork-ends.

To re-tension the secondary chain, slacken off the hand adjuster for the rear brake, loosen both rear-wheel spindle nuts, and then turn the spindle clockwise, with the appropriate spanner applied to the flats on the off-side end of the spindle, until the chain has a total up-and-down movement of about three-quarters of an inch at the centre of the bottom chain run with the chain in its tightest position; turn the wheel over slowly. Both cams must press against the stops, and when the chain is correctly tensioned, re-tighten both rear-wheel spindle nuts, tightening the off-side nut last. Finally adjust the rear brake (*see* page 139). An alignment check for the

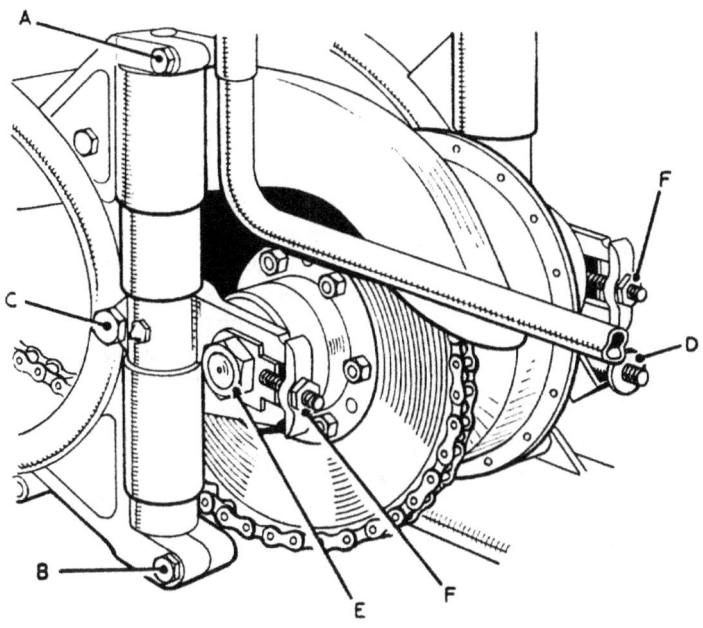

Fig. 82. Secondary Chain Adjustment (Spring-Frame Models C10, C11, 1945-53)

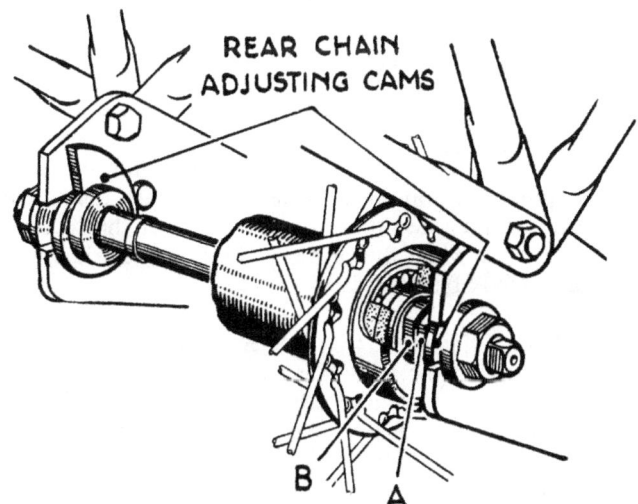

Fig. 83. B.S.A. Cam Adjustment for Re-tensioning Secondary Chain (All "B" Series Rigid-Frame Models)

At A and B are shown the lock-nut and adjuster respectively for adjusting the hub roller bearings. (*See* page 139.)

two wheels should not be necessary, as the cams maintain permanent alignment if the adjustment is made with proper care.

Secondary Chain Adjustment (Rigid-Frame Models, M20, M21, M33). On these models a single cam is provided on the near-side end of the wheel spindle. This cam bears against a stop on the frame stay. The tension of the chain should periodically (say, every 1,000 miles) be inspected and, if necessary, adjusted. As on all rigid-frame models, the chain should be kept adjusted so that there is about three-quarters of an inch up-and-down movement at the centre of the bottom run, with the chain at its tightest.

To tension the secondary chain first slacken the rear-brake adjustment and two wheel spindle lock-nuts. Then with a suitable spanner applied to the spindle head (see Fig. 84), turn the spindle clockwise until correct chain tension is obtained. Rotate the wheel slowly while checking the tension. Now screw in the chain adjuster on the off-side until correct wheel alignment is obtained as indicated with a straight edge or board (see page 131). Finally tighten the cam lock-nut on the near-side and the wheel spindle-nut on the off-side. Also adjust the rear brake (see page 139). It should be noted that an adjustment of the secondary chain is invariably called for when the primary-chain tension has been altered by moving the gearbox backwards.

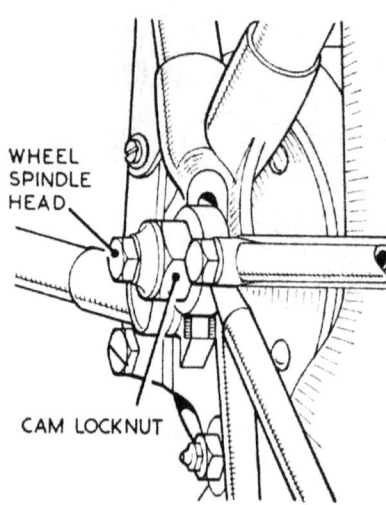

FIG. 84. B.S.A. CAM ADJUSTMENT FOR SECONDARY CHAIN "M" SERIES RIGID-FRAME MODELS

This shows the adjustment on the near-side. On the off-side there is an adjusting screw.

Secondary Chain Adjustment (Plunger-type Spring-Frame "B," "M" Series Models). On plunger models, check the tension of the secondary chain about every 1,000 miles and effect an adjustment if the chain has stretched. An adjustment is also called for if the primary chain has been re-tensioned. To check the adjustment, place the machine on its central stand so that the wheel is in the lowest position and note whether the total up-and-down movement at the centre of the bottom run, with the chain in its tightest position, is correct. This movement should be about half an inch.

To re-tension the secondary chain, with the machine on its central stand, slacken off the hand adjuster for the rear brake. Then slacken hexagon A

(*see* Fig. 85) with the appropriate spanner, and with the tommy-bar applied at *C*, loosen the spindle. Next loosen the hexagon *B* on the near-side spindle end, and then with a screwdriver or spanner screw the adjusters *D evenly* in or out as required, to obtain the correct chain

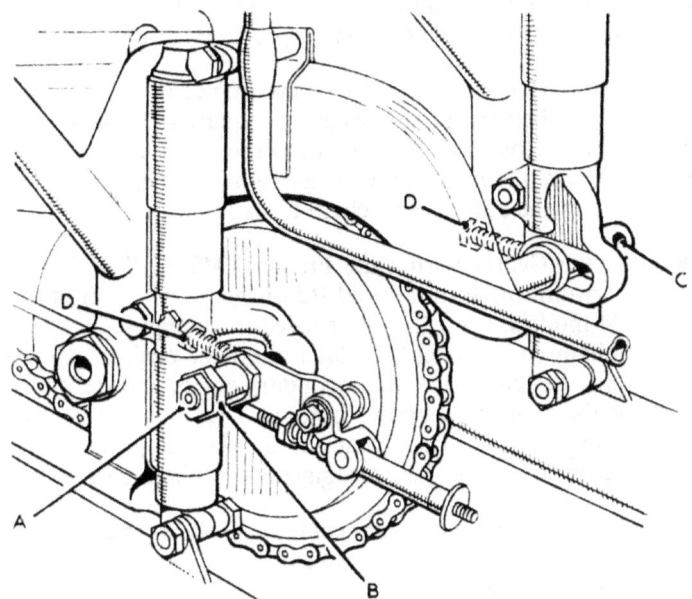

Fig. 85. Secondary Chain Adjustment on Plunger-type Spring-Frame "B" and "M" Models

tension. Finally re-tighten hexagons *B*, *A*, adjust the rear brake, and check wheel alignment.

Secondary Chain Adjustment (1954-9 "Swinging Arm" Models). Check the tension of the secondary chain about every 1,000 miles, with the machine on its central stand and the chain in its tightest position. Where a chain case is fitted, remove the two rubber plugs.

Referring to Fig. 91, unscrew slightly with a tommy-bar or a spanner (1956-9) the spindle (*B*) and then loosen the hexagon on the near side of the wheel hub. Slacken the lock-nuts (*D*) and screw the adjusters (*E*) evenly in or out as required until the chain has in its tightest position a total up-and-down movement (whip) of $1\frac{1}{4}$ in. at the centre of the bottom chain run. If in doubt as to the alignment of the wheels, it is advisable to check their alignment (*see* page 130) after adjusting the secondary chain.

Primary Chain-case Removal ("Swinging Arm" Models). To withdraw the outer cover from the aluminium oil-bath chain case (*see* Fig. 38) it is only necessary to remove the near-side footrest and the fifteen cover-securing screws. Prior to any further dismantling, remove the engine sprocket and the clutch. The back half of the chain case is secured to the crankcase by three bolts behind the engine sprocket. Remove these three bolts after breaking the locking wire passed through the heads of the bolts. Also remove the single bolt (stud, pre-1954) at the rear of the case.

Chain Stretch. It is advisable to renew immediately any primary or secondary chain when the stretch exceeds a quarter of an inch per foot. To test for stretch, close up a foot length of the chain, measure the length, pull the links apart, and measure the length again. The difference between the two lengths is the amount the chain has stretched.

To Remove the Gearbox from the Frame (1945-53 "B" Models). To remove the constant-mesh four-speed B.S.A. gearbox* from the frame on all B31 to B34 models, the following procedure is required. First remove the oil-bath chain case, the entire clutch, and the cush drive. Also disconnect the speedometer drive, the secondary chain, and the clutch cable. Now remove the gearbox securing bolts and remove the gearbox from the frame, being careful to see that the gearbox adjuster bolt, for retensioning the primary chain, is disengaged from the lug on the frame.

Gearbox Repairs. It is not recommended that the average B.S.A. owner should strip down his gearbox completely and attempt major repairs. Considerable experience and skill are needed to do this work which is best entrusted to the makers or a B.S.A. repair specialist.

TYRES, WHEELS, AND BRAKES

To Obtain Good Tyre Mileage. Always maintain the correct tyre pressures and keep the wheels in alignment. Avoid fierce acceleration, violent braking, and stunt cornering. Handle the clutch gently, remove flints which bed into the cover, and keep oil or paraffin from the treads. Fit a rubber tube to the breather pipe and position so that any oil emerging drips clear of the wheel track.

Maintaining Correct Tyre Pressures. Over-inflation causes vibration, strains the cover, and can cause concussion bursts; under-inflation produces a tendency for tyre creep, rolling, instability of steering, and cracking of the cover. All of these things are objectionable and you should therefore always run with the tyres inflated to the correct pressures and check the pressures weekly with a pressure gauge.

The correct inflation pressures for all 1945 and later solo and sidecar models are given in Tables VII, VIII, and these recommendations should

---

* All instructions concerning the gearbox apply to "B" models up to Engine No. ZB-101.

GENERAL MAINTENANCE

be strictly adhered to. Where a pillion passenger is carried, it is usually advisable to add at least 7 lb per sq in. to the solo rider rear-tyre pressure. Make a practice of inspecting the front and rear tyres weekly for embedded flints and cuts. This often saves a puncture, and takes far less time to attend to!

Concerning Tyre Pressure Tables. Note that the tyre pressure recommendations given in Tables VII and VIII are correct for a rider weighing not more than 140 lb. If you are heavier than 140 lb, or carry a pillion

TABLE VII
CORRECT TYRE PRESSURES FOR 1945-59 B.S.A.
MODELS (SIDECAR)

Model	M20 (rigid)	M21 (rigid)	M33 (plunger)
Front	22 lb per sq in.	22 lb per sq in.	23 lb per sq in.
Rear	26 lb per sq in.	22 lb per sq in.	23 lb per sq in.
Sidecar	17 lb per sq in.	17 lb per sq in.	18 lb per sq in.

TABLE VIII
CORRECT TYRE PRESSURES FOR 1945-59 RIGID, PLUNGER, AND "SWINGING ARM" MODELS (SOLO)
(Shown in lb per sq in.)*

Model	C10	C11	B31	B32	B33	B34	M20	M21	M33
Front	18	18	17	20	17	22	16	16	17
Rear	24	24	23	16	19	16	22	18	19

passenger, heavy luggage, or have any doubt about tyre pressures, use the tyre pressures in accordance with Table IX which shows the minimum pressures recommended for individual tyres subjected to specified loads.

Where the load is abnormal, the most satisfactory method of determining the correct tyre pressures is to take or ride the B.S.A. to the nearest weighbridge (provided at most large transport depots and railway stations) and check individually the fully laden weight (with passenger(s) seated)

* On rigid and plunger-type spring-frame models where a solo rider exceeds 140 lb in weight, it is advisable to increase the front tyre pressure by 1 lb per sq. in. for every 28 lb above 140 lb. For the rear tyre the pressure increase should be 1 lb per sq in. for every 14 lb increase above 140 lb.

on the front, rear, and sidecar tyre (where appropriate). Then consult Table IX for the recommended tyre pressures.

TABLE IX
MINIMUM TYRE PRESSURES FOR SPECIFIC LOADS

Nominal Tyre Section (Inches)	Inflation Pressures—lb per sq in.					
	16	18	20	24	28	32
	Load per Tyre—lb					
2·375	120	140	160	185	210	240
2·50	120	140	160	185	210	240
2·75	140	160	180	210	250	280
3·00	160	180	200	240	300	350
3·25	200	240	280	350	400	440
3·50	280	320	350	400	450	500
4·00	360	400	430	500	—	—

(*By Courtesy of The Dunlop Rubber Co., Ltd.*)

Mending Punctures. On some spring-frame models with quickly-detachable wheels a portion of the rear mudguard is hinged to facilitate rear wheel removal; on other models part of the rear guard is detachable. The hinged or detachable portion is held by the lower rear-chain stays. Wheel removal is dealt with in later paragraphs.

When removing a cover with tyre levers, start near the valve and push the opposite side of the cover into the base of the rim. Test for a puncture by submerging the tube in water. Clean the tube with sandpaper and rub off all dust. Next select a suitable auto-vulcanizing patch such as the "Vulcafix" and remove its linen backing. If solution is *not* used, rub the prepared face of the patch with a cloth moistened in petrol and transfer the brown deposit on the cloth to the punctured area. Repeat this operation and allow the patch and transferred deposit to dry for one minute. If solution *is* used, apply it to the *tube only* and allow it to become "tacky." Now affix the patch to the tube, using slight pressure, particularly at the edges, and apply french chalk.

Alignment of Wheels. In order to obtain maximum tyre life and good steering, the wheels must always be kept in perfect alignment. Moving the rear wheel in order to re-tension the secondary chain should not upset the alignment, except possibly on spring-frame models and rigid-frame

GENERAL MAINTENANCE

"M" models, which do not have a twin cam adjustment of the wheel spindle giving automatic alignment.

If desired, it is easy to check the alignment of the motor-cycle wheels by placing a straight-edge or board alongside the two wheels, with the handlebars in their normal position. It should, of course, touch the tyres at *four* points, with the handlebars "square."*

Some riders use a taut piece of string attached to an anchorage post. Where a sidecar is fitted, the sidecar wheel should "toe-in" to the extent of about 1 in. (*see* Fig. 87) and the motor-cycle itself should *lean slightly*

FIG. 86. CHECKING WHEEL ALIGNMENT ON A SOLO

The straight-edge should contact the tyres at four points. Before checking the alignment, see that the rear wheel is hard up against the adjusters.

outwards away from the sidecar. The exact dimensions vary slightly according to the design of sidecar fitted, and the maker's instructions should be closely followed.

To Remove Front Wheel (1945-54 "B," "C," "M" Models). These models have 7 in. diameter brakes.

To remove the front wheel from the telescopic-type forks, first disconnect the front-brake cable. Uncouple the cable first, at the lever on the brake cover-plate, and then unscrew the cable adjuster from the stop. Then referring to Fig. 88, slacken the pinch-bolt A, situated at the front of the near-side fork leg. Now unscrew the wheel spindle with a tommy-bar inserted through the hole B in the spindle end. On "C" series models apply a spanner to the spindle head (no hole is provided). Turn the tommy-bar or spanner *clockwise*, as the spindle has a *left-hand thread*. Withdraw the spindle from the nearside while supporting the weight of

* Assuming, of course, that the tyres are of the same section. If the rear tyre is of larger section than the front one, due allowance must be made for this.

the wheel with the hand, and slide the distance bush *C*, in the fork end, outwards to its full extent. The front wheel should then come away.

After replacing the wheel spindle, *before* tightening the pinch bolt *A* depress the forks sharply several times. This permits the near-side fork leg to position itself properly on the distance bush. Unless this is done, the near-side leg may not align itself properly and the forks may not function satisfactorily. Be sure to re-tighten the pinch-bolt *A* firmly. The above instructions are important.

To remove the front wheel on 1945-7 machines not fitted with telescopic-type forks (e.g. 1947 Models M20, M21), support the front of the machine

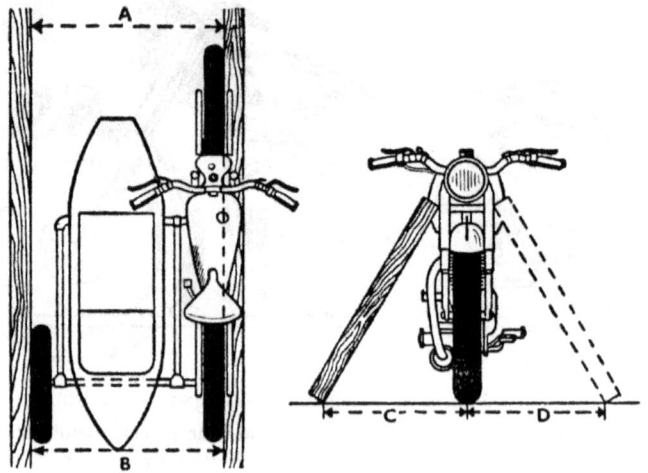

FIG. 87. CHECKING WHEEL ADJUSTMENT OF A SIDE-CAR OUTFIT

If adjustment is correct, dimension *A* is about 1 in. less than dimension *B*, and dimension *C* slightly more than dimension *D*.

by placing a box or other packing beneath the crankcase. Detach the front-brake cable and the speedometer drive. Then undo both spindle nuts and the wheel should come away from the forks. Also see that the stud on the brake cover-plate "beds" home into its socket.

To Remove Front Wheel (1955 Model B33, 1956-8 "M" Models). First remove the nut (*C*, Fig. 89) securing the lower end of the brake anchorage-strap to the brake cover-plate. Also loosen the nuts securing the upper end of the strap. Next disconnect the brake-cam operating lever, and then detach the cable by unscrewing the adjustable cable-stop from the bracket.

Now, referring to Fig. 88, slacken the pinch-bolt *A* and unscrew *clockwise* the wheel spindle *B* with a tommy-bar inserted through the hole in the end of the spindle which has a left-hand thread. While supporting the

GENERAL MAINTENANCE 133

weight of the wheel, withdraw the spindle from the near-side and remove the wheel. No distance-tube is provided on the near-side, but a bush projects from the brake-drum side of the hub. Do not allow the wheel to fall over on to this bush. Although the bush is pressed in, a sharp blow on it may force the bush back into the hub. The remedy in this case is to retrieve and re-position the bush by means of the front-wheel spindle.

To Remove Front Wheel (1956-7 "B" Models). Referring to Fig. 89, to remove the front wheel, first remove the nut (C) from the brake cover-

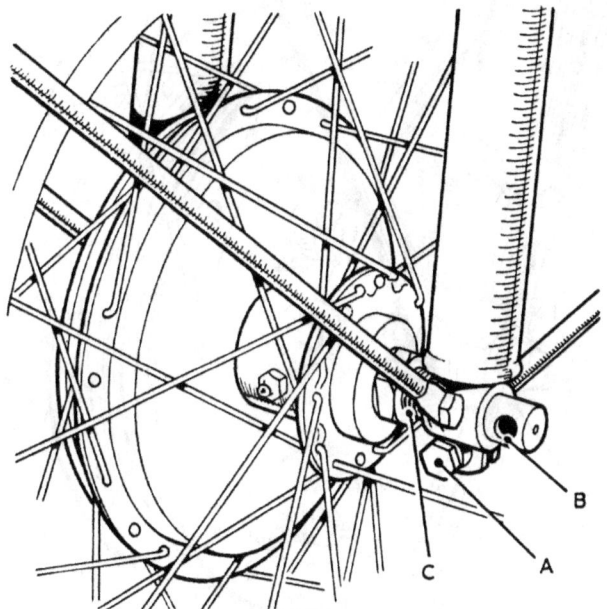

FIG. 88. B.S.A. FRONT WHEEL REMOVAL (1945-54 "B," "C," "M" MODELS)

On "C" series models the spindle has a hexagon head instead of the tommy-bar hole shown at *B*.

plate; also disconnect the brake cable. Now slacken the pinch-bolt (*A*) and remove the nut (*E*) on the opposite side. It has a normal right-hand thread. Then with a tommy-bar inserted into the hole on the head of the wheel spindle (*B*), pull the spindle out. When doing this, support the weight of the front wheel. As the spindle emerges, pull the wheel away from the off-side fork leg and remove it. Be careful not to allow the wheel to fall on the bush projecting from the brake-drum side.

When replacing the front wheel, see that all nuts and the pinch-bolt (*A*) are firmly re-tightened. *Before* tightening the pinch-bolt and *after* tightening the spindle nut (*E*), it is essential to depress the forks once or twice to enable the near-side fork end to position itself on the spindle shank. Failure to observe this precaution may cause the near-side fork leg to be clamped out of position, thereby preventing the forks from functioning correctly.

To Remove Front Wheel (1958-9 "B" Models). Referring to Fig. 90, first disconnect the front brake cable. Then remove the four bolts *A*

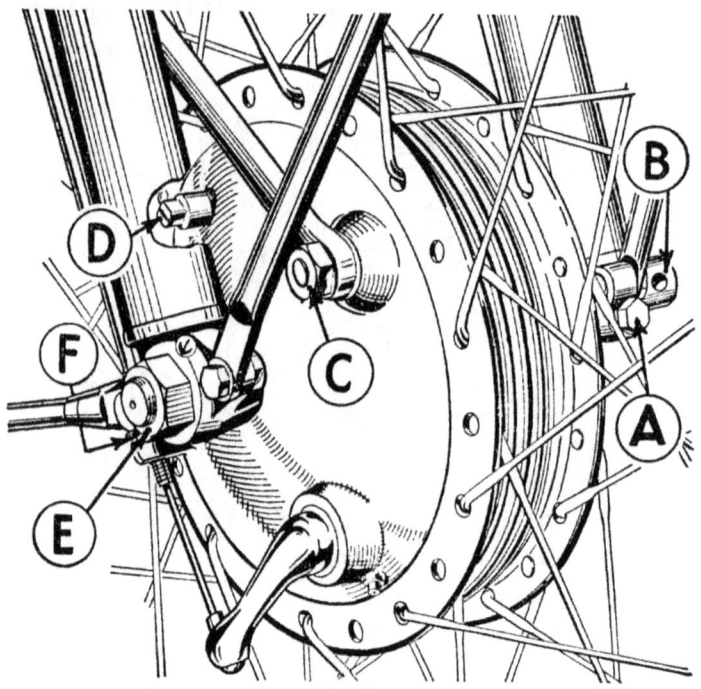

FIG. 89. FRONT WHEEL REMOVAL AND BRAKE ADJUSTMENT (1956-7 "B" MODELS)

On late 1956-7 models the front brake has a modified cam and a detachable cam-operating lever.

which secure the caps to the bottom ends of the telescopic fork legs. It is then possible to withdraw the wheel from the machine.

Replace the front wheel in the reverse order of removal. Note that it is most important to engage properly the brake anchorage peg on the off-side fork leg with the slot in the brake cover plate.

To Remove the Rear Wheel (Rigid-Frame "B," "C," 1949-57 "M" Models). To remove the rear wheel (not quickly-detachable), first place the machine on its stand and disconnect the secondary chain (do not

GENERAL MAINTENANCE 135

unwind it from the gearbox sprocket). Also remove the nut securing the brake anchor-strap, and on "C" models disconnect the speedometer-drive cable E (Fig. 92) from the speedometer gearbox F. Disconnect the tail-lamp lead and, after removing or slackening the appropriate nuts and bolts, withdraw or lift up the detachable or hinged mudguard tail-piece.

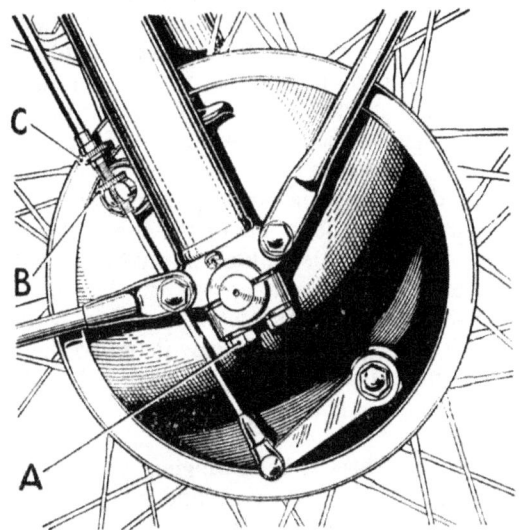

FIG. 90. FRONT WHEEL REMOVAL AND BRAKE ADJUSTMENT (1958-9 "B" MODELS)

At B and C are shown the lock-nut and adjuster for the front brake.

Then remove the knurled adjuster-nut on the brake rod, loosen both rear-wheel spindle nuts, and remove the rear wheel.

To Remove the Rear Wheel (Spring-Frame "C" Models). Remove the rear wheel (Fig. 82) as just described for the rigid-frame "C" models (250 c.c.).

To Remove the Rear Wheel (1945-8 Rigid-Frame M20, M21, M33). 1945-8 500, 600 c.c. S.V. models with rigid frame have a quickly-detachable rear wheel with the roller bearings contained within the hub. Rear wheel removal is very simple after detaching the rear portion of the mudguard as just described for "B" and "C" models. First remove the three retaining bolts, remove the nut on the off-side, and withdraw the spindle (a push fit in the hub) from the near-side. If necessary, tap the spindle out gently from the off-side. Afterwards detach the distance piece on the off-side and ease the hub off the driving studs to the right. Then lift the rear wheel rearwards clear of the machine.

If the rear wheel is not of the quickly detachable type, remove it as previously described for the rigid-frame "B" and "C" models.

To Remove the Rear Wheel (Plunger-type Spring-Frame "B" and "M" Models). On "B" and "M" models having the *plunger* type rear suspension the rear wheel is *always* of the quickly-detachable type, and its removal is perfectly straightforward. Disconnect the tail-lamp cable connexion, assuming that a touring form of rear mudguard is provided, and remove the nuts and bolts which secure the mudguard to the rear stays (slacken nuts, later models). Then lift the rear portion of the guard upwards about its hinge, so that it is well clear of the wheel.

Referring to Fig. 85, undo the outer nut A on the near-side extremity of the rear-wheel spindle, using the appropriate spanner. Do not touch nut B (the inner nut retains the whole of the brake assembly and should not be disturbed). Now with a suitable tommy-bar applied to the hole C in the off-side extremity of the spindle, pull out the spindle. Remove the distance piece between the hub and wheel bracket, withdraw the wheel sideways from its driving splines, and draw it out to the rear. Note that on some 1952 and subsequent models a re-designed brake cover plate is fitted, and the distance piece is omitted.

To Remove the Rear Wheel (All "Swinging Arm" Models). The rear wheel is of the quickly-detachable type and has ball journal-type non-adjustable bearings. Referring to Fig. 91, to remove the rear wheel, first jack the machine up on its central stand.

On 1956-9 models with full-width light-alloy rear hub, remove the nut (A) so as to free the brake anchor-strap. Also disconnect, as shown, the rear-brake operating cable (F). Remove the four nuts (G) which secure the light-alloy hub to the boss of the chain sprocket. These nuts are accessible on the near-side, and on machines provided with a chain case can be removed individually with a box spanner after first withdrawing the rubber plug (the rear one).

Now on all models apply a tommy-bar (1954-5) or spanner (1956-9) to the end of the rear-wheel spindle (B), and unscrew it *anti-clockwise* until it can be pulled clear. Remove the distance-piece (C), ease the hub to the off-side until it clears the brake drum (1954-5) or the sprocket boss (1956-9), and withdraw the wheel downwards and to the rear.

Note that when removing the rear wheel on all models, *do not disturb the large nut on the near-side*; this nut secures the brake drum or sprocket (1956-7). Also note, when replacing the rear wheel on 1956-7 models, that it is extremely important to *tighten firmly the four nuts securing the light-alloy hub to the sprocket boss*.

Replacing the Rear Wheel ("B," "C," "M" Models). The procedure is the reverse order of dismantling. When replacing the rear wheel, make

GENERAL MAINTENANCE 137

certain that the shoulders of the spindle nuts are properly located in the rear-fork ends.

Checking for Play in the Wheel Bearings. It is advisable about every 1,000 miles to check for play in the wheel bearings. The wheels should

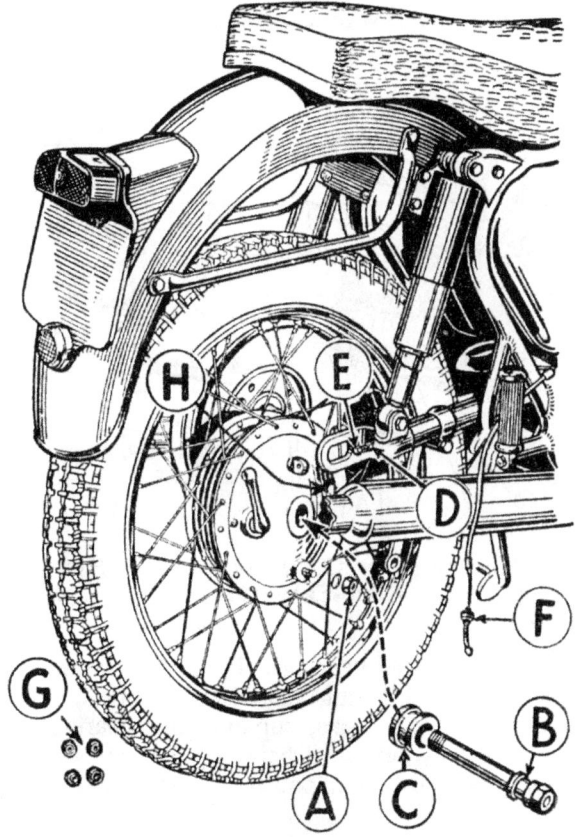

Fig. 91. Secondary Chain Adjustment, and Removal of 1956-9 Quickly-Detachable Rear Wheel

On 1954-5 "B" models the hub is not of the full-width type and the brake drum is on the opposite side, the hub being located on the drum and sprocket assembly by splines; on the pre-1956 machines spindle B has a hole for tommy-bar application but no hexagon.

always have some just perceptible side play at the rims when an attempt is made to shake them, but excessive play must never be permitted, because this subjects the ball or roller bearings to excessive stresses and can spoil good road-holding.

Except on most 250 c.c. "C" series and some earlier "M" series models, the front-hub bearings are not adjustable, but on all rigid frame "B," "C," "M" models an adjustment is possible for the *rear* wheel bearings in accordance with the instructions which follow. Where a spring frame is provided, there is *no adjustment* for the rear wheel bearings.

Adjusting Front Wheel Bearings (Models C10, C11). On the earlier 250 c.c. coil-ignition models with telescopic-type front forks, the front hub

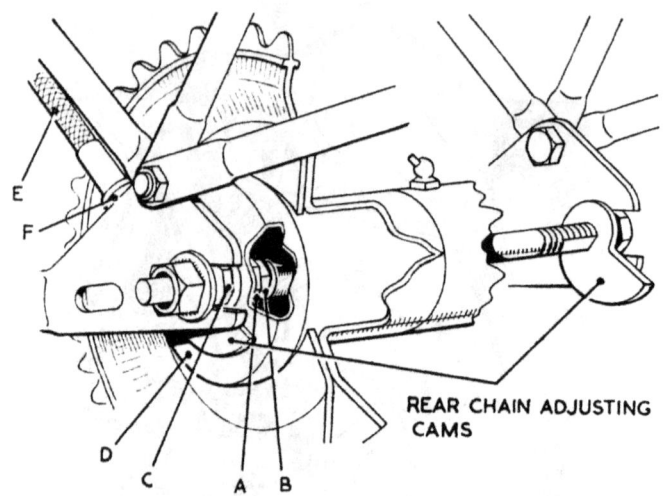

FIG. 92. ADJUSTMENT OF CUP-AND-CONE REAR HUB BEARINGS ON B.S.A. RIGID-FRAME MODELS C10, C11

is provided with ball-journal bearings. For these bearings *no* adjustment is provided or necessary. On all later 250 c.c. models, and some earlier ones with girder-type front forks, cup-and-cone bearings are provided. Adjust these bearings as described below for the rear-wheel bearings of Models C10, C11, disregarding, of course, the reference to the speedometer drive.

Adjusting the Front Wheel Bearings (Earlier Models M20, M21). Some 500, 600 c.c. S.V. models have roller bearings which should be adjusted as described later for the rear wheel bearings of these two models. Later Models M20, M21, M33 have journal-type bearings which are *not* adjustable.

Adjusting the Rear Wheel Bearings (Models C10, C11). Adjustment of the rear-wheel bearings should be effected with the wheel removed from the machine. Referring to Fig. 92, where a rear hub speedometer-drive *E* is used as shown, access to the lock-nut *A* and bearing-adjustment nut *B* is not possible, even after the nut F has been disconnected and the wheel removed, until the speedometer-driving unit D is detached. Remove nut C (and washer) and then lift off the speedometer unit D. On the four-speed models the removal of a cup washer (fitted instead of the speedometer gearbox) exposes the bearing adjustment nut B and lock-nut A. Now with the appropriate spanner turn the bearing-adjustment nut B as required.

On spring frame C10, C11 models the journal ball bearings have *no* adjustment.

Avoid tightening the adjusting nut excessively, because, when the rear wheel is replaced, there *must* be some perceptible side play at the rim. When the required adjustment has been obtained, tighten the lock-nut A against the adjusting nut B.

Adjusting the Rear Wheel Bearings (Rigid-frame Models B31, B32, B33, B34). All these "B" models have taper-roller hub bearings, and their adjustment should be effected with the wheel removed from the frame.

To adjust the wheel bearings, unscrew the wheel spindle nut on the off-side (*see* Fig. 83) and withdraw the cam and cap. This exposes the lock-nut A. Loosen this lock-nut and turn the adjuster B in or out as required in order to obtain a trace of play at the wheel rim when the wheel is subsequently replaced and the spindle nuts are firmly re-tightened.

Adjusting the Rear Wheel Bearings (Rigid-frame Models M20, M21, M33). Taper roller bearings are used on the rigid-frame models. In all cases it is desirable to remove the rear wheel to effect bearing adjustment. Referring to Fig. 93, unscrew the off-side nut A and withdraw cap B (this cap replaces the speedometer-drive unit provided on earlier machines). The lock-nut C is now exposed. Loosen the lock-nut and screw the adjuster D in or out as needed. Avoid over-tightening the bearings, otherwise the rollers may be damaged by the excessive load imposed on them. When the rear wheel is replaced some perceptible side-play must be present and felt at the wheel rim.

On spring frame "M" models *no* adjustment of the journal-type ball bearings is possible.

Wheel Alignment. After re-tensioning the secondary chain, or after removing and replacing the rear wheel, it is advisable on some machines to check the alignment of the front and rear wheels with a straight-edge or a piece of string in the manner referred to on page 130.

Brake Adjustment. For the benefit of yourself, your "next of kin," and the general public, always maintain the brakes so as to give maximum leverage and efficiency. Adjustment of the rear brake is by means of a thumb-nut at the rear end of the brake rod. Front brake adjustment is by means of a knurled thumb-nut on the cable stop, fitted to the front forks or front brake cover-plate. The 1954-5 "B" models have an adjustable stop for setting the rear-brake pedal to the most advantageous position; adjust this before adjusting the brake rod.

All 1956-7 "B" models have a brake-shoe adjustment in addition to the knurled finger adjusters. The latter are designed for cable adjustment

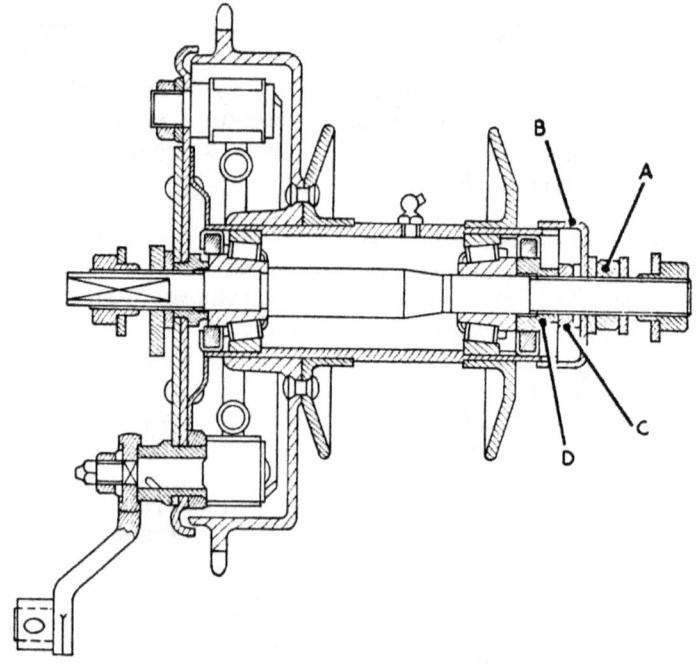

FIG. 93. ADJUSTMENT OF REAR HUB ROLLER-BEARINGS ON B.S.A. RIGID-FRAME "M" SERIES

during *initial assembly*. All subsequent brake adjustments should be effected at the brake-shoe fulcrums shown at (*H*) and (*D*) in Figs. 91 and 89 respectively. To compensate for wear of the brake linings (front or rear), apply a screwdriver or a small spanner to the fulcrum adjuster-pin (e.g. (*D*), Fig. 89), and turn *clockwise*. A series of clicks is audible as the adjuster pin is turned; each click corresponds to *one-twelfth of a turn*. To ensure correct brake adjustment, turn the adjuster pin fully clockwise, and then turn back until the front or rear wheel is just able to spin freely.

If grease gets on brake linings, remove the shoes and wash the linings in petrol. If the linings become glazed, roughen with a wire brush or a file. Do not adjust brakes too closely, as this will cause friction and heat, and possibly cause the grease in the hubs to melt, quite apart from impairing performance.

GENERAL MAINTENANCE

About every 2,000 miles check the tightness of the lock-nut on the brake cover-plate on 1954-5 "B" models and "M" models with 7-in. brakes. In the case of the 7-in. brakes, occasional centralizing is desirable. Loosen the lock-nut on the brake cover-plate so as to slacken the fulcrum pin in its slotted hole. Then apply the brake, when the fulcrum pin will automatically centralize the assembly. Now with the brake kept on, re-tighten the lock-nut.

Removal and Replacement of Brake Shoes. With the wheel removed, slacken fully the brake-shoe adjuster, and remove the brake plate from the wheel. Then grasp the shoes firmly, pulling them outwards to allow the shoes to clear the fulcrums and come away. Replace the brake shoes in the reverse order of removal. Hook the springs on to the shoes and place the ends of the shoes in position on the fulcrum pins. Push the brake shoes outwards until they are pulled into the correct position by the springs. The springs are strong and care must be taken to avoid getting the fingers trapped during shoe assembly. Note that brake shoes with new linings fitted are obtainable through the Exchange Replacement scheme.

STEERING HEAD AND FRONT FORKS

Adjustment of the Steering Head (All Models). About every 1,000 miles lift the machine and place a box beneath the crankcase to raise the front wheel clear of the ground. Then check that there is no friction in the ball bearings and that no up-and-down movement is possible. Also verify that the steering is true.

Where telescopic-type front forks are fitted, unscrew the damper knob with stem where fitted, and remove the steering head lock-nut shown at B in Fig. 94. Then loosen the clip bolt C and tighten the adjusting sleeve D* until all slackness in the steering head disappears. Be sure not to over-tighten the bearings and cause stiffness. Finally, re-tighten the clip bolt C and fit and tighten the lock-nut B.

Where girder-type front forks are fitted (i.e. on some pre-1948 models) loosen the clip bolt shown at C in Fig. 94, and then gently tighten the adjusting nut D until no appreciable slackness can be felt in the steering head. As in the case of the telescopic-fork machines, avoid excessive tightening of the bearings, otherwise the balls may be damaged and perhaps broken. When the adjustment has been completed, re-tighten the clip bolt C.

Adjusting the Girder Front Forks (1946-7 Models C10, C11, B31, B33). About every 1,000 miles check for side play in the links of the front forks.

* The sleeve can be turned by using a hammer and a $2\frac{1}{2}$ in. length of mild steel strip 1 in. wide and $\frac{1}{16}$ in. thick. The use of a punch is likely to damage the threads.

Where telescopic-type front forks are fitted, no actual adjustment is provided or necessary.

On Models C10, C11 having girder-type front forks, first slacken the shock-absorber at the side, so as to render the fork movement absolutely free. Referring to Fig. 95, then loosen the lock-nuts *A* on both sides of

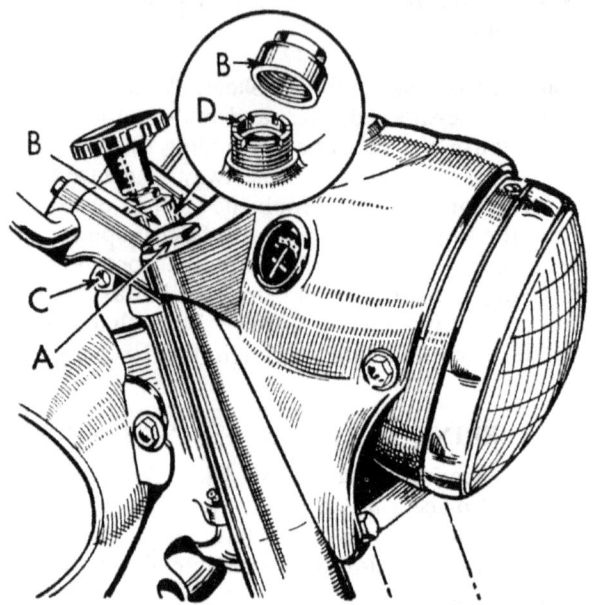

FIG. 94. STEERING HEAD ADJUSTMENT ON B.S.A. MODELS WITH TELESCOPIC-TYPE FRONT FORKS

No steering damper is fitted on later models.

the fork links. With a spanner applied to the flats on spindles *B*, screw the spindles in a counter-clockwise direction to take up slackness, and in the reverse direction to increase play. It is advisable to adjust each spindle separately and to check the effect of the adjustment before dealing with the second spindle. Only a slight adjustment should be required, as both spindles engage in tapers.

Adjusting the Girder Front Forks (1945-8 Models M20, M21). Check for side-play about every 1,000 miles. Keep the link bolts sufficiently tight to prevent this side-play. Slacken off the fork-damper adjuster and also all spindle lock-nuts. Then tighten each spindle as required. Check the fork action as each spindle is tightened and tighten the lock-nuts.

Telescopic Front Forks. 1948-59 telescopic front forks require no maintenance other than the routine checking of nuts for tightness and the

GENERAL MAINTENANCE 143

replenishment of the fork legs with suitable oil (*see* page 66) after a very considerable mileage. The time when replenishment is called for is

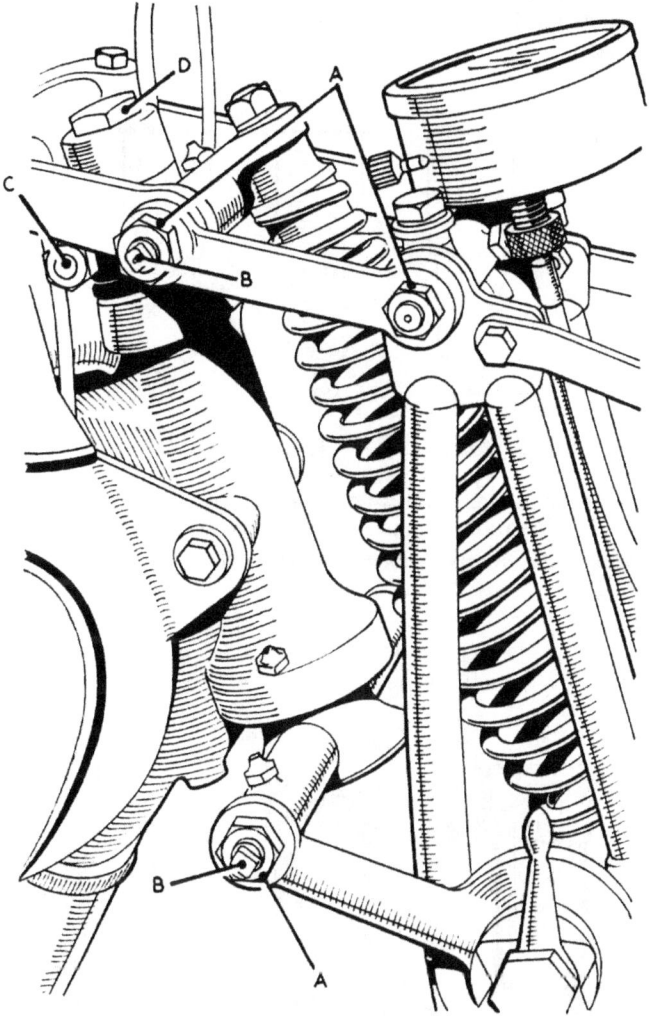

Fig. 95. Steering Head and Front-fork Adjustment on B.S.A. Models C10, C11, with Girder-type Forks (Earlier Models)

indicated by excessive up-and-down movement. Actual replenishment, not merely topping-up, as on 1945-7 forks (*see* page 64), is advised.

The "Swinging Arm" Rear Suspension. The self-contained hydraulic dampers require no topping-up or other maintenance, and the "swinging arm" pivots have "silentbloc" bushes requiring no lubrication. The springs in each suspension unit are, however, adjustable for load by means of adjustable cams which can be turned to one of the three alternative positions shown in Figs. 96, 97. The normal position (set by the makers) is shown at (A).

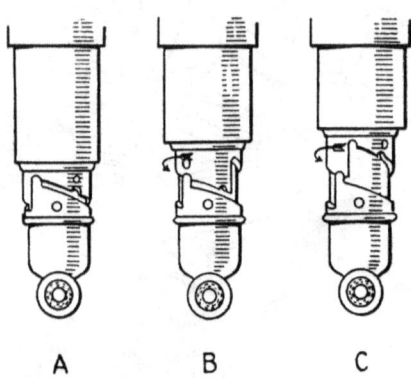

FIG. 96. ALTERNATIVE SPRING-LOADING ADJUSTMENTS FOR THE EARLIER "SWINGING ARM" REAR SUSPENSION UNITS

Progressively stiffer springing is obtained by setting the adjuster cams in the positions A, B, C.

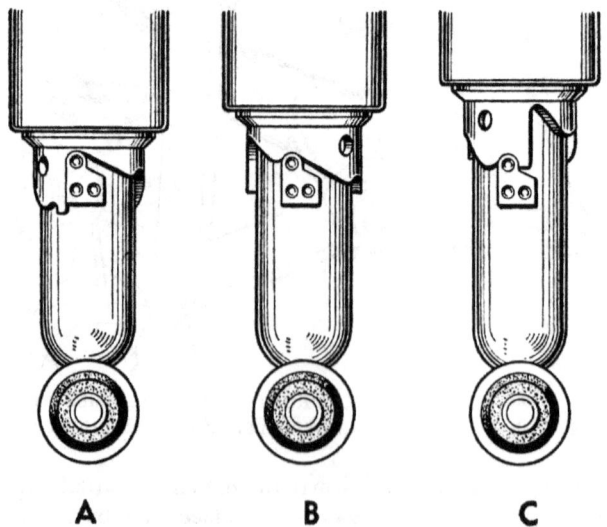

FIG. 97. ALTERNATIVE SPRING-LOADING ADJUSTMENT FOR THE LATER "SWINGING ARM" REAR SUSPENSION UNITS

Where the rider's weight is above average or the machine is being used habitually over rough terrain, slightly stiffer springing may be desirable and the required adjustment can be made in a few seconds; with the Cee-spanner in the tool kit, turn the adjuster cams to the position shown at (*B*). Adjustment is facilitated by the application of a little thin oil. Where a pillion passenger or heavy luggage is carried, it is advisable to set the suspension unit in the highest position by turning the cams to the position shown at (*C*).

To Remove Rear Suspension Units. As previously mentioned, the hydraulic dampers require no maintenance attention whatever. During manufacture they are sealed and if they become ineffective or damaged, it is necessary to renew them.

After detaching the two pivot bolts the complete suspension units can be removed from the frame. Two collets retain each top spring-housing and before the collets can be removed it is necessary to compress the spring. To do this it may be necessary to obtain the help of a second person.

Replacing Fork Top Caps. Lack of alignment (especially on cowled-headlamp models) can cause difficulty in screwing home the telescopic-fork upper caps after replenishing the fork legs with oil (page 66), or after fitting windscreen brackets (as used on the "Unicorn") to the forks. Referring to Fig. 94, the remedy is to slacken the headlamp mounting bolts, and the two nuts on the fork-crown pinch-bolts, *before* tightening the caps *A*.

INDEX

ACCESSORY firms, 69
Air filter, 25-6
Alignment, wheel, 130
Alternator, Lucas, 30
Ammeter, 30
Automatic ignition-advance, 82

BATTERY—
   connexions, 36
   filler, Lucas, 34
   removal, 32
   storage, 36
   topping-up, 32
Brake—
   adjustment, 139-41
   shoe removal, 141
Bulb renewal, 37-9

CARBON, removing, 97
Carburettor—
   assembling, 23-5
   flange, 23
   maintenance, 20-3
   tuning, 18-20
   working of, 13-18
C. & W. air filter, 26
Chain stretch, 128
Changing engine oil, 54
Cleaning—
   chromium, 72
   contacts, 79, 81
   enamel, 72
   engine and gearbox, 70-1
   "Magdyno" contacts, 78
   sparking plugs, 74-7
Clutch—
   adjustment, 114-18
   dismantling, 119-22
   spring pressure, 118-19
Coil, attention to, 81
Commutator—
   brushes, 27
   cleaning, 29
Compensated voltage control, 29
Condenser, faulty, 82
Contact-breaker gap, 77, 80

Control layout, 3-6
Cylinder—
   barrel removal, 89, 92, 94
   head removal, 89-94

DECARBONIZING, 86-106
Draining—
   crankcase, 54
   gearbox, 60
Dry sump lubrication, 50
Dynamo—
   chain adjustment, 82
   maintenance, 27-9
   terminals, 29

ELECTRIC horn, 48
Engine—
   number, 1
   oils, suitable, 49
Exhaust-valve lifter adjuster, 86

FILTER, oil, 55
Float chamber, inspecting, 23
Focusing headlamp, 36
Footrest adjustment, 3
Frame number, 1
Front forks, 64-6, 141-2
Front-wheel removal, 131-4

GAP—
   contact-breaker, 77, 80
   sparking plug, 74
Gaskets, 106
Gear changing, 9-11
Gearbox repairs, 128
Greases, suitable, 59
Grinding-in—
   cylinder head and barrel, 101
   valves, 99

H.T. pick-up, 79

IGNITION—
   timing, 106-11
   warning lamp, 81

JET-NEEDLE position, 20

LAMPS, cleaning, 37
Lighting switch, positions, 36
Lubrication—
  automatic ignition advance, 57
  brake, 67
  chain, 62-4
  chart, 59
  clutch control, 60
  dipper switch, 68
  dynamo, 57
  dynamo chain, 58
  front forks, 64
  gearbox, 59
  hub bearings, 64
  "Magdyno", 56
  shock-absorber, 64
  speedometer drive, 66
  spring frame, 67
  steering head, 64
  trouble, rectifying, 50-4

MAINTENANCE, items for, 69
"Monobloc" Amal carburettor, 16-18

NEUTRAL, obtaining, 11

OIL—
  circulation, checking, 50
  leakage, 57
  level in tank, 49
  tank, cleaning, 55
  tank removal, 56
Overhead rockers, fitting, 101

PETROL—
  tank removal, 87-8
  taps, 6-8
Pilot jet, obstructed, 20
Piston—
  removal, 94-5
  rings, 96-7
Preliminaries, 1
Primary—
  chain adjustment, 122-3
  chain-case removal, 127

Pump filters, cleaning, 55
Punctures, mending, 130

REAR—
  suspension, 68, 143-5
  wheel removal, 134-6
Rebores and oversize pistons, 101
Rectifier, Lucas, 31
Riding position, 2
Running-in, 11, 49

SECONDARY chain adjustment, 123-7
Slip-ring "Magdyno" 79
Slow-running—
  adjustment, 18
  poor, 20
Spares and repairs, 69
Sparking plugs, suitable, 73-4
Specific gravity, checking, 34
Speedometer trip, 12
Standard Amal carburettor, 13-15
Starting up, 8
Steering head—
  adjustment, 141
  lock, 12, 64

TAPPET adjustment, 82-6
Telescopic front forks, 142-3
Topping-up battery cells, 32
Tyre pressures, 128-30

UPPER cylinder lubricant, 12

VALVE—
  guides, fitting, 100
  spring renewal, 101
  timing, 111-14
Valves, removing, 98-9
Vokes air filter, 25

WHEEL—
  alignment, 130
  bearings, play in, 137-9
  removal, 131-6
Wiring—
  diagrams, 41-7
  of equipment, 39

VELOCEPRESS MANUALS - MOTORCYCLE

1930'S BRITISH MOTORCYCLE CARBS & ELEC COMPONENTS (BOOK OF)
1930'S BRITISH MOTORCYCLE ENGINES (OVERHAUL & MAINTENANCE)
1930'S BRITISH MOTORCYCLE GEARBOXES & CLUTCHES (BOOK OF)
AJS 1932-1948 SINGLES & TWINS 250cc THRU 1000cc (BOOK OF)
AJS 1945-1960 SINGLES 350cc & 500cc MODELS 16 & 18 (BOOK OF)
AJS 1955-1965 SINGLES 350cc & 500cc (BOOK OF)
ARIEL UP TO 1932 (BOOK OF)
ARIEL 1932-1939 PREWAR MODELS (BOOK OF)
ARIEL 1933-1951 (WORKSHOP MANUAL)
ARIEL 1939-1960 4 STROKE SINGLES (BOOK OF)
ARIEL 1958-1964 LEADER & ARROW (BOOK OF)
BMW R26 R27 (1956-1967) FACTORY WORKSHOP MANUAL
BMW R50 R50S R60 R69S (1955-1969) FACTORY WORKSHOP MANUAL
BRIDGESTONE 90 SERIES FACTORY WSM & PARTS CATALOGUE
BRIDGESTONE 175 SERIES FACTORY WSM & PARTS CATALOGUE
BSA BANTAM ALL MODELS FROM 1948 ONWARDS (BOOK OF)
BSA SINGLES & V-TWINS UP TO 1927 (BOOK OF)
BSA SINGLES & V-TWINS UP TO 1935 (BOOK OF)
BSA SINGLES & V-TWINS 1936-1939 (BOOK OF)
BSA SINGLES & V-TWINS 1936-1952 (BOOK OF)
BSA OHV & SV SINGLES 250-600cc 1945-1959 (BOOK OF)
BSA OHV & SV SINGLES 250cc 1954-1970 (BOOK OF)
BSA OHV SINGLES 350 & 500cc 1955-1967 (BOOK OF)
BSA TWINS 1948-1962 (BOOK OF)
BSA TWINS 1962-1969 (SECOND BOOK OF)
CYCLEMOTOR (BOOK OF)
DOUGLAS 1929-1939 PREWAR ALL MODELS (BOOK OF)
DOUGLAS 1948-1957 POSTWAR ALL MODELS FACTORY SHOP MANUAL
DUCATI 160cc, 250cc & 350cc OHC MODELS FACTORY SHOP MANUAL
HONDA 50 ALL MODELS UP TO 1970 INC MONKEY & TRAIL (BOOK OF)
HONDA 90 ALL MODELS UP TO 1966 (BOOK OF)
HONDA 125-150cc TWINS C/CS/CB/CA FACTORY WORKSHOP MANUAL
HONDA 250-305 TWINS C/CS/CB FACTORY WORKSHOP MANUAL
HONDA C100 SUPER CUB FACTORY WORKSHOP MANUAL
HONDA C110 SPORT CUB 1962-1969 FACTORY WORKSHOP MANUAL
HONDA TWINS & SINGLES 50cc THRU 305cc 1960-1966 (BOOK OF)
HONDA TWINS ALL MODELS 125cc THRU 450cc UP TO 1968 (BOOK OF)
J.A.P. ENGINES 1927-1952 & MOTORCYCLES 1934-1952 (BOOK OF)
LAMBRETTA 1947-1957 ALL 125 & 150cc MODELS (BOOK OF)
LAMBRETTA 1957-1970 LI & TV MODELS (SECOND BOOK OF)
MATCHLESS 1931-1939 ALL MODELS 250cc THRU 990cc (BOOK OF)
MATCHLESS 1945-1956 350 & 500cc SINGLES (BOOK OF)
MATCHLESS 1955-1966 350 & 500cc SINGLES (BOOK OF)
NEW IMPERIAL ALL SV & OHV FROM 1935 ONWARDS (BOOK OF)
NORTON 1932-1939 PREWAR MODELS (BOOK OF)
NORTON 1932-1947 (BOOK OF)
NORTON 1938-1956 (BOOK OF)
NORTON 1955-1963 MODELS 19, 50 & ES2 (BOOK OF)
NORTON 1955-1965 DOMINATOR TWINS (BOOK OF)
NORTON 1957-1970 TWINS FACTORY WORKSHOP MANUAL
NSU PRIMA 1956-1964 ALL MODELS (BOOK OF)
NSU QUICKLY 1953-1963 ALL MODELS (BOOK OF)
PANTHER 1932-1958 LIGHTWEIGHT MODELS 250 & 350cc (BOOK OF)
PANTHER 1938-1966 HEAVYWEIGHT MODELS 600 & 650cc (BOOK OF)
RALEIGH MOPEDS 1960-1969 (BOOK OF)
RALEIGH MOTORCYCLES 1919-1933 (BOOK OF)
ROYAL ENFIELD 1934-1946 SINGLES & V TWINS (BOOK OF)
ROYAL ENFIELD 1937-1953 SINGLES & V TWINS (BOOK OF)
ROYAL ENFIELD 1946-1962 SINGLES (BOOK OF)
ROYAL ENFIELD 1958-1966 250cc & 350cc SINGLES (SECOND BOOK OF)
ROYAL ENFIELD 736cc INTERCEPTOR FACTORY WORKSHOP MANUAL
RUDGE 1933-1939 (BOOK OF)
SUNBEAM 1928-1939 (BOOK OF)
SUNBEAM 1946-1957 S7 & S8 (BOOK OF)
SUZUKI 50cc & 80cc UP TO 1966 (BOOK OF)
SUZUKI T10 1963-1967 FACTORY WORKSHOP MANUAL
SUZUKI T20 & T200 1965-1969 FACTORY WORKSHOP MANUAL
TRIUMPH 1935-1939 PREWAR MODELS (BOOK OF)
TRIUMPH 1935-1949 (BOOK OF)
TRIUMPH 1937-1951 (WORKSHOP MANUAL)
TRIUMPH 1945-1955 FACTORY WORKSHOP MANUAL
TRIUMPH 1945-1958 TWINS (BOOK OF)
TRIUMPH 1956-1969 TWINS (BOOK OF)
VELOCETTE 1925-1970 ALL SINGLES & TWINS (BOOK OF)
VESPA 1951-1961 (BOOK OF)
VESPA 1955-1963 125 & 150cc & GS MODELS (SECOND BOOK OF)
VESPA 1955-1968 GS & SS (BOOK OF)
VESPA 1963-1972 90, 125 & 150cc (THIRD BOOK OF)
VILLIERS ENGINE UP TO 1959 INC. 3 WHEELERS (BOOK OF)
VILLIERS ENGINE UP TO 1969 (BOOK OF)
VINCENT 1935-1955 (WORKSHOP MANUAL)

VELOCEPRESS TECHNICAL BOOKS – MOTORCYCLE

CATALOG OF BRITISH MOTORCYCLES (1951 MODELS)
INDIAN PONYBIKE, BOY RACER & PAPOOSE ILL PARTS LIST & SALES LIT
MOTORCYCLE ENGINEERING (P.E. Irving)
SPEED AND HOW TO OBTAIN IT (Motor Cycle Magazine UK)
TUNING FOR SPEED (P.E. Irving)

VELOCEPRESS MANUALS - THREE WHEELER'S

BSA THREE WHEELER (BOOK OF)
VINTAGE MORGAN THREE WHEELER (BOOK OF)

VELOCEPRESS MANUALS - AUTOMOBILE

ALFA ROMEO GIULIA WORKSHOP MANUAL 1300 TO 2000cc 1962-1975
ALFA ROMEO GIULIA TECH MANUAL CARBURETED CARS FROM 1962
ALFA ROMEO GIULIA TECH MANUAL FUEL INJECTED CARS FROM 1969
AUSTIN-HEALEY 6-CYLINDER WORKSHOP MANUAL
AUSTIN-HEALEY SPRITE & MG MIDGET WORKSHOP MANUAL 1958-1971
BMW 600 LIMOUSINE FACTORY WORKSHOP MANUAL
BMW 600 LIMOUSINE OWNERS HAND BOOK & SERVICE MANUAL
BMW 2000 & 2002 1966-1976 WORKSHOP MANUAL
BMW ISETTA FACTORY WORKSHOP MANUAL
CORVAIR 1960-1969 WORKSHOP MANUAL
CORVETTE V8 1955-1962 WORKSHOP MANUAL
FIAT 500 FACTORY WORKSHOP MANUAL 1957-1973
FIAT 600, 600D & MULTIPLA FACTORY WORKSHOP MANUAL 1955-1969
JAGUAR E-TYPE 3.8 & 4.2 SERIES 1 & 2 WORKSHOP MANUAL
JAGUAR MK 7, 8, 9 & XK120, 140, 150 WORKSHOP MANUAL 1948-1961
METROPOLITAN FACTORY WORKSHOP MANUAL
MGA & MGB OWNERS HANDBOOK & WORKSHOP MANUAL
MG MIDGET TC, TD, TF & TF1500 WORKSHOP MANUAL
PORSCHE 356 1948-1965 WORKSHOP MANUAL
PORSCHE 911 2.0, 2.2, 2.4 LITRE 1964-1973
PORSCHE 912 WORKSHOP MANUAL
TRIUMPH TR2, TR3, TR4 1953-1965 WORKSHOP MANUAL
VOLKSWAGEN TRANSPORTER, TRUCKS & WAGONS 1950-1979 WSM
VOLVO 1944-1968 ALL MODELS WORKSHOP MANUAL

VELOCEPRESS TECHNICAL BOOKS - AUTOMOBILE

FERRARI 250/GT SERVICE AND MAINTENANCE
FERRARI GUIDE TO PERFORMANCE
FERRARI OWNER'S HANDBOOK
FERRARI TUNING TIPS & MAINTENANCE TECHNIQUES
HOW TO BUILD A FIBERGLASS CAR
HOW TO BUILD A RACING CAR
HOW TO RESTORE THE MODEL 'A' FORD
MASERATI OWNER'S HANDBOOK
OBERT'S FIAT GUIDE
PERFORMANCE TUNING THE SUNBEAM TIGER
SOUPING THE VOLKSWAGEN
SOLEX CARBURETORS (EMPHASIS ON UK & EU AUTOMOBILES)
SU CARBURETORS (EMPHASIS ON UK AUTOMOBILES)
WEBER CARBURETORS (EMPHASIS ON ALFA & FIAT)

VELOCEPRESS BOOKS & GUIDES - AUTOMOBILE

ABARTH BUYERS GUIDE
COMPLETE CATALOG OF JAPANESE MOTOR VEHICLES
FERRARI 308 SERIES BUYER'S AND OWNER'S GUIDE
FERRARI BERLINETTA LUSSO
FERRARI BROCHURES AND SALES LITERATURE 1946-1967
FERRARI BROCHURES AND SALES LITERATURE 1968-1989
FERRARI OPP, MAINTENANCE & SERVICE H/BOOKS 1948-1963
FERRARI SERIAL NUMBERS PART I - ODD NUMBERS TO 21399
FERRARI SERIAL NUMBERS PART II - EVEN NUMBERS TO 1050
FERRARI SPYDER CALIFORNIA
HENRY'S FABULOUS MODEL "A" FORD
MASERATI BROCHURES AND SALES LITERATURE

VELOCEPRESS BOOKS – RACING

CARRERA PANAMERICANA – MEXICAN ROAD RACE (BOOK OF)
DIALED IN - THE JAN OPPERMAN STORY
IF HEMINGWAY HAD WRITTEN A RACING NOVEL
VEDA ORR'S NEW REVISED HOT ROD PICTORIAL

AUTOBOOKS WORKSHOP MANUALS & BROOKLANDS ROAD TEST PORTFOLIOS

FOR A COMPLETE LISTING OF THE AUTOBOOKS & BROOKLANDS TITLES THAT WE CURRENTLY HAVE AVAILABLE, PLEASE VISIT OUR WEBSITE.

For a detailed description of any of the titles listed above please visit our website at;
www.VelocePress.com

www.ingramcontent.com/pod-product-compliance
Lightning Source LLC
Chambersburg PA
CBHW070551170426
43201CB00012B/1801